At home, all I really care about is how delicious something is.

If the goal of eating out is to indulge in something you can't have at home, shouldn't eating at home be a celebration of the dishes that are at their very best there? This collection of recipes is designed to offer flavours and textures that are easier to achieve at home than in a restaurant, to be enjoyed at your table with the people you care about most.

Some of the best dishes around the world have been created from a place of scarcity, whether that be time, money or the ingredients available. This book respects the best ingredients, and yet also finds use for those that may need a little help. From abundance to restraint, from big flavours to delicate refrains, this is a book for all occasions. Every idea is designed to help you find happiness in your kitchen.

A lifetime of
beautiful home cooking
starts here.

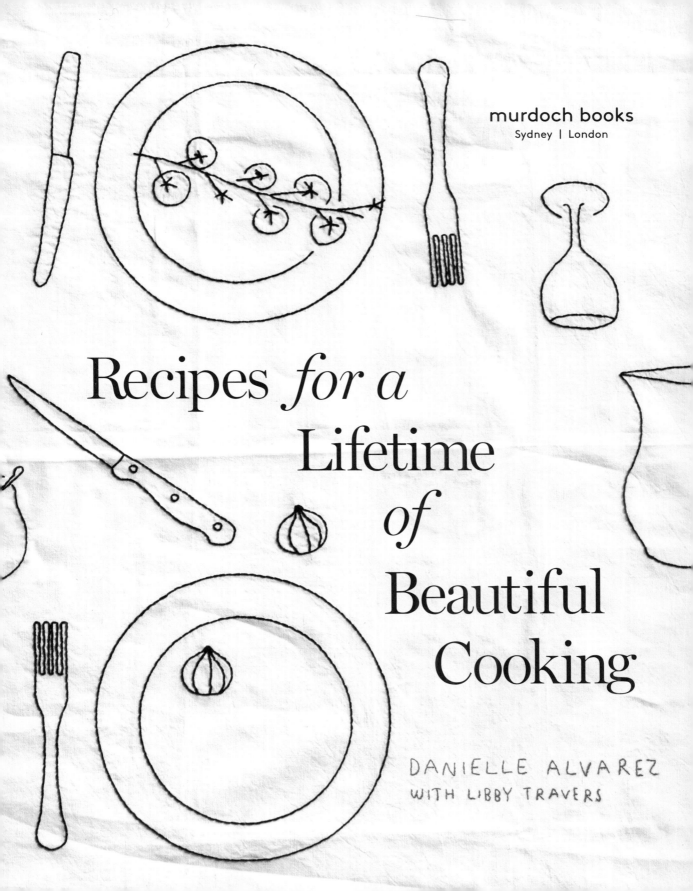

murdoch books
Sydney | London

Recipes *for a* Lifetime *of* Beautiful Cooking

DANIELLE ALVAREZ
WITH LIBBY TRAVERS

Contents

With abandon and restraint

Beautiful cooking is the simplest way to bring happiness to any home.

Food has always brought out the romantic in me: the smell of tomatoes on the vine, the flavour of the first asparagus, the juicy bite of a perfectly ripe peach. I find more joy shopping at farmers' markets, and cooking and sharing food with friends and family, than almost anything else.

This book is about the joy of cooking at home. It's about cooking with both abandon and restraint. However, this is not just about a delicious surplus of plums or a careful hand with, say, the vinegar; I'm not even thinking about the balance within each recipe. Rather, I think this balance runs across all the decisions that make your kitchen wonderful: strong, punchy dishes and the shy, quiet ones; the financial extravagances and the frugal meals; long afternoons of leisurely cooking and quick mid-week sustenance. With abandon and restraint, you can make a kitchen that ebbs and flows with the weather, with your mood, with your budget and with your tastes.

It is with both knowledge and wisdom that we can wrangle meals from the inevitable hodgepodge of ingredients we have at our disposal. In writing this book, I wanted to share the ideas and techniques I've been lucky to glean over the years from great chefs and great producers – but I'm also hoping I can help you feel confident to play the cards you've been dealt.

In Australia and many parts of the US, particularly where I grew up in Miami, the seasons aren't as pronounced as they are in the countries of Europe. This is both a blessing and a curse! We can find many ingredients, well grown in healthy soils, for the most part of the year. While this means that a lot of these recipes are available to cook year-round, it can make it harder to spot (or smell) a perfect tomato. When a tomato is at its peak, a sprinkle of salt is often enough, but this isn't really a book for those tomatoes. Rather, this is about the fruit and vegetables you can find at your local grocer or supermarket. These are the vegetables that may need a warm bath with some aromatic friends to get the best of them; these are the ingredients that benefit from some of the rules and regulations that govern good cooking.

When it comes to time in my kitchen, I never think to save it, only spend it. But then, I learnt to cook with the luxury of time: years, months, hours ... so many hours! While many of them were hard fought in busy kitchens, I had the time each day to watch ingredients transform, to peel away the outer leaves of artichokes, to gently wash thousands (millions?!) of lettuce leaves, to watch sinews give way to unctuous morsels of deep, rich umami. I also had time to think – not just about the technique I was using, or the beauty of the produce in my hands, but about balance – about the moments of abandon, and just as important, those of restraint.

This is not a book of big proteins and expensive cuts; where I suggest you spend your money is on good pantry ingredients – particularly anchovies, a good olive oil and the extenders such as pasta and risotto rice.

Taking a step up in the quality stakes will pay big dividends in your meal – the simpler the dish, the more important this balance.

A well-stocked pantry, bunches of herbs and a measured, but unfearful, use of fats will all help. Some things, a great chicken for example, should never be skimped on, but can be stretched in a number of ways to give extra value to the investment; one night you could enjoy a fantastic roast chicken, but instead of scraping those bones into the bin, you scrape them, along with the little bits of meat left behind and a few aromatics, into a pot to create the building blocks for your next meal. That, for me, is home cooking.

A carefully stocked larder becomes your toolbox of flavours. I've tried to keep this pantry list tight, as no one likes to shop for a million ingredients they may not use again, just to make one dish. Another excellent lesson in restraint. In a restaurant we have rooms filled with ingredients; at home it should mostly fit into one cupboard. You need to choose wisely, and, for this, you will find my suggestions on page 15–20. Likewise, I like to keep my kitchen toolbox to a minimum – you'll find my most-loved "kitchenalia" items that I use to turn my pantry and produce into the dishes throughout these pages on page 21.

It is from a place of adversity that some of my favourite dishes have been created. I want to arm you with some classics inspired by the best *cucina povera* dishes from around the world: *bagna cauda*, *pappa al pomodoro*, *pan bagnat*, the use of tinned fish – from sardines in pasta to mackerel in *polpette*. Traditionally pasta, rice and noodles were used to lengthen a meal so no one would go hungry. You simply cannot convince me that slices of zucchini fried with olive oil and garlic and tossed through hot spaghetti, using pasta water and a bit of parmesan cheese to make a creamy sauce, is not one of the most elegant solutions to this problem. This is my idea of grace under pressure.

I believe that our interaction with food is one of the most important things we can do for ourselves, for those we love and for our community. The world is a fragile, precarious place. The ability to feed ourselves well and economically is a skill that should be learned by all.

These are recipes I hope you will enjoy following – a collection of ideas and tiny adjustments to your approach that will form a delicious meal. Some steps may seem superfluous: a pinch of bicarbonate of soda (baking soda) here, a combination of two or three spices there, how long your onions really need to draw out their flavour, or when to turn off the heat to arrest the garlic in that precious golden moment before it turns bitter. Pay attention to these little details.

These are also recipes that I have compiled with the aim to teach. Every step has been considered – applying the economy of movement in the restaurant kitchen to the economy of movement in the home kitchen. If a recipe is in this book, it's because I think it's important, and it's also because it's delicious. These are my favourites. I'm not going to wax on too much about how good I think each dish is – you can rest assured that it's in here because I think it's good.

That said, the one thing I can't do is taste for you. Constantly tasting and adjusting is the only way to make something as good as it can be. Taste the tomato before you commit it to a dish, breathe in the garlic as you crush it with the back of your knife – is it strong, meaning you will only need one clove, or will you need a few? Try a morsel of the chilli – how piquant is it? I often ask you to add pinches of salt throughout the cooking process. The result of this continuous seasoning is more depth and, in my experience, less salt. This will all inform your meal.

In a quest for constant perfection and the big flavour bombs, I fear we've lost sight of the joy and simplicity that is only found when cooking at home. I think we were wrong to let the desire for sameness seep out of restaurants and sully the home kitchen. It makes no sense. This is about relearning how to taste, without prejudice.

Although I am a restaurant chef, this book is very much about the food I cook at home. It draws on my Cuban roots, my time spent cooking in California and then in Australia, my love of Italian and French food, and all the incredible Asian influences that have coloured my time here. The recipes are eclectic because my interests in flavour are eclectic. We are so lucky to live in a world where one night we might be cooking something Indian, the next something Italian and then something Australian. This is a luxury to be used to our advantage. Even if you live somewhere remote, if you have a basic grocery store, you can make most of the recipes in this book. These ideas and recipes are designed to help you find joy in your kitchen with the best that is available to you. A lifetime of beautiful home cooking starts here.

—Danielle

Between the bookshelf and the kitchen

While my food education was also borne of a thousand repetitions, I didn't learn to cook in a restaurant kitchen. My lessons have largely come from cookbooks and food literature; from indulging in the ideas of M.F.K. Fisher, Elizabeth David, Patience Gray and Claudia Roden. Through the pages of their books, these women taught me much of what I know.

I have also been fortunate to eat at many wonderful restaurants, from the elaborate to the humble bistros. I have travelled, visiting markets from Morocco to Marseille; I have eaten octopus plucked from the rocks of Pantelleria, sea urchins in the port of Cassis, wild weeds collected from the plateaux of Crete. I learnt to taste at the tables of others.

I admit my skills are dull. I know the theory, that I should curl my fingers up over the vegetable I am cutting. I know I should let the knife be guided by my knuckles, and yet I rarely do it. A dirty secret, but the truth of my cooking.

I have been a more attentive student when it comes to the wonder of fabulous produce – at times frugal, at times indulgent, but always thoughtful. I have learnt that no two seasons will ever be the same, no two harvests, not even two fruits from the same tree. I have learnt when to leave a tomato alone, and when it needs time and company to bring out its inherent flavours. Sameness and exactitude are not found in nature. I have learnt to respect that.

Scattered among these pages, you will find wise words gleaned from some of my most treasured cookbooks. These are the food writers who have taught me so much. There are also occasional histories and anecdotes, or sometimes an explanation of an ingredient or technique, nestled alongside Danielle's wonderful recipes. These little "romance notes", as we came to call them, add to the experience of cooking for me – the context that will transport you while chopping, kneading or stirring.

I am lucky to count among my dearest friends some wonderful chefs. This has allowed me to delight in the most brilliant conversations, to question out loud something I have read. I haven't absorbed their skills in the kitchen, but I have absorbed their thoughts. I didn't get to steal with my eyes, but with my ears.

Danielle is one of the most thoughtful chefs I know. We've shared many excellent meals together, and some beautiful bottles. There's been a lot of laughter, and she's borne the brunt of my endless questions – her answers to which were always considered and often profound. My job, on these pages, has been to take you with me into Dani's kitchen – one of my favourite places to be.

—*Libby*

My pantry and other kitchenalia

Before you begin

Each recipe in the book lists both "active" and "inactive" cooking times. "Active" is the time you spend chopping, slicing, dicing and standing at the stove, oven or grill, stirring and actively cooking. "Inactive" is the time when something is in the oven, quietly simmering on the stove, marinating in the fridge or even cooling on your benchtop. These should be used as a guide; it may take you slightly more or less time and that's okay. If you need a round of pastry or to make and roll your pasta dough for a recipe, this is included in the given cooking times. The "Before you begin" section will help you plan so things go smoothly.

The recipes also list the servings a recipe makes. Most savoury recipes can be scaled up or down. This is a bit trickier with dessert, but where applicable, I've given instructions.

In my pantry

I have, perhaps unusually, put a bit of thought into my desert island pantry. The minimalist in me thinks she can get it down to seven: good olive oil, anchovies, red or white wine vinegar, sea salt, black pepper, chilli flakes and tinned tomatoes. But then I think, *Well, if I have the tinned tomatoes, surely I need the pasta … and who could possibly have pasta without parmesan?* A few seconds later my tastebuds niggle, *I'd better just add capers and olives, too.* That's when the incredible Asian staples – the soy sauces, sesame oil, fish sauce, miso and rice wine vinegar – start jostling for my attention. *Oh, and dried beans – how could I forget dried beans?* Gosh, and that's before I've even started on the spices, flours, sugars, vanilla, baking powder …

A well-stocked pantry or larder is the key to making everyday food interesting, diverse and flavourful. We are so lucky that in most major cities around the world you can find these ingredients without too much trouble (or, for those further afield, even have them sent to your door). Here are the seven (plus a few) I can't imagine being without:

SALT: I always have both fine sea salt and flaked sea salt in my kitchen. It's the fine sea salt that works hardest: it's added to blanching water for vegetables and pasta cooking water, as well as soups and sautées. Its job is to dissolve evenly and rapidly, which is the reason I use it in my baking, too. I do also use it on just-fried items – it sticks better. Delicate flaked salt is precious and treated accordingly. It's known as fleur de sel in France for the way the delicate crystals bloom on the water's surface before being hand harvested. It offers distinct flavour and texture to finished dishes. The form of the salt varies – from the little pyramids of Maldon to the flakes of Murray River – depending on both the region and process of evaporation. I reserve flaked sea salt for salads and for finishing a dish.

OILS: I have at least three types on hand – **extra-virgin olive oil**, a **neutral oil** and a **toasted sesame oil**. With olive oil, I will keep one less expensive (but good) option for cooking with, and one really-good-quality olive oil just for finishing and dressings. If you live in a country that produces olive oil, seek out one that's locally made. This is not just about food miles, but also about freshness: olive oil is pressed annually in late autumn and should be used within that year; left too long, it can become flabby and even rancid. I prefer the fruity, floral notes as opposed to the hot, peppery and spicy notes, but taste around and see what you like.

As for neutral oils, they are essential for making mayonnaise and chilli oil, and for any sort of cooking outside of the western palate. They're also handy for deep-frying. I like avocado oil for its mild, buttery flavour, super high smoke point and healthful properties, and grapeseed oil (not to be confused with rapeseed or canola) for its clean flavour and similarly high smoke point. Find a neutral oil that suits you, ready to turn to when I call for neutral oil in these recipes.

Toasted sesame oil, which has a strong, nutty flavour, is great for finishing dishes. I think sesame oil should also be removed from the shackles of only being used in Asian-leaning dishes. I love a little sesame oil in my tahini dressings or in my coleslaw for its depth of flavour. A little drizzle goes a long way.

SPICES, DRIED HERBS AND CHILLIES: To think wars were fought, and lives lost, over cinnamon! While I understand the obsession, I'm glad I don't need to live and die by it (but I do take spices very seriously). In order to have a good spice cabinet, you need to use your spices regularly – buy them fresh (ideally from a good spice retailer) and keep rotating them. They work magic when they are lively and aromatic. It's so important to make your spices accessible. Get them organised – get them out of those little plastic sachets and into sealed glass jars and use them up!

My most-used dried spices: freshly cracked white and black pepper, coriander seeds, cumin seeds, fennel seeds, cayenne pepper, chilli flakes (Aleppo or Korean and standard – see opposite page), smoked paprika, ground turmeric, mustard seeds, sesame seeds, allspice, cardamom pods, cinnamon (ground and quills), cloves, Szechuan pepper pods, star anise, za'atar, yellow curry powder (I like Keen's!). I keep many more obscure spices because I love them so much, but I recognise they are a little less used in my kitchen.

With most spices, I prefer to buy the whole version that I then toast and grind myself. Simply toast them in a hot pan until perfumed then crush them in your mortar and pestle. One exception is cinnamon, which is very hard to grind finely, so I keep it in powdered form too. As for cloves – I get around the lack of powdered clove by studding whole cloves into a piece of celery or onion (to benefit from the flavour, while avoiding wasted time fishing around for them later).

There are a few dried herbs I also adore: mint, oregano, thyme and dill. These don't usually take the place of fresh herbs, but instead add something really delicious all of their own.

To make a simple coleslaw:
Thinly slice a medium-sized head of cabbage and toss it together with half a red onion (thinly sliced) and two carrots that have been peeled and grated on the large holes of a box grater. Give that a good few pinches of fine sea salt, a good crack of black pepper and about 2 teaspoons of white (granulated) sugar. Add ¼ cup (60 ml) of apple cider vinegar, 2 tablespoons of Dijon mustard and ½ cup (120 g) of mayonnaise, finishing with 1 teaspoon of toasted sesame oil. Toss well to combine, then serve cold.

THE SPECIAL CASE OF CHILLI: The world of dried chillies is vast and varied. It is also confusing, in part due to the use of the word "pepper". What started out as a rather ingenious marketing suggestion from Columbus and his gang, who had in large part gone in search of a rival product to the black peppercorn, does complicate matters here.

The standard **Italian-style chilli flakes (pepperoncini)** are a mix of chopped chilli flakes and seeds – the seeds give them the extra kick and they are often very spicy. They are a good multipurpose option. **Aleppo** chilli flakes are a coarsely ground, seedless chilli flake found in a lot of Syrian, Turkish and Middle Eastern cooking. They give a beautiful red colour and a mild heat, which is why I love to use them for garnishing – they are particularly striking scattered over feta, scrambled eggs or a citrus salad. **Korean chilli flakes, or gochugaru,** have also become a staple in my kitchen for their important role in chilli oils. Like Aleppo chilli flakes, they exclude the chilli seeds and give a beautiful red colour to chilli oils without too much heat. They are essential for your kimchi and are the main ingredient in gochujang, the Korean answer to miso. I always combine standard chilli flakes with Aleppo and/or Korean chilli flakes for making chilli oils.

Harissa hails from the Maghreb (more specifically Tunisia), the name deriving from the Arabic "to pound" or "to break apart". This prepared paste of chilli, salt and olive oil may also include garlic, caraway and coriander seeds. In rose harissa, dried and crushed rose petals are added for a wonderful perfume. Happily, harissa is now available in those lovely little aluminium tubes. The quality is surprisingly good and they last a long time in the fridge, so I rarely make my own.

CAPERS AND OLIVES: Capers are the preserved buds from the caper bush. Before the buds turn into flowers, they are preserved in either brine or salt (the latter being my preference). They are piquant, slightly horseradish-y and salty. When dealing with salted capers, most people will tell you it's important to soak the capers in water for 30 minutes to remove some of their saltiness, but I've learned that if you just adjust your seasoning slightly in your dish, you can skip this step and simply give them a good rinse to remove the salt crystals. I find the easiest way to do this is to sit the capers in my hand and run cold water over them, letting the salt crystals wash off and drop down through my fingers.

Olives are a world unto themselves and there is probably an encyclopaedia's worth of things to be said about them. My quick take is that I prefer to use whole olives and pit them myself. They are much better than pitted olives which, to me, should be reserved for nothing more than stuffing. Recipes will specifically call for black and green olives because they are quite different in flavour. The only place I note where they are interchangeable is in Tapenade (see page 34): black for something much punchier and green for something a little more subtle and meaty tasting. Look for varieties like gordal, picholine, Gaeta, green mammoth, Castelvetrano, Lucques, Niçoise or a mix of local table olives.

PARMIGIANO REGGIANO: The most wonderful of cheeses. My favourite. It's the act of fermentation that binds Parmigiano Reggiano to its place of origin, and only raw milk produced in the provinces of Parma, Reggio Emilia, Modena, Bologna to the left of the River Reno, and Mantua to the right of the river Po, is used to produce Parmigiano Reggiano cheese. It's a special milk, characterised by the unique and intense bacterial activity of its indigenous microbial flora, and is influenced by environmental factors, especially the local grass and hay that constitutes the main feed of the cows. I can't imagine my kitchen without it.

Grana Padano is a close relative of Parmigiano Reggiano. Coming from the Po river valley, it is Italy's most produced cheese. Very similar to Parmigiano in style and process, it is more delicate, with less fat due to being made with partially skimmed milk and a shorter maturation time. It is also less expensive. For all intents and purposes, it is interchangeable with Parmigiano – but my preference is still for the king of cheeses.

ANCHOVIES: A really good anchovy is one of the greatest flavours on the planet: briny, meaty, and deliriously happy with a lick of good butter on fresh bread, or straight from the tin or jar. Conversely, a poor-quality or cheap anchovy is horrible, so bad it can put you off anchovies forever. Don't risk it.

Good anchovies are also wonderful cooked, imparting an umami richness that complements tomatoes, garlic, lamb and olive oil so well. The best anchovies come from the Cantabrian Sea, off the north coast of Spain, where they're preserved in salt and either sold whole in salt or rinsed, filleted and preserved in oil. My preference is for those filleted and preserved in oil, not just for flavour but for ease of preparation. Price is often an indicator of quality, or at least of time spent on the part of the artisan perfecting their craft. This doesn't always mean the most expensive is best, but it does most often mean the cheapest is not the best! Spend the money on the good ones or don't use them at all.

White anchovies are the pickled version of the salted "brown" anchovies, their colour relating only to their treatment, not the species. They are quite different and not to be used interchangeably except in their raw form on salads or on crostini.

VINEGAR: The vinegars I keep on hand are: white wine vinegar, red wine vinegar, sherry vinegar, balsamic vinegar, black vinegar, apple cider vinegar and rice wine vinegar. They all bring something different, and I have been known to mix different vinegars to get the right flavour and level of acidity in a dish. Like anchovies, the good vinegars cost more and are worth it.

WINE: When a dish needs a little wine, my first question is always, "What do we have open?" If it's something I'm happy to drink, then I'm happy to cook with it (this works both ways – as it's often only a glass or two in a recipe, it's worth considering whether you will enjoy the rest). That said, if it's a very special wine, I'll think twice about the need for it.

If I'm buying a bottle for the purpose of cooking, I will choose neither the cheapest nor the most expensive, rather something in the lower-mid range. In terms of flavour, whether it's red or white, I'm generally looking for something dry without being overly acidic or oaky – strong flavours that might get in the way of the dish. It's also nice to think about what you're making. If it's something Italian, I like to choose an Italian wine, or a domestic wine made from an Italian grape; with French-leaning dishes, I will consider the same. Often dishes from specific regions will be best with wines from that region – not just for the splash you will add to the meal, but for the glass that will accompany your dinner!

MUSTARD: Dijon, named for the town in northern Burgundy, France, is my favourite mustard. It's made with the addition of local white wine (varying from wine to verjus to vinegar, depending on the producer), which is what gives it its unique flavour. **Wholegrain mustard** is made from whole mustard seeds, instead of finely ground. I love its popping texture and how it looks when it's dressing something. I also think its coarse texture means its flavour is less pervasive. Like anything, there are better-quality mustards out there and often they are not much more expensive.

TOMATOES: My preference is for peeled and whole San Marzano tomatoes. San Marzano is a variety of plum tomato that has a long cylindrical shape. Originally grown between Naples and Salerno, near the Amalfi Coast, the San Marzano tomato is praised for its thick flesh and intense (read: not watery), sweet flavour. Although you can grow this variety of tomato anywhere, the original San Marzano, grown in Valle del Sarno, will include a DOP (Protected Designation of Origin) distinction. Like Parmigiano Reggiano, this means that the product comes from a particular region and meets the highest standards of quality, flavour and texture. After years of overly sour or flavourless tinned tomatoes, I finally realised these were always going to be the best. I also love to buy passata from local small farms when possible. Passata is a purée made from fresh tomatoes, which many tomato farmers will then jar over summer and keep for themselves, while maybe selling a few bottles at farmers' markets (if we're lucky).

SOY SAUCE: One of the oldest and most used (and adored) condiments in the world, at its most basic, soy sauce is made from a fermented paste of cooked soybeans, roasted wheat and a salty brine. Over millennia its culinary influence has spread through Asia, finding gentle adaptation in its travels, from China to Japan to Korea.

For most of my life I only knew about all-purpose soy sauce, mainly via that ubiquitous, red-topped brand. My time in Australia has really opened my eyes (and palate) to the subtleties found in the many varieties we can access. Without delving too deeply into the confusion between dark Japanese soy and dark Chinese soy, light soy that isn't necessarily "light" at all (rather, first pressed), and tamari, a gluten-free option that isn't a soy sauce at all, it's sufficient to say that there is a world of wonder here if you're interested! As a rule of thumb, I use all-purpose (or light) soy sauce in most of my cooking. Dark soy sauce is thicker, deeply coloured and a little sweeter. This is the soy sauce that coats stir-fried noodles with an appealing rich colour and deep flavour. I love the deeply burnished look it gives – it makes a fantastic marinade for pork ribs or chicken wings, or a glaze for lamb. It sticks to whatever you put it on – just be mindful that a little goes a long way.

To make miso eggplant (aubergine):

Heat your oven to 200°C (400°F). Take 3–4 Japanese eggplants and cut them in half lengthways. Score the flesh in a diamond shape, making deep cuts but not piercing the skin. Place the eggplant halves on a baking tray, brush them with toasted sesame oil and flip them over to be cut-side down. Bake for 15–20 minutes, until soft and tender throughout. In a small bowl, combine 3 tablespoons of white miso with 1 tablespoon of white (granulated) sugar, 1 tablespoon of mirin and 1 tablespoon of sake or water. Stir to dissolve and combine well. Remove the tray from the oven. Turn the oven onto grill (broiler) function. Flip the eggplant over and spoon some miso glaze onto each half. Grill, cut-side up, until browned and bubbly – this will only take a couple of minutes. Garnish with sliced spring onion (scallion) and toasted sesame seeds.

MISO: This fermented rice and soybean paste, introduced to Japan from China some 1,300 years ago, adds a deep, baseline saltiness and umami to dishes. It's one of those culinary wonders that crosses the sweet-salty divide. I find it works particularly well with sweet things like corn, sweet potato and chocolate. Perhaps it's for this reason that I prefer to keep the more delicate white miso in my fridge. Compared to its red cousin, white miso is fermented for a shorter period, with a greater ratio of rice (less soybeans). Conversely, red miso is deeper, saltier and has a richer flavour, but it would also work for all the recipes in this book.

FISH SAUCE: As counter-intuitive as it may seem, given fish sauce's punchy olfactory notes, I find fish sauce a more amenable ingredient than soy sauce if I feel something needs a little umami kick. I love adding it to hearty pasta sauces like Bolognese (sacrilege aside!) because you wouldn't even know it was there. I try to think of it like colatura, an ancient Italian version of fish sauce, to give myself a free pass. This cheeky addition can replicate the taste of an hour's cook time, or a more reduced sauce – there's a little magic in those bottles.

PLAIN (ALL-PURPOSE) FLOUR, BREAD FLOUR, SEMOLA RIMACINATA AND 00 FLOUR: Plain flour, also known as "all-purpose" or "AP-flour", is the most commonly used flour. It's best for cakes, quick-breads and biscuits, as well as for a frying batter or for dredging. It has a lower protein percentage than other flours, ensuring you will get a delicate and tender crumb when baking with it. The higher protein percentage in **bread flour** allows for better stretch and a chewy texture when baked, making it excellent for breads and pizza dough. You can use plain (all-purpose) flour in place of bread flour and sacrifice a little texture, but you shouldn't swap bread flour for recipes calling for plain (all-purpose) flour. **00 flour**, often labelled as "tipo 00", has been specially milled to the finest degree. Typically, it is also high protein, making it excellent for pasta dough – just how much protein depends on the wheat and the brand. **Semola rimacinata** is a twice-ground, hard durum wheat; it's yellow in colour and contains high amounts of protein. It gives wonderful texture to finished pasta and gnocchi.

DRIED PASTA, RISOTTO AND POLENTA: The shapes I keep on hand are spaghetti, pappardelle, rigatoni and casarecce. But this is one area where you can, and should, use shapes that bring you joy. In most cases, long pastas like linguine, spaghetti and spaghettini are interchangeable, and the same goes for short pastas like rigatoni, penne, fusilli, orecchiette and casarecce. Most suggestions and pairings relate to how the sauce will cling to the given pasta shape. Quality, however, cannot be overstated here. Different producers use different machinery and flours: these nuances contribute to a pasta with better "al dente" chew (in contrast to something mass-produced using cheaper flours, which will be flabbier). Buy the better pasta if you can. Same goes for **polenta** and **risotto rice**. Skip instant polenta, which is never the right consistency when cooked, and look for a coarse-ground cornmeal. A quality risotto rice is also a game changer; the best ones are worth a trip to a specialty shop because, like pasta, a good risotto rice keeps its chew when cooked for longer.

Kitchenalia

These are your kitchen tools, and my most-loved kitchenalia:

- Small chopping board for fruit only (garlic and fruit do not mix – it's amazing how wooden boards hold onto flavours)
- Large chopping board
- Chef's knife
- Paring knife
- Serrated bread knife
- Microplane
- Box grater
- Vegetable peeler (a cheap little metal number)
- Mortar and pestle
- Measuring spoons
- Measuring jug
- Assorted mixing bowls

- Assorted wooden spoons (you can never have too many!)
- Whisk
- Rolling pin
- Tongs
- Rubber spatula
- Fish spatula (or palette knife)
- Fine mesh sieve
- Colander
- Salad spinner
- Small non-stick frying pan for cooking eggs
- Sauté pan (large and small)
- Small saucepan (about 1.5 litres/52 fl oz)

- Medium saucepan (about 3 litres/100 fl oz)
- Stock pot (about 6 litres/ 200 fl oz)
- Large enamel-lined Dutch oven or heavy-based pot with lid
- Cast-iron frying pan (skillet)
- Baking tray (baking sheet)
- Baking pan
- Cooling rack
- Baking paper
- Aluminium foil

The tools and equipment I don't assume that you have, but may have called for in recipes (if any of these items appear in a recipe, they will be listed in "kitchenalia"):

- Blender
- Stick blender
- Food processor
- Stand mixer (electric mixer) with dough hook, paddle and whisk attachments
- Potato ricer
- Butcher's string
- Toothpicks or skewers
- Outdoor grill or indoor grill pan
- Wok
- Deep-fry thermometer

- Internal meat thermometer
- Bench scraper
- Pasta machine
- Pastry brush
- Offset spatula
- Round pizza baking tray
- Cake tins of various sizes
- Bundt (ring) tin
- Fluted tart tin with removable base
- Loaf tin
- Trifle bowl

A note on ovens:
All oven temperatures listed are fan-forced unless otherwise stated. If you require the conventional oven temperature, increase the given temperature by 15–20°C (25–35°F) degrees, according to the manufacturer's instructions.

A note on eggs:
All recipes have been tested and developed using large, 600 g (1 lb 5 oz) per dozen eggs unless otherwise specified.

Aperitivo

"… something *raw*, something *salt*, something *dry* or *meaty*, something *gentle* and *smooth* and possibly something in the way of fresh fish."

Elizabeth David, *French Provincial Cooking*

Each year, towards the end of our summer holidays, my family would gather at a basic little motel in Naples (Florida, not Italy) called The Tides. Days were sunburnt and salty, filled with swimming, shuffleboard and shell-hunting on beach walks. It was the place I saw my parents truly exhale.

Every afternoon, around 5pm, we would retreat from the beach. My grandfather would pour the adults two fingers worth of Scotch over ice and add a splash of water. Mom would prepare a little platter of snacks – in her words "saladitos"– roasted peanuts, pimento-stuffed olives and a tin of sardines with saltine crackers.

At some point, with alarming regularity, Mom would reach over and offer me a bite of her sardine, just one, to see if I'd come around. I was years away from becoming a chef, and I was also years away from liking tinned fish. Back then, you couldn't have paid me in hours at the beach just to try one.

Food-entangled memories are so deliciously potent. Sardines, which I never liked, and hadn't even tasted back then, still remind me of that beautiful time. Whenever I make My sardine pasta (see page 122), or simply open a tin of sardines, I think of my family and those utopian days. More and more, I gravitate towards food that makes me feel something. If I'm going to cook, I want it to be great. I want it to feel good.

In Europe, it seems that not just every country, but every region, almost every town, has its own traditions of the apéritif – at their heart a salted, cured or tinned wonder that works with their local tipple. While you can still find these precise (and entirely romantic) odes to the *comarca*, or *terroir*, there is also great liberty in breaking free of these shackles! In the following pages you will find Gildas and marinated mussels from Spain, gougères, radishes, rillettes, tapenade and pissaladière inspired by France, Italy's burrata and a smoky eggplant (aubergine) with harissa from the Levant. When considering a combination, think of contrast – texture, taste, time and colour.

A wonderful accompaniment to your aperitivo can be as simple as some saucisson or thinly sliced prosciutto, a nice cheese and a good baguette. Serve these with some fresh crunchy radishes and salted room-temperature butter, the crunchy piquant nature of the radish contrasted by the salty, sweet and creamy butter, and you have a little feast!

Olives are another great and simple treat when entertaining guests at home. The little bit of extra effort it takes to marinate your own olives is a gesture to show you care (without really doing too much!). A little plate of something made ahead, like olives, and a batched cocktail or mocktail, relieves some of the pressure from you having to cook in front of people, meaning you can get straight to the point of enjoying each other's company. Add in any of the recipes that follow, and you are putting just a little bit more of yourself into the preparation. That care and attention is what sharing food is all about.

And, as much as I love a big feast and cooking everything from scratch, this is a great way of sidestepping the exhaustion of cooking, while spending far less money and still enjoying the wonder of feeding friends and family. Depending on the collective energy, your aperitivo might turn into a party, or you could be in bed by 9pm. I welcome either option.

My favourite apéro snack is so simple it doesn't even warrant a recipe: fresh bread, slathered with room-temperature butter and a fillet of really good-quality, oil-packed anchovy. The ultimate celebration of our little fishy friend (although the anchovy sneaks its way into a lot more in my kitchen).

To dress up a bowl of olives:
Choose olives with pits still in them. Heat a saucepan with a generous amount of olive oil. Use a vegetable peeler to scrape two strips of zest from a lemon or orange, or both, and add them to the olive oil. Add a crushed garlic clove, with an optional pinch of chilli flakes. Add the leaves from a branch of rosemary or thyme. Let that sizzle for a few seconds to infuse the oil, then toss in your olives. Put a lid on the pan and shake it every now and then to warm the olives through. Serve the olives warm or at room temperature, alongside a little dish for the pits.

My Gilda

Makes: 8 skewers
Active time: 5 minutes

Kitchenalia: 8 toothpicks
   or skewers

16 pieces Quick pickled celery
   (see below)
8 pickled guindilla chillies
4 large green olives (e.g.
   gordal), pitted and halved
8 good-quality anchovy fillets
2 thin slices of lemon, each
   cut into 4 wedges

This perfect aperitivo bite was named for Rita Hayworth's signature role in the classic film noir *Gilda*. A case of culinary synaesthesia, this small bite incorporates a smoky anchovy (she was nothing if not sultry), salty olive (for her wit) and spicy guindilla chilli (for that intriguing addiction to the small burn). These three ingredients are all found in their finest form on the Basque Coast, where this tapa originated. I have added a little pickled celery because I think a little acid never goes astray.

Onto each toothpick, thread a slice of celery, one chilli, half an olive, an anchovy (folded into a little zigzag snake) and a wedge of lemon, finishing with another piece of pickled celery.

Serve at room temperature. This can be made ahead and kept refrigerated – just remember to remove from the fridge 20 minutes before your guests arrive.

Makes: 1 jar
Active time: 10 minutes
Inactive time: 1 hour

Kitchenalia: Glass jar

4 celery stalks, sliced
   on the bias (around 3 mm/
   ⅛ inch thick)
1 garlic clove, split in half
1 bay leaf
1 teaspoon black peppercorns
1 teaspoon fine sea salt
2 teaspoons white
   (granulated) sugar
½ cup (125 ml) white wine
   vinegar (no need for your
   fanciest here!)
½ cup (125 ml) water
2 tablespoons extra-virgin
   olive oil

Quick pickled celery

Pickled celery is fabulous in the Radicchio chopped salad with chickpeas and Italian dressing (see page 82) and the Tarragon and celery chicken sandwich (see page 110); in fact, it's friends with salads and sandwiches of all kinds! Also, the addition of this little wonder will turn a beef tartare with olive oil and Parmigiano from the simple to the sublime.

Place the celery, garlic, bay leaf and peppercorns into a clean glass jar.

Combine the salt, sugar, vinegar and water in a small pot and bring to a boil. Once boiling, pour it over the celery and leave to cool, uncovered, at room temperature.

Once cool, top with the olive oil, seal the jar and refrigerate. The pickle will last in the fridge for several months.

Note: This is a quick pickle that must be kept in the fridge. A clean jar will suffice, no need to boil and sterilise your jar.

Parmesan and thyme biscuits

As perfect with a cocktail as they are for afternoon tea, these little biscuits are incredibly moreish and so easy to bring together.

Combine the butter, thyme and flour in the bowl of your food processor and pulse until the mixture resembles sand.

Add in the parmesan and pulse another three times.

Add in 1 tablespoon cold water and pulse a few more times. Open the food processor and grab a small amount of dough in your hand. If the dough holds together, you've added enough water; if not, add another tablespoon and test again.

Dump the dough out onto a dry, clean bench and bring it together, pressing it into a rough square without kneading. Wrap the dough in baking paper and chill for at least 30 minutes in the fridge (this can all be done a day ahead).

Preheat your oven to 175°C (345°F).

Unwrap your dough and top it with another sheet of baking paper so the dough is sandwiched between two sheets. Using a rolling pin, roll it out to about 3 mm (⅛ inch) thick. Remove the top sheet of baking paper and, with a knife or a pizza wheel, cut the dough into squares of around 3 x 3 cm (1¼ x 1¼ inches), taking care to leave the bottom piece of baking paper intact. Sprinkle the squares with salt and pepper.

Use the paper to lift the dough onto a baking tray. Bake for 15 minutes then flip the biscuits to brown the undersides. Bake for a further 5–10 minutes until golden.

Allow to cool completely on a cooling rack before serving.

Makes: 12 biscuits
Active time: 10–15 minutes
Inactive time: 1 hour

Kitchenalia: Food processor

35 g (1¼ oz) cold unsalted butter
1 teaspoon chopped fresh thyme
50 g (⅓ cup) plain (all-purpose) flour
50 g (½ cup) freshly grated Parmigiano Reggiano or Grana Padano
1–2 tablespoons cold water
Flaked sea salt
Freshly cracked black pepper

As with Parmigiano Reggiano, Grana Padano is produced in a specified region, however its borders are widened to incorporate the Po River Valley. It's estimated that 24 per cent of Italy's milk production is used to make Grana Padano. While there are a number of differences between the two cheeses – Grana Padano's lower fat content and shorter maturation generally results in a milder, less nuanced cheese – both cheeses will eventually form those fabulous little crystalline deposits. These are not (as commonly thought) salt deposits, but rather an amino acid that when metabolised by the body, produces certain chemicals, including dopamine – these cheeses are scientifically proven to make you happy! I always use Parmigiano Reggiano for grating over pasta, however, Grana Padano is more economical and, generally, a pretty great option for baking.

Crisp, bubbly fried crackers
with herbed chèvre and salumi

Makes: Enough to serve 6,
 or 30+ crackers
Active time: 45 minutes
Inactive time: 1 hour

Kitchenalia: Deep-fry
 thermometer (or follow
 the visual cue in the recipe),
 pasta machine (optional),
 fluted pasta wheel
 (alternatively, use a knife)

Crackers
150 g (1 cup) plain (all-purpose)
 flour, plus extra for dusting
½ teaspoon fine sea salt
½ teaspoon white
 (granulated) sugar
60 ml (¼ cup) warm water
1 tablespoon extra-virgin
 olive oil
500 ml (2 cups) neutral oil,
 for deep-frying

Herbed chèvre
2 tablespoons chopped chives
2 tablespoons chopped
 flat-leaf parsley
1 tablespoon chopped dill
1 teaspoon dried or fresh
 chopped thyme
150 g (5½ oz) log fresh chèvre
2 tablespoons extra-virgin olive
 oil, plus extra for drizzling
Freshly cracked black pepper

To serve
Slices of prosciutto, mortadella
 or any good, freshly sliced
 salumi you can find

These fried, unsweetened crackers are the ideal accompaniment to fresh cheese, salumi and charcuterie. Not only do they taste great, but they look fantastic. They are similar to the gnocco fritto of Emilia-Romagna, however this dough is unleavened, so the result is not as puffy but rather flatter and more bubbly and crisp. This is an incredibly versatile recipe, and one I cherish.

Place the flour, mixed with the salt and sugar, in a medium-sized mixing bowl and add in the water and olive oil. Mix until you have a sticky dough and tip out onto a lightly dusted bench. Knead until the dough is uniform, about 5–7 minutes. Put this back into the mixing bowl and cover with a damp tea towel. Allow to rest at room temperature for 1 hour.

Place the dough on a lightly dusted bench. Using a rolling pin, roll out to a thinness of about 2–3 sheets of paper thick. Alternatively, a pasta machine makes quick work of this. Cut into 3 x 10 cm (1¼ x 4 inch) rectangles using either a fluted pasta wheel or a knife. Use a fork to poke holes into each cracker (this will prevent the dough from puffing up too much).

To make your herbed chèvre, sprinkle the chopped herbs onto a sheet of baking paper and give them a good mix. Roll the log of cheese over the herbs. Drizzle with the olive oil and sprinkle with pepper.

Heat your neutral frying oil to 180°C (350°F). Ideally, use a deep-fry thermometer here. Alternatively, place the handle of a wooden spoon into the oil and if bubbles appear immediately, it's ready; if not, continue to heat the oil until they do. Add a few pieces of dough at a time and fry until bubbly and golden on both sides, about 2–3 minutes per side. Allow to drain on a cooling rack. Proceed with the remaining pieces. The crackers can be fried and kept in a warm and dry place for several hours before serving.

Serve the crackers with the herbed chèvre and slices of salumi.

Notes: The beauty of this dough is how versatile it is: make it into savoury lavosh by cutting it into sheets and baking it at 175°C (345°F) for 10–12 minutes; alternatively, for something sweet, toss the crackers (after frying) into icing sugar for a sweet fritter to serve with ice cream.

Try to find salumi that you can get a butcher or deli to slice for you. The pre-sliced stuff in packages is convenient, but it's not great. Not only does the flavour take a hit, but I find it's rarely as thin as I would like it. I am always so sad when all that work maturing cured meat is ruined by chewy, rubbery slices – the ultimate culinary crime. There's a reason the good salumerie in Italy only slice to order.

Sweet, salty and spicy nuts

Makes: 2 cups (280 g)
Active time: 5 minutes
Inactive time: 25 minutes

3 tablespoons water
¼ cup (55 g) white
   (granulated) sugar
2 tablespoons extra-virgin
   olive oil
2 cups (280 g) mix of your
   favourite raw nuts (almonds,
   cashews, pecans, walnuts,
   peanuts, hazelnuts)
½ teaspoon fine sea salt
¼ teaspoon freshly cracked
   black pepper
1 teaspoon Spanish smoked
   paprika (pimentón de La Vera)
¼ teaspoon cayenne pepper
   (or a pinch)
Flaked sea salt, for finishing

Note: These nuts can be stored in an airtight container in your pantry for a few days before needing a freshen up. Re-toast them by placing them on a tray in a 165°C (320°F) oven for 5 minutes.

Is there a more perfect bar snack than a bowl of nuts? The days of communal bowls on bar tops and pub tables may be gone, and so it's up to you to preserve their love affair with a beer at home. Every time I serve these to friends and family, they always want to know how I made them. So here is the recipe, for everyone.

Preheat your oven to 165°C (320°F).

In a small saucepan, combine the water, sugar and olive oil. Bring to a boil and cook until the sugar is dissolved.

In a mixing bowl, combine the nuts with the sugar-water. Toss together with the fine sea salt and pepper and spread out on a baking tray.

Bake for 20–25 minutes, stirring halfway through, until the nuts are toasted and fragrant.

Remove the nuts from the oven, place them back in the mixing bowl and toss with the paprika and cayenne pepper, then allow to cool. Taste for seasoning, adjusting with the flaked sea salt.

Back when stories and ideas travelled with bolts of silk and sacks of nutmeg, cinnamon and cloves, it was the peppercorn that reigned supreme. When Christopher Columbus returned from the Americas and presented the spicy, piquant chilli "pepper" to the Spanish royal court, they believed they had finally found a competitor. The peppers were entrusted to a monastery in Extremadura and, to this day, pimentón de la Vera can only be grown and produced in this region. The red peppers are harvested by hand and slowly dried, using green oak to smoke them dry. Finally, they are crushed by stone mills – a process that has barely changed over the centuries. While the pimentón de la Vera is considered one of the best spices in the world, just like the peppercorn before it, pimentón (paprika) travelled with the people. Its smoky, spicy hues are particularly celebrated in Portuguese, Hungarian and Serbian cooking.

Tapenade

Makes: 1 cup, enough to serve
    8–10 for aperitivo snacks
Active time: 10 minutes

Kitchenalia: Food processor

Heaped 1 cup (200 g) black
    olives (see note), pits
    removed (alternatively,
    1¼ cups/150 g pitted
    black olives)
2 tablespoons salted capers,
    rinsed
8 good-quality anchovy fillets
    (optional)
2 garlic cloves, grated on
    a microplane
½ cup (125 ml) good-quality
    extra-virgin olive oil
1 tablespoon lemon zest
1 tablespoon lemon juice
1 teaspoon fresh thyme leaves
2 tablespoons flat-leaf parsley
    leaves

To serve
Grilled or toasted croutons
    (see opposite page)
Stracciatella cheese

This tapenade is great friends with grilled bread or toasted crostini, but equally enjoys the company of grilled fish or lamb. It's highly flavourful and highly seasoned, so no need to add salt.

Combine the olives, capers, anchovies (if using) and garlic in the bowl of a food processor and pulse until everything is chopped finely. Add in the remaining ingredients and pulse a few more times until it comes together to form a chunky paste.

Serve with grilled or toasted croutons and stracciatella cheese.

Note: If it's an option, try to make this with Niçoise (Nice being a neighbour to Marseille – the birthplace of tapenade) or Gaeta olives. Of course, good-quality Kalamata olives will also work. For a milder tapenade, to serve with fish for example, I use green olives like Castelvetrano, picholine or gordal.

Smoked trout rillettes

The key to this recipe is the hot-smoked trout. While most rillettes are made using meat confit (slowly cooked in its own fat), here we rely on the combination of fatty trout and its long, hot smoking to provide a similar malleable texture. Cold-smoked fish is essentially cured (think smoked salmon), meaning it retains a firm, somewhat bouncy texture that won't flake apart, nor play nice with the other ingredients. Serve this with croutons or lavosh, on lettuce cups or even with fresh radishes to dip into the rillettes.

Preheat your oven to 175°C (345°F).

For the croutons, drizzle a large baking tray with half the olive oil. Slice your baguette into thin slices, about 5 mm (¼ inch) thick, and lay them on the tray in a single layer (you may need two trays). Drizzle the baguette slices with the remaining olive oil and bake for 6–10 minutes, or until they are golden and crunchy, but not completely crisp (rotate the trays halfway through baking if using two trays). Once cool, these croutons will keep in an airtight container for up to 3 days.

To make the rillettes, combine all the remaining ingredients, except for the salt and pepper, in a bowl and stir to combine. Taste and season with salt and pepper.

Spoon the rillettes into a nice dish, garnish with the extra chives and finish with a crack of pepper. Serve with the croutons and cornichons.

Makes: 1½ cups, enough to serve 6–8 for aperitivo snacks
Active time: 20 minutes
Inactive time: 10 minutes

2 tablespoons extra-virgin olive oil
1 baguette
250 g (9 oz) hot-smoked trout
2 tablespoons chopped dill
1 tablespoon chopped chives, plus extra to garnish
½ teaspoon lemon zest
1 teaspoon lemon juice
150 g (5½ oz) crème fraîche
Fine sea salt
Freshly cracked black pepper

To serve
½ cup (60 g) cornichons (about 12 cornichons) or other pickles

When considering food to accompany your aperitivo, it's important to think not just of taste but of texture. Rillettes – whether pork, duck, rabbit or fish – are a great way to bring softness and a little subtlety to your collection of culinary wonders. As they are traditionally slow-cooked in their own fat (confit), they also tend to bring a gentle flavour, and work well to balance the spike of vinegar that will come from your cornichons or other pickles.

Comté gougères

Makes: 6 large gougères
Active time: 30 minutes
Inactive time: 50 minutes

Kitchenalia: Stand mixer fitted
   with the paddle attachment,
   pastry brush

180 ml (¾ cup) whole milk
60 g (2¼ oz) unsalted butter
110 g (¾ cup) plain
   (all-purpose) flour
3 eggs, plus 1 extra for
   egg wash
½ teaspoon fine sea salt
150 g (5½ oz) Comté
   finely grated
Extra-virgin olive oil,
   for greasing
1 teaspoon water
Freshly cracked black pepper

Note: I have used milk instead of
water as it gives a wonderful colour
to the baked puffs. As with all simple
things, the smallest tweaks can make
a big difference! You can freeze the
dough after you've scooped it onto
the baking tray, egg washed and
topped with cheese, and bake from
frozen when ready – just extend the
bake time at the higher temperature
by 5–7 minutes. This recipe can
happily be doubled for that purpose.

These are the gougères of my dreams: crisp, crunchy cheese on the outside
and custardy on the inside. The benefit of making these at home is that you
can time them perfectly, serving them straight out of the oven. It's the best
way. It's the only way.

Combine the milk and butter in a small saucepan and place over a low heat.
Once the butter has melted, add in the flour. Use a whisk to stir, switching
to a wooden spoon when the mixture becomes thick. Stir the dough until
you can see that a film has stuck to the bottom of the pan. Immediately
transfer the dough to the bowl of a stand mixer fitted with a paddle
attachment.

Preheat your oven to 230°C (450°F) and line a baking tray with
baking paper.

Turn the mixer on to a medium–high speed and let it run for about
a minute to cool the dough down slightly. Add the eggs, one at a time,
waiting for each egg to be completely incorporated before you add
the next.

Add the salt and half of the grated cheese and mix on a medium speed
until well combined, about 30 seconds.

Grease a ¼ cup measuring cup with a little olive oil and use it to scoop
the dough into balls, completely filling the cup. Flip the gougère out onto
the baking tray. Repeat with the remainder of the dough, being sure to
leave a 5 cm (2 inch) space between the gougères to allow for the dough
to expand as it bakes.

Mix the remaining egg with 1 teaspoon water and beat well with a fork.
Use a pastry brush to brush the tops of the gougères with the egg wash
and sprinkle them with the remaining cheese. It will look like a lot, and
some will fall onto the tray, but that's okay. Crack black pepper over the
top of each gougère and place the tray in the oven.

Bake for 10–15 minutes, until the dough puffs and turns lightly golden, then
reduce the heat to 150°C (300°F) and bake for a further 30–35 minutes,
until the gougères are nicely golden and crisp all over.

Remove the tray from the oven and serve the gougères warm.

The gougère is an ode to the Alpine regions where France meets Switzerland,
a taste of the verdant highlands that's traditionally made with either Swiss Gruyère
or French Comté. As with most European cheeses, the names and provenance are
carefully controlled, while the reality is that for centuries the Swiss and French
farmers who were making these cheeses were closer to each other than they were
to those with whom they shared a flag. These long-matured cheeses could be stored
until there was an opportunity to take them to market, while the farmers themselves
were more likely to live on fresh cheeses made with the leftover whey. A gougère is
the way to make those windswept mountains and valleys travel to your home, their
light airiness only adding to the whimsy.

Fried zucchini blossom fritters

These feel like an Italian summer, which is always welcome.

Add your frying oil to a heavy-based saucepan and place over a medium–high heat. Heat to 190°C (375°F). Ideally, use a deep-fry thermometer here. Alternatively, place the handle of a wooden spoon into the oil and if small bubbles appear immediately, the oil is ready; if not, continue to heat the oil until they do.

Cut each zucchini flower in half through the stem and the flower, and gently pull off and discard the stamen.

In a small mixing bowl, combine the flours, bicarbonate of soda and salt. Stir in the olive oil and sparkling water, followed by the garlic and thyme. The consistency should be like that of single (pure) cream (it's okay if there are some lumps). Prepare this batter *just* before frying – it should not be done ahead.

Take a flower, dip it into the batter and use your fingers to open up the flower to make sure it's completely coated inside before dipping it into the batter again. Let it drain over the bowl for a couple of seconds so it's not heavily coated, then (carefully!) drop it straight into the hot oil. Only do as many as you and your pan can manage at a time without overcrowding. Flip the flower over to crisp up the other side. Once crisp and golden all over, lift the flower out of the oil and place it directly onto a cooling rack set over a tray. Sprinkle the flowers with salt immediately after they come out of the oil to ensure the salt sticks.

Fry the remaining flowers, then serve with wedges of lemon.

Notes: Rice flour absorbs less moisture than wheat flour, resulting in something more crisp and less greasy. Meanwhile, the gluten in wheat flour helps the batter cling. Always scoop just-fried items directly onto cooling racks instead of paper-towel-lined plates. It allows the moisture to evaporate, rather than steam your fresh and crisp fried item, making it soggy.

Across the Mediterranean, it's the male flower you will find in the markets, still attached to the stalk, as opposed to the female flower attached to the young fruit, which is considered a waste of the zucchini. In Australia, you can track down zucchini flowers at local farmers' markets in season, and at selected grocers. If you can only find female flowers (pictured) attached to baby zucchini, simply slice the flower and fruit in half as you would the male flower, and proceed with the recipe.

Makes: 24 fritters
Active time: 30 minutes
Inactive time: 10 minutes

Kitchenalia: Deep-fry thermometer (or follow the visual cue in the recipe)

300 ml (10½ fl oz) light extra-virgin olive oil for frying, or a neutral oil
12 zucchini (courgette) flowers (see notes)
¼ cup (35 g) plain (all-purpose) flour
2 tablespoons (30 g) rice flour
A pinch of bicarbonate of soda (baking soda)
½ teaspoon fine sea salt, plus extra for finishing
1 teaspoon extra-virgin olive oil
100–120 ml (3½–4 fl oz) cold sparkling water
1 garlic clove, grated on a microplane
1 tablespoon chopped thyme leaves
Half a lemon, cut into wedges

Shallow or deep-frying was quite common in our house, as it is in most Cuban households. I remember the greasy tin under the cupboard that housed the oil for frying. Frugality meant that it was strained and reused several times before being discarded. Through spending time in other people's homes, I've recognised similar greasy tins under cupboards around the world, from Italy to Mexico to Japan. I try to use as little oil as possible and always strain it and reuse it again. Frying isn't for everyday, but every now and then it's wonderfully uplifting!

Burrata with better tomatoes

Makes: 1 cup roasted tomato
   halves, enough to serve
   4–6
Active time: 5 minutes
Inactive time: 3 hours

500 g (1 lb 2 oz) tomatoes
   (see note), split in half
½ teaspoon fine sea salt
½ teaspoon white
   (granulated) sugar
Freshly cracked black pepper
1½ tablespoons extra-virgin
   olive oil
1 tablespoon thyme leaves (or
   leaves from a few sprigs)
1 × 100 g (3½ oz) ball fresh
   burrata

To finish
Good-quality extra-virgin
   olive oil
Basil leaves, to garnish
   (optional)

Note: Any large variety of tomato, such as Roma or large heirlooms (not cherry tomatoes), will work well here. Heirloom varieties will take longer to cook than Romas as they contain more water, so if using those, add an extra hour onto the cooking time (4 hours in total).

Serving suggestion: Serve this dish with Yoghurt flatbreads (see page 45) to mop up the olive-oil-spiked creaminess from the burrata.

I think we all know that gorgeous, juicy tomatoes at their peak are unbeatable with a drizzle of olive oil and a pinch of flaked sea salt. But for all the other times, when the tomatoes are lacking, you're going to need to give them a hand. This is a recipe for those tomatoes.

Preheat your oven to 120°C (235°F).

Place your tomatoes on a baking tray, cut-side up. Sprinkle them with the salt, sugar, a good crack of pepper, olive oil and thyme.

Slowly soften the tomatoes in the oven for 2½–3 hours, until they are juicy, concentrated and beginning to brown at the edges. Remove and allow to cool.

Serve the cooled tomatoes with the burrata and a drizzle of good-quality olive oil. A garnish of fresh basil leaves is a nice touch to finish, if you have them on hand.

Burrata is a variation on mozzarella, most often made with cow's milk. It was born of a desire to manage the wasteful scraps of torn "rags" of mozzarella, known as stracciatella. The stracciatella is combined with cream before being committed to a little pouch of mozzarella that is then knotted shut to form the burrata. Not to be confused with standard mozzarella, which is all cheese and no cream; mozzarella may weep a little when split in two, but will not pour forth its contents like burrata.

Pickled mussels on buttered bread

Buttered bread with something salty and pickled on top is a love affair for the ages. This pickle is particularly good for mussels, as they remain so tender.

Rinse your mussels under cold running water and set aside.

Heat a pot (with a tight-fitting lid) over a high heat. Add the mussels and cover with the lid, giving them a shake every now and then, allowing them to steam open in their own liquid for about 3–4 minutes. Have a look inside the pot: if they are all open, then turn off the heat; otherwise cook for another 1–2 minutes. Once most mussels are open, turn off the heat, remove the lid and leave to cool. Discard any mussels that didn't open.

Once cool enough to handle, pick the mussels out of the shells and remove and discard any straggling beards that might still be attached by gently pulling them off (see note). Set the mussels aside in a heatproof dish.

For the pickle, heat a small (non-reactive) pot over a high heat and add the 2 tablespoons of olive oil. Sizzle the garlic and chilli together until the garlic is beginning to brown. Add in the remaining pickle ingredients, except for the extra olive oil, and bring to a boil. Boil for at least a minute to dissolve the sugar and salt and allow the flavours to meld.

Pour the hot liquid over the mussels and leave to cool.

Once cool, pour the remaining olive oil over the mussels. If you are making these in advance, you can store them in an airtight container in the fridge. They will keep for about a week.

Serve the pickled mussels with slices of fresh bread and soft butter so that everyone can create their own little tartines.

Note: The "beard" is made up of the elastic strands that the mussel produces to attach itself to rocks (and now, the long pieces of rope that mussel farmers hang in the ocean). I find the beard easier to remove after cooking, which is no problem when pickling as the mussels don't have to be served hot. If preparing mussels for a hot dish, remove any beards when washing the mussels before cooking.

Makes: 2 cups, enough to serve
  6–8 for aperitivo snacks
Active time: 25 minutes
Inactive time: 1 hour

Kitchenalia: Mandoline
  (alternatively, a very sharp
  knife to thinly slice)

1 kg (2 lb 4 oz) blue mussels

Pickle
2 tablespoons extra-virgin
  olive oil, plus an extra ½ cup
  (125 ml)
8 garlic cloves, thinly sliced
  on a mandoline
  (or with a very sharp knife)
1 long green chilli,
  thinly sliced
2 bay leaves
½ cup (125 ml) rice wine vinegar
½ cup (125 ml) water
1 teaspoon black peppercorns
1 teaspoon fennel seeds
2 strips lemon zest (peeled
  using a vegetable peeler)
1 tablespoon smoked paprika
1½ tablespoons white
  (granulated) sugar
2 teaspoons fine sea salt

To serve
Unsalted butter, at room
  temperature
Good crusty sourdough
  or rye bread

The humble blue mussel has been feeding Australians for tens of thousands of years. Bizarrely maligned in the home kitchen, this wonderful bivalve is delicious, affordable and sustainable. Farmed mussels are suspended on longlines, where they get to work filtering the water around them. This also means that the harvested mussels no longer need to be purged of grit or sand – the only thing they'll give up to the pot is a tasty broth. You can buy them cleaned, largely debearded (although do check as there's always a couple of rogue stragglers) and pot-ready. As wonderful in a pickle as they are plucked warm from a shared pot in the middle of the table (and in both cases, fabulous with some buttered bread). Move over prawns …

Smoky eggplant with garlic, harissa, mint and feta, with yoghurt flatbreads

Makes: Enough to serve 6
Active time: 25 minutes
Inactive time: 30 minutes

Kitchenalia: Outdoor grill or
    indoor grill pan (optional)

2 large purple eggplants
    (aubergines)
⅓ cup (80 ml) extra-virgin
    olive oil
3 garlic cloves, minced
2 teaspoons harissa paste
1 tablespoon lemon juice
70 g (2½ oz) Greek or
    Bulgarian-style feta
¼ cup (5 g) mint leaves
    (preferably round mint)

To serve
Yoghurt flatbreads (see
    opposite)

Taking its cue from the region where the Mediterranean meets the Middle East, this simple summer snack is particularly good for those days when it's almost too hot to cook. It's a happy coincidence that a chilled glass of rosé is the perfect companion for this dish.

The accompanying flatbreads are one of the few "breads" that I believe are worth nailing at home. The absolute delight of warm, freshly baked bread, with none of the hassle. A home cooking gem.

Poke a few holes into each eggplant, using a paring knife, to allow steam to escape as they cook. Burn the eggplants until completely charred and soft all the way through – you can do this over an open gas flame, an outdoor grill, or on a grill pan over a high heat on your stove top. Once completely soft, place the eggplants in a bowl and cover tightly with aluminium foil to finish steaming as they cool.

In a small saucepan, heat the olive oil over a medium heat. Once hot, add the garlic and harissa. Allow to sizzle for a minute, then remove the saucepan from the heat and set aside.

Remove the charred skin of the eggplants, leaving the top stem attached (for presentation). Place the eggplants on a serving platter and slice them into chunks.

Spoon the garlic and harissa oil over the eggplants and add a squeeze of lemon juice. Crumble the feta over the top and sprinkle with the mint leaves. Serve with warm yoghurt flatbreads.

Yoghurt flatbreads

A flatbread that doesn't require yeast or long rising times. From start to finish, it takes about 45 minutes, with no baking skills required.

In a medium mixing bowl, combine the flour, yoghurt, baking powder and salt. Mix until a dough starts to form. Remove the dough from the bowl and knead on a flour-dusted bench for about 2 minutes. Add enough flour so the dough does not completely stick to your hands, but don't overdo it or your flatbreads will be dry.

Divide the dough into 6 pieces and shape each piece into a ball. Coat each ball with a small amount of olive oil and place them on an oiled plate. Cover with a tea towel and rest for about 30 minutes.

Take the balls of dough, one at a time, and use the palm of your hand to press them onto your bench to form flat discs or ovals, about 2–3 mm (¹⁄₁₆–⅛ inch) thick. Heat a medium-sized cast-iron or non-stick frying pan over a medium–high heat. (Alternatively, these are excellent cooked on an outdoor grill.) Brush the dough with olive oil and fry each flatbread in the pan (or on a grill) for about 2 minutes per side, until golden and bubbly. Set the cooked flatbreads aside, covered with a tea towel to keep warm while you repeat with the remaining dough.

For the optional garnish, melt the butter in a small saucepan, add the garlic and sizzle until fragrant. Remove from the heat and add the parsley. Brush this onto the cooked, warm flatbreads.

Serving suggestions: These flatbreads are excellent piled high with raw vegetables and a little hummus for a simple lunch, or are a perfect accompaniment to a bowl of soup. Try them with the Pumpkin, curry leaf and coconut soup (see page 64) or with the Chicken thighs with spiced ghee and yoghurt (see page 180).

Makes: 6 flatbreads
Active time: 15 minutes
Inactive time: 30 minutes

Kitchenalia: Pastry brush

1⅓ cups (200 g) plain (all-purpose) flour, plus extra for dusting
Scant 1 cup (220 g) Greek-style plain yoghurt
2 teaspoons baking powder
½ teaspoon fine sea salt
Scant 1 teaspoon extra-virgin olive oil, plus extra for brushing

Optional garnish
2 tablespoons unsalted butter
1 garlic clove, minced
1 tablespoon chopped flat-leaf parsley

Smoky eggplant with garlic, harissa, mint and feta, with yoghurt flatbreads

Some like it *hot*

"...they alter *slightly* each time they're prepared, by virtue of the *season, whim* and the *character* of one's very own hand."

Sean Moran, *Let it Simmer*

Thousands of precise directives and then three little words. Without being dramatic, your whole dish hangs in the hands of these three words – *season to taste* – so important and yet so vague; an instruction as simple as it is complex. So, let's start at the beginning. Season with what, and to whose taste?

Salt is the silent workhorse in every kitchen. While its skills of amplification are unsurpassed, beyond its inherent saltiness it essentially has no flavour, it just helps others. Your job is to use that salt to enhance the flavours of each ingredient to create a harmonious whole. The tastebuds, then, are yours – of course it needs to work for everyone else at the table, but as the cook, you're the yardstick. That's not meant to apply pressure, but simply to say, you need to taste.

When I'm cooking, I like to add salt all the way along, at multiple times throughout the preparation. With a pumpkin soup, it will be a pinch of salt with the onions before I leave them to cook quietly, then the pumpkin gets a pinch, and when I add the water or stock a little while later, another pinch. Sometimes it's heavy pinches, sometimes they're scant, but the cumulative effect is balanced, never salty. Perhaps, like seasoning the pasta water, that salt sneaks its way right into the heart of that pumpkin and those onions, creating a subtle, well-seasoned whole? Whatever its alchemy, it's fundamental.

Conversely, large roasts like chicken, pork shoulder, lamb leg or a standing rib of beef get seasoned 24 hours in advance to give the salt time to permeate and season through the meat. They often spend their last night in the fridge, naked, save for this good sprinkle of salt (both the dry fridge air and the salt help to dry out the skin, creating a delicious crackling). Salads and fish, the more demure and delicate of the bunch, get seasoned too, but only just before serving.

The recipes in this book will direct when and where to add salt but if you consider that each ingredient needs a little seasoning, you won't go wrong. Don't forget that our salty friends can also fill in for a pinch here and there – keep an eye on the capers, olives, parmesan and anchovies, among other saline buddies. As a rule of thumb, a pinch is a three-finger pinch between your thumb, index finger and middle finger, and is about a quarter teaspoon (but this can vary greatly between fine and coarse salt).

I find that good home cooks generally know how to taste. They have learnt the only way there is – by trial and error. My mother is incredible at this. She always seasons right to the edge; a few extra grains would make something salty, but she's always just below that, teetering on the precipice.

It is perhaps true that we recipe writers could do more, that we could give you grams or teaspoon measurements of salt, but I really can't come at it. This is not me holding out on you, rather that I know the experience of cooking would be ruined. The tediousness would rob you of the feeling of salt between your fingers and connection to your food, which is so important. Without decisions to make, you might even forget to taste along the way – this would be the real sin. The spell that makes cooking such a pleasure, the real crux of all that we do in the kitchen, is taste. I can't do that for you.

When you're at home, alone or with family, and you're sitting down to eat the meal you've created, take the time to stop and taste again. This is when you can analyse how it all played out: when you can taste all the imperceptible details you don't notice when you're standing over something, trying a tiny spoonful here, or a leaf there, to check for seasoning. How something tastes, bite after bite, changes. What may have tasted under-seasoned in one bite, after a few bites is perfect, or vice versa. There is no shame here – I find those "aha" moments particularly transformative as a cook. You are free to make little corrections and record to memory what you'll do differently next time. This is how the home cook and the professional chef alike practise and learn to taste. This is part of the wonder of it all! Don't stress, and do try to enjoy the process.

Greens, feta and ricotta pie

Flavours of spanakopita and enough greens to make this feel virtuous. I love working with this filo-style pastry, a recipe I've adapted from pastry wizard, Julie Jones. I was a little scared of it at first, thinking it would be too advanced for me, but then I felt it between my fingers, and I was hooked. There are a few little tips in here to make this easier than it might look.

Start by making the pastry. Mix the flour and salt in a small bowl and make a well in the centre. Add in the egg, water and olive oil and mix, using a fork, to make a shaggy dough. Dump out onto a floured bench and knead until smooth (about 10 minutes), using enough flour to prevent it from sticking to the bench while kneading. Alternatively, you can mix this in the bowl of a stand mixer fitted with a dough hook, mixing on a low speed for about 7 minutes. Rub the dough with a small amount of olive oil and wrap it in baking paper. Let this rest in the fridge for 30 minutes.

While your dough is resting, make the filling. Heat a wide sauté pan over a medium heat and add the olive oil. Follow with the onion, zucchini and garlic (and silverbeet stems, if using) with a pinch of salt and sweat until soft and starting to brown, about 15 minutes.

Add in the greens. Your pan will likely be overflowing, but the pile of greens will begin to soften and shrink quickly. It's helpful to put a lid on the pan to press the greens down so they begin to steam. Once they've started to wilt, remove the lid, add in the herbs and cook everything down until it's starting to brown, and very little liquid remains. Tip the greens out onto a tray to cool. Once cool, squeeze out any remaining liquid.

Mix the feta, ricotta, eggs and a good crack of pepper in a bowl and add in the cooled greens. Stir to combine. Set this aside while you prepare the dough.

Preheat your oven to 180°C (350°F) and line a baking tray with baking paper.

Clear a large area on your clean, dry bench (or table) and lightly dust it with flour. Begin rolling out your dough with a rolling pin. When you've gotten the dough as thin as possible, move it aside and lay out a tablecloth (this will help you flip the thin dough later). Lightly dust your tablecloth with flour and place the dough onto the tablecloth. Begin using your hands to stretch the dough to its absolute maximum, paper-thin level. Small tears are okay. If an area won't stretch completely, let it rest for a couple of minutes and come back to it. Once the dough is paper-thin, leave it to dry for 45 minutes. After drying, use a paring knife to trim the thick edges away. Sprinkle 1 tablespoon of flour over the dough, brushing your hand over to make sure it's evenly coated. Use a pastry brush to brush the entire sheet with about half of the butter, then evenly sprinkle it with salt and pepper.

Makes: Enough to serve 4–6
Active time: 1 hour 15 minutes
Inactive time: 2 hours

Kitchenalia: Stand mixer fitted with the dough hook (optional), pastry brush

Before you begin: You'll need a lot of bench space, about 1 square metre (1 square yard), and a clean tablecloth to help with filling and rolling the pie.

Pastry
250 g (1⅔ cups) plain (all-purpose) flour, plus extra for dusting
1 teaspoon fine sea salt
1 egg, lightly whisked
100 ml (3½ fl oz) warm water
1 tablespoon extra-virgin olive oil, plus extra for coating dough

Filling
¼ cup (60 ml) extra-virgin olive oil
1 brown onion, diced small
1 large zucchini (courgette), grated using large holes of a box grater
4 garlic cloves, minced
500 g (1 lb 2 oz) mixed greens (spinach, silverbeet/Swiss chard, cavolo nero) (see note over page)
¼ cup (15 g) chopped dill
¼ cup (10 g) chopped flat-leaf parsley
200 g (7 oz) Greek or Danish-style feta, crumbled
150 g (5½ oz) ricotta
3 eggs, lightly beaten
70 g (2½ oz) unsalted butter, very soft for brushing dough
Fine sea salt
Freshly cracked black pepper

Dill yoghurt
1 cup (250 g) Greek-style
 plain yoghurt
¼ cup (15 g) chopped dill
1 garlic clove
Pinch of fine sea salt
Good crack of black pepper
Hot sauce (optional)

Note: Strip the leaves from the silverbeet stems, but don't throw the stems away – they are sweet and delicious. Dice them up and sauté with the onions, zucchini and garlic. Strip the leaves from the cavolo nero stems – unfortunately these stems should be composted as they can be quite fibrous. If using spinach, use both the leaves and stems; just give them a good wash before using, as spinach is often sandy.

Serving suggestions: Serve this with the Salad of red capsicum, feta and white anchovies with za'atar pita (see page 89), the Fennel and pumpkin caponata (see page 96) or a simply-dressed green salad (see page 71) for a complete, and lovely, meal.

Place the greens in a thin log at the bottom edge of the dough and use the tablecloth to help you roll the dough over the filling. Use a pastry brush to brush the top of the log with butter and flip again, brushing the top with butter each time you roll until you reach the end. Trim and pinch the edges shut. Carefully turn the left end of the log inward to the centre and the right end down and inward to the centre to meet and form a figure of eight. Gently lift the roll and place it seam-side down on the baking tray. Finally, brush the top with the remaining butter and transfer it to the oven.

Bake the pie for 50–60 minutes, until golden brown. Allow it to cool slightly before cutting into it.

To make the dill yoghurt, combine all the ingredients except for the hot sauce (if using). The hot sauce is optional, but I like to squeeze it onto the yoghurt at the end. Serve with the pie.

Bagna cauda with vegetables

It's tempting to suggest that all vegetables should be dunked into a warm bath of anchovy at some point. I like a mix of boiled and raw vegetables here, relishing in the simplicity of delicate, yielding vegetables with a luscious buttery, silky, salty and garlicky sauce. Simple luxuries. The bagna cauda recipe can be halved for an intimate meal with the person you love – it's excellent rainy-night food. Use the best-quality anchovies that you can get your hands on.

Add the potatoes to a small pot and cover with cold water. Add a pinch of salt and bring to a boil. Cook until they are completely tender. Drain and cool.

Fill a medium-sized pot with water and season it well with salt (you want it to be almost as salty as the sea). Bring it to the boil.

Cut the fennel into wedges 2–3 cm (about 1 inch) thick. Slice the cauliflower into bite-sized little trees. Peel the outside of the celery, cut in half lengthways and then into 7–8 cm (about 3 inch) lengths. Peel the carrots and leave them whole. Wash the radishes, leaving their tops on if the leaves are fresh.

Begin boiling each of the vegetables (except the radishes) in the salted water. Start with the fennel, which will take about 5 minutes to become tender. Scoop it out of the water and onto a plate to cool. Then proceed with the cauliflower, which will take about 2 minutes. Follow with the carrots for 4–5 minutes, and finally the celery, which only needs 30 seconds. Leave all the vegetables at room temperature. Do not rinse! You want to keep the vegetables seasoned from the salted water.

To make the bagna cauda, crush the garlic in a mortar and pestle until it's smooth, add the anchovies and crush together to form a paste. Combine the garlic-anchovy paste with the olive oil in a small saucepan and heat over the lowest heat possible on your stove for about 10 minutes, stirring with a whisk every now and then to emulsify. There should be no bubbling and you should be able to touch the pan and only just feel warmth, not heat. If your stove doesn't go so low, you may need to turn the stove on and off a couple of times in that 10-minute period. Remove the pan from the heat and add in the cold, diced butter, whisking to combine. You may be able to keep the bagna cauda emulsified if the temperature stays consistent (just warm) but if it splits, just give it a stir – it will still be delicious. Taste for seasoning and finish with a crack of pepper.

Warm a bowl for the bagna cauda in a 50°C (120°F) oven for 10 minutes. Pour the bagna cauda into the warmed bowl and serve surrounded by the cooked and raw vegetables.

Makes: Enough to serve 4–6 as an entrée
Active time: 45 minutes

6 small potatoes (kipfler/ fingerling or new potatoes are great here)
1 fennel bulb
2 heads fioretto cauliflower (or half a head of regular cauliflower)
2 stalks celery
6 small heirloom (or Dutch) carrots
6 radishes
Fine sea salt

Bagna cauda
8 large garlic cloves, peeled
100 g (3½ oz) oil-packed, good-quality anchovy fillets (about 2 tins)
¼ cup (60 ml) extra-virgin olive oil
60 g (2¼ oz) cold unsalted butter, diced
Freshly cracked black pepper

Note: *Fioretto*, translating to "little flower" in Italian, is flowering cauliflower. Its sweet, delicate flavour makes it perfect for crudités.

Originating in Piedmont, this was a simple way to dress up ordinary winter vegetables while warming the hands and souls of those at work in the fields. It is a wonderful example of making the most of what you can get; the Piedmontese traded their butter and wheat with the Ligurians' salt and, seeking a way to circumvent the carefully regulated salt tax, they would pack the untaxed anchovies over the top of the salt barrels to sneak the salt through. As for the olive oil? Apparently, it wasn't olive oil at all, but rather walnut oil. You'll often see crushed walnuts added to the bagna cauda, with all this beauty still found on Piedmontese tables on Christmas Eve.

Korean vegetable pancake

Makes: Enough to serve 2–3
Active time: 25 minutes

2 tablespoons neutral oil,
   for frying

Vegetables
200 g (7 oz) thinly-sliced
   cabbage (about ⅛ head of
   cabbage)
1 teaspoon fine sea salt
80 g (2¾ oz) spring onions
   (scallions) (about 1 bunch)
70 g (2½ oz) carrot, grated
   (about half a large carrot)
80 g (2¾ oz) chopped kimchi

Batter
80 g (2¾ oz) plain
   (all-purpose) flour
35 g (1¼ oz) rice flour
½ teaspoon baking powder
15 g (½ oz) cornflour
   (cornstarch)
¼ teaspoon ground turmeric
160 ml (5¼ fl oz) water
1 tablespoon kimchi juice

Dipping sauce
½ small French shallot,
   finely diced
1 green chilli, deseeded and
   finely chopped
1½ tablespoons light soy sauce
1 tablespoon rice wine vinegar
1 teaspoon white
   (granulated) sugar
1 teaspoon sesame oil

A quick, but deeply satisfying dinner, late-night snack, breakfast or lunch. It uses up all the bits in the fridge – almost any combination works. I'm fascinated by savoury pancakes: okonomiyaki in Japan or yachaejeon in Korea, spring onion (scallion) pancakes from China and even corn johnnycakes from America. A wonderfully clever use of vegetables, and great inspiration for a different type of meal, this is my take on a Korean-style vegetable pancake.

Mix the cabbage with the salt and squeeze it well with your hands, crushing the cabbage as hard as you can. Allow it to sit while you gather the remaining ingredients, at least 10 minutes.

Slice the spring onions into 3 cm (1¼ inch) lengths and combine with the carrot and kimchi in a mixing bowl.

In a separate mixing bowl, combine the dry batter ingredients, then add in the water and kimchi juice. Whisk until smooth.

Rinse the cabbage in cold water to remove the salt. Squeeze out all the water and combine with the other veggies, giving them a toss before adding them to the batter mix. Stir to combine and set aside.

Combine the dipping sauce ingredients in a small bowl and set aside.

Heat a small non-stick frying pan over a medium–high heat. Add the oil and, once the pan is hot, add a large scoop of the pancake batter. Cook for 2–3 minutes on each side, until browned and crisp. Continue with the remaining batter. To keep the cooked pancakes warm, place them on a rack sitting over a baking tray in a 60°C (140°F) oven until ready to serve.

Cut the warm pancakes into rough wedges and serve with the dipping sauce.

Note: As with the Fried zucchini blossom fritters (see page 38), the combination of rice flour and plain flour in the batter creates a better consistency for frying. Cornflour (cornstarch) also aids in this – both cornflour and rice flour absorb less moisture than wheat flour, resulting in something more crisp and less greasy. Wheat flour still has a role to play, as its gluten helps the batter cling to whatever it is you're frying. The mix of all three is crucial to this recipe.

Pumpkin, leek and Gorgonzola galette

Makes: 1 galette, enough
  for 8–10 slices
Active time: 50 minutes
Inactive time: 1 hour 30 minutes

Kitchenalia: 30 cm (12 inch)
  round pizza tray, pastry brush

Before you begin: You'll need one
prepared round of Flaky pastry (see
page 254) for this recipe. This can
be made a day ahead and kept in the
fridge. If you're making the dough
on the day, prepare it an hour before
starting this galette so it has time to
rest in the fridge.

1 round Flaky pastry (page 254),
  rolled out to a thickness of
  3–4 mm (about ⅛ inch)
2 tablespoons extra-virgin
  olive oil
1 brown onion, thinly sliced
1 large leek, thinly sliced
  and washed well
2 teaspoons plain
  (all-purpose) flour
300 g (10½ oz) pumpkin
  (squash), deseeded,
  thinly sliced, skin left on
2 tablespoons rosemary or sage
  leaves (or a combination of
  the two), chopped, plus extra
  to serve
¼ cup (60 ml) single
  (pure) cream
1 egg
50 g (1¾ oz) Gorgonzola Dolce
Fine sea salt
Flaked sea salt
Freshly cracked black pepper

Gorgonzola plays the part of seasoning here, so be mindful not to use too much salt on the toppings of the galette. If Gorgonzola is not a cheese you love, swap it for Parmigiano Reggiano or Fontina.

Prepare one round of Flaky pastry and leave it, rolled out, on a baking tray lined with baking paper in the fridge.

Heat a large sauté pan over a medium heat and add the olive oil. Sweat the onion and leek with a good pinch of fine sea salt and a good crack of pepper. Sweat until they are soft and sweet but have no colour, about 10–15 minutes. Scoop out onto a plate or tray and cool in the fridge until you're ready to assemble your galette.

Preheat your oven to 200°C (400°F).

Remove the pastry round from the fridge and spread the flour across the base (this will absorb the moisture from the onion and leek to prevent the base from going soggy). Top the pastry with the cooked onion and leek, leaving a 5–6 cm (2–2½ inch) border around the entire edge.

In a mixing bowl, combine the pumpkin slices with the rosemary and/or sage leaves, cream, Gorgonzola, a pinch of fine sea salt and a crack of pepper. Lay this mixture on top of the onion and leek, then pour any excess cream or cheese in the bowl over the pumpkin.

Fold the edges of the galette up over the pumpkin in as rustic or pretty a shape as you like, leaving the filling exposed in the middle.

Mix the egg with a teaspoon of water and use a pastry brush to brush the crust of the galette with the egg wash. Finish with a sprinkle of flaked sea salt and cracked pepper over the crust.

Place the galette in the oven and immediately turn the temperature down to 180°C (350°F). After about 40–50 minutes the crust should be deeply golden, and the pumpkin browned.

Transfer the galette to a cooling rack without the baking paper underneath so the pastry remains crisp on the bottom while it cools slightly. Serve warm, scattered with the extra rosemary and/or sage.

Over the years I have experimented with many different combinations for savoury galettes. Some of my favourites include:

Stewed onion + tapenade + tomatoes
Stewed onion and leek + blanched kale + Parmigiano Reggiano
Stewed onion + sliced zucchini (courgette) + thyme + toasted pine nuts
Stewed onion + pancetta + sage
Stewed onion and leek + crème fraîche + smoked trout (added after baking)

Broccoli and white bean soup

Makes: Enough to serve 2–3
Active time: 30 minutes
Inactive time: 10 minutes

Kitchenalia: Blender or
  stick blender

2 tablespoons extra-virgin
  olive oil
2 tablespoons unsalted butter
1 brown onion, sliced
3 garlic cloves, minced
Pinch of chilli flakes (optional)
1 teaspoon fennel seeds
1 tablespoon chopped rosemary
3 cups (750 ml) chicken stock
  or water, or a mix of both
1 x 400 g (14 oz) tin cannellini
  beans, drained and rinsed
2 heads broccoli, finely chopped
Fine sea salt
Freshly cracked black pepper

To serve
Good-quality extra-virgin
  olive oil
Parmigiano Reggiano
Freshly cracked black pepper

A creamy soup, without the cream. This soup can be adapted to suit the season or the produce you have on hand. While normally I prefer freshly soaked and cooked-at-home beans, this is one of those moments where you should take the shortcut, as it really doesn't make a difference – their role here is to add creaminess and body.

In a large enamel-lined Dutch oven or heavy-based pot, heat the olive oil and butter. Add the onion and the garlic, with a pinch of salt and a crack of pepper. Sweat over a medium heat until the onion and garlic are soft and sweet and beginning to brown. Add in the chilli flakes (if using), fennel seeds and rosemary and sizzle for 30 seconds. Add in your stock or water and beans and bring to a simmer.

Once simmering, add in the broccoli and cook until the broccoli is very soft, about 10 minutes.

Blend the soup with a stick blender, or in a blender, until it's smooth.

At this point, you can either chill the soup down to reheat and serve later, or return it to the pot and bring it to a simmer. Ladle the soup into bowls, add a drizzle of olive oil, a (heavy) sprinkle of parmesan and more pepper.

Seasonal adjustment: During the warmer months, replace the broccoli with a 400 g (14 oz) tin of whole peeled San Marzano tomatoes and follow the recipe exactly as is, just replacing the broccoli with tomato. It's oh-so-good, especially with a grilled cheese sandwich for dipping!

Other alternatives to broccoli (simply substitute one of the following for the broccoli and continue as per the recipe):

Fennel (1 large fennel bulb, finely chopped)
Kale (1 bunch, stems removed)
Broad beans (1½ cups/280 g, podded and peeled)

Cavolo nero and farinata soup

This is a real stick-to-your-ribs, warm-you-to-your-core kind of soup. It's deeply satisfying to cook, as well as to eat. This soup is similar to the Tuscan ribollita but is thickened with polenta instead of bread, hence the name "farinata", which not to be confused with the pancake-like dish that you'll find in Liguria.

In a large enamel-lined Dutch oven or heavy-based pot set over a medium heat, add the olive oil, onion, garlic, celery and carrot with a pinch of salt and drop the heat to low. Sauté until the soffritto (see notes) is very soft and starting to brown, about 20 minutes.

Next, add in the pancetta and rosemary and sizzle for 2 minutes. Follow with the cavolo nero leaves and cook until they've wilted.

Add in the beans, parmesan rind (if using) and the stock or water and bring to a simmer. Once simmering, whisk in the polenta and leave it to continue to simmer, with the lid ajar, for about 30 minutes, giving it a stir every few minutes.

While the polenta is cooking, make your chilli oil by combining the chilli flakes and olive oil in a small saucepan. Set it over the lowest possible heat and warm the oil for about 5 minutes. Turn the heat off. At no point should the chilli flakes be sizzling – that's too hot.

Taste the soup for seasoning and adjust as needed before ladling it into bowls. Top with a crack of pepper and a good spoonful of the chilli oil. Serve piping hot.

Notes: Once the chilli oil is cool, you can store in a clean glass jar in the fridge. It's great drizzled on eggs, wilted greens, pizza, pasta or ricotta on toast. Try it on Crostini (see page 104), the Rigatoni with cime di rapa and sausage (see page 129) or the Sheet pan pizza (see page 190). If you sterilise the jar, your oil will keep for up to six months.

It's good to get into the habit of freezing parmesan rinds for a rainy day. A rind will add body and flavour to your next Bolognese or stock. If you find yourself with a little collection of them, you can make a quick parmesan broth by generously covering a few rinds (or as many as you have stocked up) in about 3 cups (750 ml) cold water in a stock pot or pan. It's not necessary, but you can also add any stock vegetables you might have on hand: celery, carrot, onion, garlic. Bring to a simmer for 30 minutes, stirring occasionally to ensure the rinds don't stick to the base of the pot. Strain the broth and pour into a freezer-safe container to leave in your freezer, ready to use as needed. A little of this broth can be used to add extra oomph to your risottos, soups and beans. It works beautifully in place of stock or water to cook polenta, too.

Soffritto is the Italian term given to the aromatic mix of finely diced carrot, celery and onion (I often add garlic) that is sautéed to create a flavour base for dishes, such as soups, stews and slow-cooked pasta sauces. The word comes from the verb *soffriggere*, meaning "to sauté" or "to brown". For further reading on this fundamental combination of humble ingredients, see page 124.

Makes: Enough to serve 4
Active time: 30 minutes
Inactive time: 50 minutes

⅓ cup (80 ml) extra-virgin olive oil
1 brown onion, finely diced
3 garlic cloves, minced
1 celery stalk, finely diced
1 carrot, finely diced
50 g (1¾ oz) pancetta, diced
1 branch rosemary, leaves picked and chopped
1 bunch cavolo nero, leaves pulled off the stem
1 x 400 g (14 oz) tin white beans (such as cannellini beans) or borlotti beans, drained and rinsed
1 parmesan rind (if you have it)
6 cups (1.5 litres) chicken stock or water, or a mix of both
¼ cup (50 g) polenta
Fine sea salt

Chilli oil
1 tablespoon chilli flakes (I like Aleppo or Korean for their bright red colour)
¼ cup (60 ml) extra-virgin olive oil

To serve
Freshly cracked black pepper

Pappa al pomodoro

Makes: Enough to serve 4
Active time: 30 minutes
Inactive time: 20 minutes

800 g (1 lb 12 oz) ripe (or even
    overripe!) tomatoes
    (see note)
400 g (14 oz) stale bread
    (about one small loaf),
    crusts removed but saved
    for croutons, bread cut into
    large chunks
¼ cup (60 ml) extra-virgin
    olive oil, plus an extra
    2 tablespoons if
    making croutons
1 small brown onion, diced
4 garlic cloves, minced
Pinch of chilli flakes
4 cups (1 litre) chicken or
    vegetable stock
    (preferably homemade)
½ cup (30 g) basil leaves,
    firmly packed
Fine sea salt

To serve
Parmigiano Reggiano
Good-quality extra-virgin
    olive oil
Freshly cracked black pepper

Note: This soup is wonderful served
hot but, amazingly is also very
good served cold, if the tomato glut
appears before the weather turns.
Any heirloom variety is perfect
here – non-heirloom varieties, for
example Roma, aren't right for this
dish as they won't be juicy enough.

Pappa al pomodoro is a brilliant example of stretching what you have to feed many. Some versions are so thick and concentrated that you can fry them in olive oil like a pancake; this version is hearty, but it's still meant to be eaten with a spoon. Don't skimp on the olive oil either; like cream is to cake, the olive oil is the luxurious blanket that wraps around this soup, making it silky, glossy and pure summer heaven to eat.

Bring a medium-sized pot of water to the boil. Cut out the stem end of the tomatoes and cut a small "X" into the base of each tomato. Prepare a bowl of ice water and keep it near the stove. Drop your tomatoes into the boiling water until you see the skin begin to peel back, about 1 minute. Immediately scoop out the tomatoes and dunk them into the ice water. Once cold, the skins should peel off easily. Discard the skins, roughly chop the tomatoes and set them aside, being sure to retain any juices.

This step is optional but recommended to minimise waste: Preheat your oven to 170°C (340°F). Cut the crusts from the bread into large-bite-sized pieces. Fill a bowl with cold water and dunk the stale crusts quickly into the water (to soften them and prevent broken teeth!). Place the crusts on a baking tray and toss with the extra olive oil and a sprinkle of salt. Bake in the oven until golden and crisp, about 12–15 minutes. Allow to cool and set aside.

Heat a medium-sized pot over a medium heat and add the olive oil. Add the onion with a pinch of salt and sauté until soft and sweet, about 10–15 minutes. Add in the garlic and chilli flakes and sauté for another minute. Next, add the tomatoes, their juices and the stock. Bring this up to a gentle simmer, then cook for about 10 minutes. Taste for seasoning and adjust with salt as needed.

Add in the chunks of crustless bread and half the basil leaves and let them slowly simmer for 10 minutes. Use your spoon or a fork to help break up the bread as it cooks. Taste for seasoning once more and adjust.

Spoon the soup into bowls and top with grated parmesan, a glug of good-quality olive oil, a good crack of pepper and the remaining basil leaves. Use the croutons (if you made them) to scoop into the soup.

This soup is a love letter to Italy. The idea of *cucina povera*, or peasant food, celebrates simple, seasonal, vegetable-forward, waste-eliminating cooking, and it was, like many great things, born out of necessity. Its beauty and sophistication lie in the belief that no matter what you do or don't have, you are going to eat well. These are the values of Italian cooking that I love the most; it's a cuisine that celebrates the simple, seasonal and local. This (and an addiction to Parmigiano Reggiano) is the reason I will forever be in love with the food of Italy.

Pumpkin, curry leaf and coconut soup

Makes: Enough to serve 4
Active time: 20 minutes
Inactive time: 20 minutes

Kitchenalia: Blender or
stick blender

2 tablespoons coconut oil
or neutral oil
1 large brown onion, sliced
¼ teaspoons chilli flakes
(optional)
1½ teaspoons yellow curry
powder
½ teaspoon fennel seeds
700–800 g (1 lb 9 oz–1 lb 12 oz)
butternut pumpkin (squash),
peeled and cut into 2 cm
(¾ inch) dice
2 tablespoons water (if needed)
1 × 400 ml (14 fl oz) tin coconut
milk
Fine sea salt

Temper
1½ tablespoons coconut oil
or neutral oil
2 teaspoons brown mustard
seeds
¼ cup (6 g) fresh curry leaves

To serve
1 lime, cut into 4 wedges

Note: If you have leftover curry
leaves – often the case as they usually
come in larger bunches! – see pages
180, 202 and 242 for other recipes
that use them.

Curry leaves have such a unique and interesting flavour. An essential
ingredient in Sri Lankan and Indian cooking, their nutty and savoury
qualities remind me of buttered popcorn – you would be surprised how
well that flavour complements dishes and ingredients of all sorts. This
soup is still delicious without curry leaves, but they're worth seeking out.

In a large enamel-lined Dutch oven or heavy-based pot, heat the
2 tablespoons of oil over a medium heat. Add the onion and a pinch of salt
and cook until soft, sweet and starting to caramelise, about 10–15 minutes.
Add the chilli flakes (if using), curry powder and fennel seeds. Stir to
combine and cook for another minute.

Next, add the pumpkin and place a lid on the pot, turning the heat to low.
Cook until the pumpkin has softened, about 15 minutes, stirring every few
minutes. If you notice it browning in the pan, add 2 tablespoons water to
deglaze and steam.

Add in the coconut milk, then fill the tin with water and add that in, too.
This should cover the pumpkin, but if it doesn't, add another half tin
of water and see if that does it – you want the liquid to just cover the
pumpkin. Season with a pinch of salt.

When everything is soft, remove the pot from the heat and blend (using
a stick blender or blender) on high to produce a silky-smooth texture.
Taste and adjust the seasoning before returning the pot to a low heat.

To temper the spices, place the oil in a small sauté pan over a medium–
high heat. When hot, add in the mustard seeds. They will begin to pop as
they heat. Once the popping starts to slow, add in the curry leaves, which
will splatter when they hit the oil – be careful! Once the sizzling has begun
to ease, remove the pan from the heat and set aside.

Serve the hot soup in bowls, drizzled with a spoonful of the temper
(including mustard seeds and crisp curry leaves). Squeeze in a wedge
of lime just before eating.

Seasonal adjustment: Replace the pumpkin with 8 ears of corn with their husks
removed. Strip the kernels from the cob and add these to the pot in place of the diced
pumpkin. Add the stripped cobs in when you add the coconut milk and water to
impart flavour while cooking. Remove and discard the cobs before blending. This
is the most delicious summer or early-autumn version of this soup.

Noodles with pork mince and black vinegar, chilli and soy dressing

We all need recipes like this in our repertoire. Easy to knock together, faster than takeaway, while still being deeply comforting. Replace the pork with tofu, chicken or cabbage, or even scrambled egg. As with all quick cooking, it's important to have your ingredients prepped and at hand before you begin. This comes together so fast that there's no time to stop and chop or slice in between!

Before you begin: Double the dressing recipe to have an extra batch ready to go for next time, or to dress up other dishes (see note).

Combine all the dressing ingredients in a small pot. Bring to a boil, turn off the heat and cover the pot. Allow everything to steep for about 10–15 minutes. Strain and reserve the liquid, discarding the spices.

Bring a pot of water to the boil and cook your noodles according to package instructions, usually about 2 minutes. Drain the noodles, run them under cold water and set aside.

Set a wok or sauté pan over a high heat and add the oil. Once the oil is hot, add the pork and cook, stirring often, until the pork starts to brown. Add in the garlic and chilli flakes and cook until the garlic starts to brown. Continue to cook until the pork is deeply golden and crisp.

Add the noodles to the wok, along with the sesame seeds, sesame oil, about 4 tablespoons of the dressing and the spring onions. Toss to combine. Divide the noodles into bowls and spoon a touch more dressing over each bowl. Finish with a drizzle of your favourite chilli oil, if using, and sprinkle with the extra sliced spring onions. Keep any remaining dressing in a glass jar in your fridge (see note).

Note: Save any excess dressing in a glass jar in your fridge to make this dish even easier next time – it gets better with age, so keep it for as long as you like. It's also excellent as a dipping sauce for dumplings or is simply delicious spooned over plain noodles combined with a spoonful of Ginger and chilli jam (see page 194).

Makes: Enough to serve 4
Active time: 30 minutes

Kitchenalia: Wok (alternatively, use a sauté pan)

200 g (7 oz) fresh Chinese egg noodles, or 2 x 80 g (2¾ oz) packets of dried instant noodles
¼ cup (60 ml) neutral oil
500 g (1 lb 2 oz) minced (ground) pork
4 garlic cloves, minced
2 teaspoons Aleppo or Korean chilli flakes (Italian chilli flakes are fine at a pinch – just reduce the quantity as they are spicier)
1 tablespoon sesame seeds
1 teaspoon sesame oil
¼ cup (15 g) sliced spring onions (scallions), plus extra to garnish
Chilli oil, optional (see page 61 or page 88 to make your own)

Dressing
¾ cup (185 ml) light soy sauce
⅓ cup (80 ml) black vinegar
2 tablespoons water
1 tablespoon oyster sauce
½ teaspoon Szechuan pepper pods
1 teaspoon white (granulated) sugar
1 teaspoon fennel seeds
1 star anise pod
3–4 cm (1¼–1½ inch) piece of fresh ginger, thinly sliced
Pinch of fine sea salt

Some like it *cold*

*The music
in my kitchen*

"Fashionable consumption oscillates violently between *gout-inducing excess* and *penitential restraint* ... In China, you can combine your *gastronomic indulgence* and its *antidote* in a *single meal*."

Fuchsia Dunlop

Most restaurants these days have a playlist, a carefully curated collection of songs that are designed to tell the musical story of the meal to come. Some are meant to take you places – the well-placed Edith Piaf or Charles Trenet – while others are designed to uplift, the balance firmly in favour of the major scales. And yet, for all the travel and all the happiness, those songs, night after night, eventually wear you down – not the guests, of course, but the people who work there. You simply cannot listen to the same music every night; we're not wired to be that predictable.

Cooking is the same, and that freedom is one of the great joys of learning how to cook well for yourself. Having a varied playlist of dishes that you can draw from – some big hitters, but also some gentle, nurturing meals – means that you can cook to match your mood.

The idea of approaching food like an operatic score – where the flavours rise and rise until they reach their crescendo and then gently fall and fall again – is distinctly European. Escoffier and his protégés would move from soup to fish and seafood, to poultry to red meat and game, and then slide back down the scale via vegetables, salad, cheese and dessert. There is no question that the melody is harmonious, but perhaps there is other music we could be playing?

In her book *Land of Fish and Rice*, Fuchsia Dunlop talks of the Chinese term "*qing dan*". Depressingly translated as "insipid" in English, its literal meaning in China, or more specifically in Jiangnan, where her book focuses, is much more romantic. The word is the combination of two characters: pure and light, "... a mildness of taste that refreshes and comforts, restoring equanimity to mind and body", explains Dunlop.

In the Jiangnan tradition, a wide variety of dishes are often served together. This allows guests to partake in the *qing dan* as they would like. The pleasure of culinary whispers tend to get forgotten in the quest for the big hitters.

To continue with the musical analogies, we can learn from these quiet pauses found within. We have the starches: a bowl of steamed rice, some crunchy bread, a bowl of homemade tagliatelle; and the greens: a simple green salad, some quickly sautéed spinach with a little garlic, bok choy flashed in the wok with a splash of oyster sauce. They all play their part. Perhaps even more valuable are the slower-cooked greens, bringing with them the subtle notes; whether it be weeds blanched so they lose their bitterness, flat beans stewed in a tomato sauce, long-cooked leeks, or zucchini (courgettes) cooked until it collapses into your pasta. While disparate in their origins, their purpose is often the same; it is among the green things you find room to breathe at a dinner table. This is where you find pause to let your palate relax.

When putting a meal together, the question of balance is relatively simple. If you're making something involved – a spiced braise or a joint of roast beef involving sauce, or even pasta as a main course – opt for very simple side dishes: greens such as spinach, silverbeet (Swiss chard) or kale, potato purée, or asparagus steamed or simply grilled with olive oil and salt. This makes sense, not just for your palate, but for your workload. Alternatively, if the main dish is quite simple, like a pan-fried trout, a roast chicken or a grilled steak or mushrooms, then we have more time and space to consider an elaborate side or two.

However, it's important to note that this balance can also play out across your week of menu planning. Life can't be all rock'n'roll, and there's beauty in slotting in some quieter dishes – a night of classical music, if you will. A bowl of noodles, a simple omelette, silken tofu or some gently cooked vegetables like the Leeks gribiche (see page 80). This is where the balance can also live.

The kitchen shouldn't be all about the so-called umami bombs (heavy metal/rock'n'roll/insert your own musical metaphor here), it should also be a place for subtlety. Some foods can elicit a quiet and peaceful feeling; clarity, a feeling of less is more. The luxury of cooking well for yourself is the ability to play the dishes to match your mood, and your sense of wellbeing each night. Be mindful to celebrate them, too.

For a simple Dijon and French shallot vinaigrette for dressing green salad leaves:
Place $\frac{1}{4}$ cup (40 g) of finely diced French shallot in a fine mesh strainer and rinse under cold water. Drain well and combine the shallot in a bowl with $\frac{1}{4}$ cup (60 ml) of sherry vinegar, 1 tablespoon water, 1 teaspoon Dijon mustard, $\frac{1}{2}$ teaspoon fine sea salt, 1 teaspoon honey and a few cracks of black pepper. Stir to combine and allow to sit for 10 minutes before slowly streaming in $\frac{2}{3}$ cup (170 ml) of extra-virgin olive oil while whisking. Pour your dressing into a sealed container and use as needed, being sure to give it a shake or stir just before pouring it onto your salad leaves. This dressing can be kept in the fridge for 2–3 days.

Pissaladière

Makes: 1 galette, enough for
    8–10 slices
Active time: 1 hour
Inactive time: 1 hour 15 minutes

Kitchenalia: 30 cm (12 inch)
    round pizza tray, pastry brush

Before you begin: Make your
Flaky pastry (see page 254) a day
ahead to give yourself a head start.
Not necessary, but helpful. If you're
making the dough on the day,
prepare it an hour before starting
this galette so it has time to rest in
the fridge.

1 round Flaky pastry (page 254),
    rolled out to a thickness of
    3–4 mm (about ⅛ inch)
¼ cup (60 ml) extra-virgin
    olive oil
3 brown onions, thinly sliced
1 tablespoon plain
    (all-purpose) flour
1 egg, beaten with 1 teaspoon
    water (egg wash)
8–12 good-quality anchovy
    fillets, cut lengthways
    down the middle
¼ cup (35 g) pitted black
    olives (preferably Niçoise,
    alternatively Kalamata)
1 tablespoon thyme leaves
Fine sea salt

A classic pastry-based pissaladière was one of the very first things I learned to make at Chez Panisse. The dish made several appearances throughout my time there – a rarity, as the menu changed every day. While I relished the seasonal spontaneity of cooking in that kitchen, I did love the opportunity to revisit this dish: to experiment by adding the thyme in with the onions or on top of the tart (I liked on top because it kept the flavours cleaner); to cook at a consistent high temperature or not (I like a high temperature to start to help the pastry puff a little, before turning it down for a lengthy baking time, allowing maximum caramelisation).

My most recent revelation, regarding the humble yet ubiquitous onion, followed a trip to Nice. Rather than being caramelised before baking, these onions were stewed much more gently. The caramelisation, instead, happened only while the tart baked, resulting in a more unctuous, savoury and juicy layer of onions, rather than a thin, dried out layer of sweetness. Another reminder why the details and technique matter.

Prepare your round of Flaky pastry and leave it, rolled out, on a baking tray lined with baking paper in the fridge.

Preheat your oven to 200°C (400°F).

Begin by placing a sauté pan (or a pot) with a tight-fitting lid on the stove over a medium heat. Add the olive oil, onions and a good pinch of salt. Cover the pan with the lid and allow the onions to sweat and steam until fully cooked, about 20 minutes; open the lid and give them a stir every couple of minutes. You are not looking for caramelised onions here, just sweet, juicy soft onions. Remove them from the pan and allow to cool.

Take the pastry round from the fridge and spread the flour over the pastry (this will absorb the moisture from the onions). Top with the onions, leaving a 4 cm (1½ inch) clean edge all the way around. Fold the clean edges up and over the onions to create a crust.

Use a pastry brush to brush the crust with the egg wash, then transfer it to the oven. Immediately turn the heat down to 180°C (350°F) and bake for 40–45 minutes, until the crust is deeply golden, and the onions have started to caramelise.

Remove the tart from the oven. Carefully lay the anchovy fillets in a lovely lattice pattern across the onions and place one black olive in the centre of each lattice diamond. Return the tart to the oven for a further 5 minutes to allow everything to become perfumed with anchovy and olive.

Remove the pissaladière from the oven and slide it onto a cooling rack without the baking paper underneath. Top with a sprinkle of thyme leaves and allow to cool slightly before serving. This is best served warm or at room temperature, but after no more than a few hours out of the oven.

Serving suggestions: As an apéro snack, I like to cut thin slices so people can eat this standing up with their hands. If you want to serve it as a simple lunch or dinner, I suggest a slice of pissaladière with a green salad with lots of raw, thinly sliced radish and dressed with a simple Dijon and French shallot vinaigrette (see page 71).

Fennel, mandarin and olive salad

Makes: Enough to serve 4
Active time: 20 minutes

Kitchenalia: Mandoline
   (alternatively, a very sharp
   knife to thinly slice)

2 tablespoons finely diced
   French shallot
Zest of half a lemon
Juice of 1 lemon
1 teaspoon honey
2 teaspoons white wine vinegar
2 tablespoons extra-virgin
   olive oil
4 mandarins
1 large fennel bulb,
   including fronds
⅔ cup (115 g) green olives
   (about 24 olives), pitted and
   torn in half (e.g. gordal)
1 large handful mint leaves
Fine sea salt
Freshly cracked black pepper

To finish
Pinch of chilli flakes (optional)

Both citrus and fennel are ingredients that ripen through the winter, making this a wonderful cold-weather salad. It's a dish that is thought to have originated in Sicily – an island that has long-benefited from influences stretching from Europe to North Africa. The anise of the fennel, the sweet tang of the mandarin and the saltiness of the olive makes for an excellent culinary dance.

First make your dressing by combining the diced shallot with the lemon zest and juice, honey and vinegar. Add a pinch of salt and a crack of pepper. Set aside for 10–15 minutes to allow the shallot to pickle slightly, before whisking in the olive oil.

Remove the skins from the mandarins, using a sharp knife to trim off the outer white membrane – they will look more beautiful. Cut each whole mandarin into eight chunks, cutting through the equator, then tearing each half into four equal pieces. Set aside.

To prepare the fennel, cut off the base and remove the outermost layer (these can both be reserved for stock). Thinly slice the fennel on a mandoline (or with a very sharp knife). Use the entire bulb, including the green tops, but excluding any pieces that look stringy or woody. Chop any fronds and mix them in with the fennel.

Combine the sliced fennel, olives, mint and dressing in a mixing bowl and toss to combine. Taste and season with salt. Lay the fennel salad onto your serving platter and top with the mandarin pieces and a sprinkle of chilli flakes (if using).

Serving suggestions: The freshness and wintry roots of this salad make it a great one to serve alongside deep, unctuous dishes: daubes, stews and all that is slow cooked. Serve it with the Beef daube and panisse (see page 221), the Bean and chorizo stew (fabada) (see page 126) or the Polenta with sweet-spiced lamb ragù (see page 152).

Baby cos Caesar salad

Makes: Enough to serve 4–6
  as an entrée
Active time: 20 minutes
Inactive time: 8 minutes

4 heads baby cos lettuce
200 g (7 oz) sourdough
  (about half a small loaf)
⅓ cup (80 ml) extra-virgin
  olive oil
2 large garlic cloves
Parmigiano Reggiano,
  for grating
Fine sea salt
Freshly cracked black pepper

Dressing
1 egg yolk
8 good-quality anchovy fillets,
  chopped (use less for a
  subtler anchovy flavour)
Zest of half a lemon
3 tablespoons lemon juice
1 tablespoon lime juice
1 teaspoon fish sauce
½ teaspoon Worcestershire
  sauce
100 ml (3½ fl oz) extra-virgin
  olive oil
100 ml (3½ fl oz) neutral oil
Fine sea salt

Note: A perfect salad relies on so little that every tiny detail counts. The crunch of dirt on a leaf and the spell is broken. A little ice bath can help to pep-up greens that are looking slightly sad – also a great way to ensure they're free of grit. Have a salad spinner at the ready – a tool I swear by (yes, you can wrap the lettuce in a tea towel, but I don't think it does the best job and you're more likely to bruise the leaves).

I've had my fair share of good and bad Caesars. I've come to know what I like: a dressing more like an anchovy vinaigrette than an anchovy-spiked mayonnaise, ice-cold little cos leaves, lots of Parmigiano Reggiano, and crunchy, chewy, garlicky sourdough croutons. As basic as this may seem, this Caesar salad took much trial and error, and many years of research to get just right.

A homemade Caesar also highlights the benefits of cooking at home. The dressing is ideally made minutes before serving, so unless you're dining at a restaurant that makes the dressing table-side (bring it back?), the way to experience the Caesar at its best is by making it at home.

Preheat your oven to 200°C (400°F).

Trim the root of each head of lettuce and separate the leaves. Wash and dry the lettuce and place the leaves in the fridge.

Tear the sourdough into bite-sized croutons and place in a bowl. Toss the bread with the olive oil, a good pinch of salt and a good crack of pepper. Place the croutons on a baking tray in a single layer and bake for 6–8 minutes, or until golden brown. Grate the garlic cloves directly over the hot croutons using a microplane and toss with tongs. Return the tray to the oven for another 2 minutes, then remove the tray and allow the croutons to cool.

To make the dressing, combine the egg yolk, anchovies, lemon zest and juice, lime juice, fish sauce, Worcestershire sauce and a pinch of salt in a small bowl and whisk to combine. Combine the oils in a measuring jug. While whisking the egg yolk mixture, slowly drizzle in the oil in a steady stream until the mixture emulsifies.

In a large mixing bowl, toss the lettuce leaves with enough dressing to coat them well. Add in the croutons and season with a pinch of salt and a good crack of pepper. Grate as much parmesan as you like (I like a lot!) into the bowl and toss to combine.

Serve the salad on a large platter, or in individual bowls, and shower with an extra shaving of parmesan.

Crisp leaves with peas and buttermilk herb dressing

A good, creamy herb dressing paired with crisp, cold, crunchy salad leaves is one of my favourite combinations – an American steakhouse staple typically known as a "wedge" salad, using a wedge of iceberg lettuce with a dressing of either ranch or blue cheese. I like to think mine is a little lighter: heavy on the fresh herbs and omitting the blue cheese for something that complements the delicate spring vegetables better. The mixture of sour cream and mayonnaise ensures you have something that feels light on the tongue but rich enough to coat the leaves. For a truly American experience, add chopped crisp bacon, tomatoes and crumbled blue cheese in place of the peas and fennel.

Bring a pot of salted water to a boil and blanch your fresh peas for about 3 minutes. Strain and shock them in an ice bath as soon as they come out. If using frozen peas, simply thaw them before using (see note).

Wash your lettuce and dry it well, either using a salad spinner or laying the washed leaves out on clean tea towels and carefully wrapping them.

To make the dressing, add all the ingredients (except for salt and pepper) to a small bowl and whisk to combine. Taste and adjust the seasoning with salt and pepper.

To serve, arrange the lettuce leaves on a large platter and top with the peas and sliced fennel. Finish by drizzling as much of the dressing as you like over the salad. Keep any excess dressing in the fridge for other uses (see serving suggestion).

Note: Frozen peas are flash steamed before freezing, consequently they don't need to be cooked, just warmed quickly, to ensure they retain their colour and pop. Simply place the frozen peas in a strainer and hold them under warm running water.

Serving suggestions: This salad dressing recipe makes more than the salad requires but it holds well in the fridge for several days. It's excellent to dip pizza into, or pizza crusts at least (hi, I'm American!), as well as crudités. It can be difficult to find buttermilk in small amounts, but any leftover buttermilk makes an excellent marinade for chicken or can be frozen to use another time.

Makes: Enough to serve 4–6
Active time: 15 minutes
Inactive time: 10 minutes

Kitchenalia: Mandoline
    (alternatively, a very sharp
    knife to thinly slice)

½ cup (75 g) fresh peas
    (or frozen works fine)
3 heads little gem lettuce
    (or other crisp lettuce
    such as cos or iceberg),
    leaves separated
1 small head fennel, thinly sliced
    on a mandoline
    (or with a very sharp knife)

Buttermilk herb dressing
Scant ½ cup (100 g)
    sour cream
Scant ½ cup (100 ml)
    buttermilk
2 tablespoons mayonnaise,
    preferably homemade
    (page 109)
Juice of half a lemon, about
    2 tablespoons
3 tablespoons chopped chives
1 tablespoon chopped dill
1 garlic clove, grated on
    a microplane
1 small French shallot,
    finely diced
Fine sea salt
Freshly cracked black pepper

Leeks gribiche

Makes: Enough to serve 4
as an entrée or side, or
a delicious lunch for 2
Active time: 30 mins

Kitchenalia: Food processor

Before you begin: You'll need
a batch of homemade Mayonnaise
(see page 109) for this recipe, or
use a good shop-bought one.

4 medium–large leeks
Juice of half a lemon
2 tablespoons good-quality
extra-virgin olive oil
Watercress, to garnish
Fine sea salt

Gribiche
2 eggs
2 tablespoons mayonnaise,
preferably homemade
(page 109)
1 tablespoon chopped French
tarragon
3 tablespoons chopped flat-leaf
parsley
3 tablespoons chopped
watercress
1 tablespoon chopped chives
1 tablespoon lemon juice
1 tablespoon seeded mustard
1 teaspoon white wine vinegar
Fine sea salt
Freshly cracked black pepper

Serving suggestion: Gribiche
also goes wonderfully with charred
lettuce, chicken in all its guises or in
place of tartare sauce with crumbed
or grilled fish.

This pared-back gribiche is inspired by a meal I had at the restaurant
La Merenda while I was on holiday in Nice. Celebrating vegetables in
simple and elegant preparations like this is sadly underrated – the kind of
dish you swoon over when you try it on holidays, but somehow fear serving
when you return. I'm convinced that this dish can taste just as wonderful
between the walls of your home as it did between those art-crowded walls
in Nice – it just requires the right mindset.

For the gribiche, bring a small pot of water to a boil and carefully lower
in your eggs. Boil for 8 minutes. Drain the eggs and cool them under cold
running water. This can be done ahead. Peel the eggs and set aside.

Fill a wide shallow pan (ideally large enough to fit your leeks) with water
and bring it to a boil. Meanwhile, prepare your leeks by trimming off the
roots and the very dark part of the tops (these can be frozen and reserved
for stock). Cut lengthways through the centre of the top third of the leeks
and rinse them under cold running water to remove any sand. If the leeks
don't fit into your pan, cut them into lengths and tie the pieces together,
side by side, using butcher's string to ensure they don't fall apart while
boiling. Add enough salt to your pan so that the water tastes salty. Drop
your leeks in and boil for 5–7 minutes, or until they can easily be pierced
with a sharp knife. Remove them from the water and allow to cool.

To make the gribiche, roughly chop the eggs and combine them with all
the remaining ingredients, except for the salt and pepper, in the bowl of
a food processor and pulse until well combined. Taste and season with salt
and pepper and adjust the thickness with a teaspoon or two of water as
needed – you want the dressing to fall from the spoon, rather than sitting
on it like a stiff mayonnaise.

Remove and discard the outer layer from the leeks, then cut the leeks into
3–4 cm (1¼–1½ inch) lengths. Place them in a bowl and toss with the lemon
juice, olive oil and salt to taste before laying them on your serving platter.
Spoon the gribiche over the top and garnish with the watercress.

Notes: Leeks, like salad leaves, need to be thoroughly washed to avoid the terrible
disappointment of a rogue grain of sand or dirt (really, it only takes one!). They
grow partly buried and the dirt can only be removed once the tops are cut. This is
a recipe for your everyday leek – no need to go hunting for elegant, sprightly leeks
of early spring (although, it works with them too; just reduce the cooking time by
2–3 minutes).

I use a little mayonnaise in the gribiche to guard against splitting and to ensure
a lovely thick consistency. If you're looking for a little extra zing, you can pep up
the gribiche by adding capers, finely diced cornichons or French shallots, but I'm
going for gentle joy here – a celebration of pure simplicity.

The quest for umami, punch, spice and zing has pushed aside the wonder of gentle
dishes. It's like living in a world where there is only jazz (often, more accurately, heavy
metal) and no classical. And yet, the delicate and humble leek is so adored in France
that "to obtain the leek" is to have been awarded their highest agricultural medal.
While they are part of the allium family, they are mild, with a delightful sweetness
and a unique soft, ribbony texture – a gentle joy.

Radicchio chopped salad with chickpeas and Italian dressing

Makes: Enough to serve 4
Active time: 20 minutes
Inactive time: 10 minutes

Kitchenalia: Glass jar

1 cup (60 g) sourdough
    breadcrumbs
2 tablespoons extra-virgin
    olive oil
1 head radicchio di Chioggia
    (the round one)
1 x 400 g (14 oz) tin chickpeas,
    drained and rinsed
¼ cup (25 g) freshly grated
    Parmigiano Reggiano, plus
    extra to garnish
¼ cup (40 g) pickled guindilla
    chillies, chopped
Fine sea salt
Freshly cracked black pepper

Dressing
240 ml (8 fl oz) extra-virgin
    olive oil
30 g (1 oz) minced garlic
    (about 6 cloves)
¼ cup (40 g) finely diced
    French shallot (see notes)
¼ teaspoon chilli flakes
1 teaspoon dried oregano
100 ml (3½ fl oz) white wine
    vinegar
Juice of 1 lemon
1 teaspoon fine sea salt
Freshly cracked black pepper,
    to taste

This salad is a real homage to the American-Italian "red sauce" restaurants of my youth. The tablecloths are red checked, the grated parmesan and chilli flakes sit in jars on the table, the dressings are sharp and the tomato sauce is sweet. And so I'm calling this dressing "Italian" for no reason other than it's the type of dressing you would find at these places. The salad would typically have been made with iceberg, but I like it with radicchio for a more adult taste and texture.

For the dressing, in a small saucepan, combine half the olive oil with the garlic and shallot and heat over a low heat. When they start sizzling, cook for a further minute, then turn the heat off and allow to cool.

Combine all the remaining dressing ingredients in a glass jar, along with the other half of the olive oil. Pour in the cooled olive oil-garlic mix and a few cracks of pepper. Close the jar and give everything a good shake. Refrigerate the finished dressing until you're ready to dress your salad.

Heat your oven to 180°C (350°F). Toss the breadcrumbs with 2 tablespoons of olive oil, a pinch of salt and a few cracks of pepper. Spread them onto a baking tray and toast until golden brown and crunchy, about 8 minutes.

Use a knife to thinly slice the radicchio, then combine it in a bowl with the chickpeas, parmesan, pickled chillies, toasted breadcrumbs and a pinch of salt. Give your dressing a good shake before pouring some of it onto the salad; use as much or as little dressing as you like and keep any leftover in a glass jar in the fridge for up to 2 weeks. Toss the salad together and serve topped with an extra shaving of parmesan.

Notes: Whenever I have leftover sourdough bread, I cut the crusts off and process the stale bread in a food processor to form breadcrumbs. I keep those in a sealed container in my freezer to use as I need. If making fresh, for 1 cup (60 g) of breadcrumbs you'll need 2 cups of torn, crustless sourdough. Toasted breadcrumbs are excellent added to salads or sprinkled on top of pasta dishes.

There's an important difference between diced (as for the French shallot in this recipe) and minced (as for the garlic). The act of dicing a vegetable is reliant on precise cuts to arrive at cube-shaped pieces (literally, dice). Mincing is the step beyond that, when you run your knife over the ingredient – aim for a see-sawing motion with the knife that will result in a mass, rather than distinct individual shapes. In the case of onion or French shallot, unless specified as "minced", it's important not to do that in order to retain the texture and bite they bring to dishes. A sharp knife is imperative for both mincing and dicing without bruising, particularly for herbs, allowing them to retain their green vibrancy and fresh flavour.

Optional add-ins to this salad:

¼ cup (40 g) diced salami
¼ cup (40 g) diced provolone cheese
¼ cup (40 g) pitted green olives
¼ cup (35 g) Quick pickled celery (see page 26)
1 x 500 g (1 lb 2 oz) shredded poached chicken breast (see page 164)

Grilled eggplant with salsa verde, pomegranate and chèvre

Makes: Enough to serve 4
Active time: 30 minutes
Inactive time: 15 minutes

Kitchenalia: Outdoor grill or
indoor grill pan (optional)

Before you begin: If you are using
an outdoor grill to grill the eggplant,
go ahead and heat that up before
you begin your prep for this salad
as it may take longer, especially if
charcoal is involved.

3 large purple eggplants
 (aubergine)
Extra-virgin olive oil, for grilling
 or frying
Seeds from half a large
 pomegranate (see notes)
70 g (2½ oz) log fresh chèvre
¼ cup (40 g) pine nuts, toasted
1 tablespoon honey
Fine sea salt

Salsa verde
2 tablespoons finely diced
 French shallot
2 tablespoons white wine
 vinegar or lemon juice
⅓ cup (80 ml) good-quality
 extra-virgin olive oil
⅓ cup (10 g) finely chopped
 soft herbs (flat-leaf parsley,
 chervil, chives, French
 tarragon, mint, dill)
 (see notes)
Fine sea salt

Seasonal adjustment: In winter,
use roasted pumpkin wedges in place
of the eggplant – you might have
to forgo the pomegranate seeds but
between the pine nuts and the
salsa verde, you'll still get a good
dose of crunch and zing.

Are pomegranate seeds the festoon lights of the culinary world? While strikingly beautiful, it's the substance that gets me here, the lovely combination of textures and flavours: silky charred eggplant (aubergine), crunchy pomegranate seeds and pine nuts, creamy goat's cheese and bright salsa verde; salty, sweet, sour and nutty. I make this in early autumn when eggplants are still at their best and pomegranates have just arrived. A dish that is as delicious as it is gorgeous.

First, make your salsa verde. Macerate the shallot in the vinegar or lemon juice with a pinch of salt for at least 15 minutes. Add in the olive oil and the chopped herbs and stir to combine. Set aside.

Using a vegetable peeler, peel your eggplants in thick stripes from the stem to the base. Trim off the stems and slice the eggplants into 1 cm (½ inch) thick rounds. Drizzle a generous amount of olive oil over the rounds and set them aside.

Grill the eggplant slices until they're well browned on both sides; you can do this on an indoor grill pan or an outdoor grill, alternatively, you can fry them in a cast-iron frying pan. This takes about 5–6 minutes, but the timing depends on your grill (or how hot your pan gets). You'll probably need to do this in 2–3 batches, again depending on your grill or pan. Drain the grilled eggplant on paper towel and season with salt.

Arrange the eggplant on a platter. Drizzle over the salsa verde and sprinkle with the pomegranate seeds and dollops of the chèvre, finishing with the pine nuts and a drizzle of the honey.

Notes: To easily remove the seeds from a pomegranate, take the tip of a paring knife and insert it into the flowering end of the pomegranate, then turn your wrist to crack it open. From there, you can break the pomegranate into quarters or smaller pieces using your hands. Fill a bowl with cold water and hold a piece of pomegranate in one hand, seeds facing down close to the water, then gently tap the skin side with the back of a wooden spoon. The seeds should tumble right through your fingers and into the bowl. The water separates any white papery bits, which surround the seeds, because they float and the seeds sink. Remove the white bits, then discard and strain the seeds from the water. Keep the seeds refrigerated in a sealed container. You can use any excess to toss through salads over the course of a week.

Salsa verde literally means "green sauce" and the term consequently encompasses the many and varied wonders of that genre: pesto, chimichurri, tomatillo, sauce verte, or a variation of this little number. I dare you to find a vegetable it doesn't like (most meats and fish will also fall under its spell). This is the little black dress of recipes, to be brought out when seeking simplicity and confidence. Use whichever herbs you have on hand, only remain wary of tarragon, as its flavours can overpower. A salsa verde is a welcome addition to everyone's repertoire.

Soba noodles with sesame dressing

I vividly recall travelling in Tokyo and stepping into beautiful soba restaurants where the noodles would come out on small woven bamboo trays with a bowl of sesame dipping sauce. I watched as business people carefully picked up the soba noodles with chopsticks and delicately dipped them into the dressing, gingerly slurping them up. It's such a fond food memory, that I had to adapt a version of it for my working lunch at home. Serve this salad cold or at room temperature.

To make the dressing, combine all the ingredients in a small bowl and whisk to combine. Add a little more water if the mixture is too thick – it should be the consistency of thick pouring cream and completely smooth.

Bring a pot of water to the boil and cook your noodles according to the package instructions. Add the bok choy into the same pot with noodles for the last minute of cooking. Strain and rinse everything under cold running water and set aside in a colander to continue to drain.

Heat a small sauté pan over a medium heat and add the neutral oil. Sauté the mushrooms in the oil until they're cooked, about 2–3 minutes. Set them aside.

To serve, place your noodles and the bok choy in a bowl and drizzle them with some of the sesame dressing and the Crunchy chilli oil (see page 88) (use as much or as little of the dressing and oil as you like and save the rest for another time). Serve the noodles either at room temperature or cold, topping them with the sliced spring onions and the sautéed mushrooms.

Makes: Enough to serve 2
Active time: 25 minutes

Before you begin: You'll have enough leftover Crunchy chilli oil to keep in a glass jar in the fridge to use next time you make this dish, or to add a little zing to other dishes. Feel free to halve the recipe if you don't want leftovers.

180 g (6¼ oz) dried soba
    noodles
1 bok choy, split in half
2 teaspoons neutral oil
100 g (3½ oz) mushrooms
    (shiitake, oyster or wood ear),
    sliced
6 spring onions (scallions),
    thinly sliced

Sesame dressing
1 teaspoon red or white miso
2 tablespoons tahini
1 teaspoon grated ginger
1 tablespoon rice wine vinegar
2 teaspoons sesame oil
2 teaspoons light soy sauce
2 teaspoons maple syrup
    or honey
2 tablespoons water
Pinch of fine sea salt

To serve
Crunchy chilli oil, to taste
    (see over page)

Japanese soba noodles are made with buckwheat flour (often with a little wheat flour to make the dough more stretchy) and have a slightly nutty taste. Long considered a spiritual food, Zen Buddhist monks would eat soba noodles before committing their bodies to a ten-day fast. They're wonderfully light and energising. It's not unusual to be served a glass of the hot soba-cooking water (*sobayu*, "*yu*" meaning "hot water") to drink at the end of your meal.

Makes: 1 cup (250 ml)
Active time: 20 minutes
Inactive time: 10 minutes

100 g (3½ oz) French shallot
  (about 2 large shallots),
  finely diced
250 ml (9 fl oz) neutral oil
40 g (1½ oz) garlic (about
  8 cloves), peeled and
  thinly sliced
40 g (1½ oz) sliced almonds,
  finely chopped
1 tablespoon sesame seeds
1 star anise pod
3 tablespoons Aleppo or Korean
  chilli flakes (see note)
A pinch of fine sea salt
2 teaspoons white (granulated)
  sugar

Note: Standard chilli flakes, as opposed to the Aleppo or Korean ones I've used here, include seeds and carry slightly more heat so if you're using these, start with 1 tablespoon to see how much heat suits your palate. Aleppo or Korean chilli flakes will give your oil a beautiful bright red colour that the standard chilli flakes won't.

Serving suggestions: This Crunchy chilli oil is so versatile. Try it on cooked green beans or soft polenta with a poached egg, and for the brave, it can even share plates with your favourite pasta. It is also great with silken tofu (see page 90).

Crunchy chilli oil

I always have this staple on hand for when something needs a little crunchy kick (which is often!).

Combine the shallot and oil in a small sauté pan and place over a medium heat. Cook until the shallot is starting to turn golden. Use a skimmer, or spoon, to scoop the shallot out of the oil and set it aside. Add the garlic, almonds, sesame seeds and star anise to the oil and let them sizzle until everything is caramelised and golden. Turn the heat off and add in the chilli flakes, salt and sugar. Set aside to cool.

Pour the chilli oil into a clean glass jar and store it in the fridge. This oil will happily keep for months.

Salad of red capsicum, feta and white anchovies with za'atar pita

This punchy salad is best served at room temperature. It's a wonderful dish for entertaining in late summer, when the sweet capsicums (peppers) are at their peak. Everyone can scoop pieces of the marinated capsicum and anchovy up and pile them onto the crisp za'atar pita.

Char your capsicums over an open gas flame, on a charcoal grill, or under a grill (broiler) in the oven (see notes). Turn them several times so they char evenly. When they are completely blackened on the outside and the flesh is soft and collapsing, place them into a bowl and cover with a plate or aluminium foil to finish steaming as they cool.

Preheat your oven to 180°C (350°F).

Split your pita breads open and use the ⅓ cup (80 ml) of olive oil to brush both sides using a pastry brush. Lay them on a baking tray in one even layer (you may need two trays) and season with salt. Transfer the tray to the oven to toast the pitas, flipping them after 5–7 minutes, or when the first side becomes golden. Continue to bake until the entire pita is completely crisp and golden, about 10–12 minutes in total. Remove from the oven and immediately sprinkle the hot pitas with the za'atar. Set aside.

Peel the charred black skin from the capsicums and scrape away any seeds or stem. Tear them into strips about 3–4 cm (1¼–1½ inches) thick and place in a mixing bowl. Add the vinegar, remaining olive oil and a pinch of salt, then grate in the garlic clove using a microplane. Toss everything together to combine.

Spread the capsicum strips on a platter and either shave or crumble the feta over the top. Drape the anchovies (if using) over the capsicum and serve with the crisp za'atar pita.

Notes: If you don't have access to an open flame or grill, you can cook these in a hot oven. Lay the capsicums (left whole) on a baking tray, drizzle with extra-virgin olive oil, season with fine salt and cook them in an oven at 250°C (480°F) until charred and collapsing, about 10–12 minutes.

When charring capsicums, it is possible to take them too far. When this happens, they almost completely disintegrate when you peel them and fall apart in tatters. When cooked just enough, the capsicum will be completely soft – the skins should come off easily, but the flesh will still be thick and juicy, and maintain its integrity. Overcooked capsicum can be puréed into a delicious romesco or muhammara.

Makes: Enough to serve 4 as an entrée
Active time: 25 minutes
Inactive time: 30 minutes

Kitchenalia: Pastry brush

Before you begin: When charring or roasting capsicums, it's always worth doing a few extra – submerged in olive oil, charred capsicum will keep for weeks in the fridge. It makes an excellent addition to salads or sandwiches like the Pan bagnat (see page 116).

3 red or yellow capsicums (peppers), or a mix of both
2 pita breads
⅓ cup (80 ml) extra-virgin olive oil, plus an extra ¼ cup (60 ml)
2 teaspoons za'atar
2 tablespoons white wine vinegar
1 garlic clove
60 g (2¼ oz) Danish-style creamy feta
8 good-quality white or brown anchovy fillets (optional)
Fine sea salt

Silken tofu with corn, garlic, chilli oil and breadcrumbs

Makes: Enough to serve 2–4 depending on whether you serve as an entrée, main, or side
Active time: 30 minutes

Before you begin: You might want to prepare a batch of Crunchy chilli oil (see page 88) to go with this, which can be done ahead and stored in the fridge. Alternatively, use your favourite shop-bought chilli oil.

1 x 300 g (10½ oz) packet silken tofu
½ cup (125 ml) neutral oil
2 cobs corn, husks peeled off and kernels cut from the cob
2 tablespoons sesame seeds
¼ cup (15 g) panko breadcrumbs
3 garlic cloves, minced
3 spring onions (scallions), white and light green parts thinly sliced, dark green parts thinly sliced and reserved to garnish
2 tablespoons light soy sauce
1 tablespoon black vinegar
½ teaspoon white (granulated) sugar
½ teaspoon sesame oil
Fine sea salt

To serve
Crunchy chilli oil (page 88) (or shop-bought chilli oil)
Minced chives (optional)

This dish is inspired by my friend Jemma Whiteman. At her wonderful restaurant Ante, in Sydney, she serves a silken tofu and corn dish that works as a side to many of the main courses. Corn and silken tofu is a classic Cantonese pairing, but Jemma adds different flavours like nori, katsuobushi or breadcrumbs (my favourite). I'm adding a toasted garlic and black vinegar dressing and imagining this as an excellent dish to serve on a hot summer's day when cold salads are all you want to eat. You could also serve it with steamed white rice for a complete, and excellent, meal.

Drain the tofu and lay it on your serving platter, then cut it into 2–3 cm (about 1 inch) slices. With it being so delicate, I slice it directly on the platter to avoid having to move it after slicing.

Add 2 tablespoons of the neutral oil to a medium-sized sauté pan and set over a high heat. Cook the corn with a pinch of salt until the kernels start to brown. Try not to stir too much, to allow for some colour to develop. Add the sesame seeds and cook for a few seconds. Remove the corn and sesame seeds from the pan and set aside. Return the pan to the stove over a medium heat. Add 1 tablespoon of the neutral oil and cook the breadcrumbs until nicely golden. Set aside.

Wipe out the pan and return it to the heat. Add the remaining 3 tablespoons of the neutral oil, along with the minced garlic and white and light green spring onion, and sizzle until the garlic is starting to turn a pale golden brown. Turn off the heat and let the garlic turn completely golden in the residual heat (this stops it from ever getting over-browned, which happens very quickly!). At that stage, add in the soy sauce, vinegar, sugar and sesame oil. Allow to cool to room temperature.

Spoon the corn over the tofu. Pour the dressing in the pan over everything and add the toasted breadcrumbs and a drizzle of the chilli oil, finishing with the reserved sliced spring onions and minced chives (if using).

Tofu is made from dried soybeans that have been soaked, crushed and boiled. The soy "milk" is curdled, separating into curds and whey – a process that is actually quite similar to that of cheese making. Defined by the amount of water that has been pressed out of it, tofu will be labelled as: silken, soft, medium, firm, extra-firm, etc. The less water there is, the higher the quantity of fat and protein. In this case, silken tofu is undrained and unpressed, with a high-water content and a custardy texture. A delicate refrain.

Shaved cabbage with pine nuts, currants and vinaigrette

Cabbage is such a wonderful salad leaf; its raw, sweet crunch is entirely enticing. While it's at its best in winter (all brassicas love a bite of frost to bring out their sugars), cabbage is pretty good all year round. Plus, it's very affordable. This simple salad is a lovely lunch on its own but also makes for a perfect and easy side to main events of meat or pasta.

For the vinaigrette, place your shallot in a bowl with the vinegar, salt and honey, then allow it to sit and pickle slightly while you prepare the rest of the salad.

Soak the currants in hot water for at least 5 minutes.

Thinly shave the cabbage using a mandoline (or with a very sharp knife) and place it in a large mixing bowl. Drain the currants and add them in along with the pine nuts, herbs and parmesan.

Whisk the olive oil into the shallot-vinegar mixture to finish the vinaigrette and pour it over the salad. Add a good pinch of salt and a good crack of pepper to the bowl and toss everything together. Taste for seasoning and serve immediately.

Notes: This is not a salad that likes to be made ahead. It's best dressed liberally, seasoned well and served immediately.

This recipe is easily scaled up or down to suit the number of people around the table.

Makes: Enough to serve 4
Active time: 20 minutes

Kitchenalia: Mandoline (alternatively, a very sharp knife to thinly slice)

¼ cup (40 g) currants
4 heaped cups (300 g) thinly sliced green cabbage (about half a large head of green cabbage)
¼ cup (40 g) pine nuts, toasted
2 tablespoons chopped mint
2 tablespoons chopped flat-leaf parsley
¼ cup (25 g) shaved Parmigiano Reggiano (use a vegetable peeler)
Fine sea salt
Freshly cracked black pepper

Vinaigrette
2 tablespoons finely diced French shallot
3 tablespoons sherry or white wine vinegar
Pinch of fine sea salt
1 teaspoon honey
5 tablespoons extra-virgin olive oil

Serving suggestions: Serve this salad with chicken, steak or alongside a bowl of pasta. Try it with the Spatchcocked roast chicken on crouton (see page 174), the Tagliatelle Bolognese (see page 144) or the Pancetta-wrapped pork neck roast (see page 210).

Crispy rice and trout salad with fish sauce dressing

Makes: Enough to serve 2–3
as a main
Active time: 40 minutes
Inactive time: 4 hours

Before you begin: This recipe is a great excuse to cook extra rice. If you have leftover steamed rice, spread it out on a plate and dry it in your fridge overnight, ready to fry. Otherwise, cook the rice as the recipe instructs – I like to do this in the morning if I know I want to make this salad at lunch time.

1 cup (200 g) jasmine rice,
  uncooked, or about
  3 cups (555 g) cooked
  jasmine rice
2 cups (500 ml) neutral oil, plus
  an extra 1 tablespoon
½ teaspoon ground turmeric
1 small (about 600 g/1 lb 5 oz)
  rainbow trout, deboned and
  butterflied, or 2 x 200 g
  (7 oz) fillets, skin on
2–3 cups (300 g) thinly sliced
  white cabbage (a quarter of a
  large head of cabbage)
⅓ cup (50 g) toasted peanuts or
  cashews, crushed (optional)
½ cup (15 g) coriander (cilantro)
  leaves
½ cup (10 g) mint leaves
Fine sea salt

Dressing
1 small garlic clove, peeled
1 teaspoon peeled and
  chopped ginger
1–2 small red birdseye chillies,
  sliced
Zest of 1 lime
Juice of 2 limes
2 tablespoons fish sauce
2 teaspoons white
  (granulated) sugar
1 tablespoon neutral oil
1 French shallot, thinly sliced

This is the salad to make if you're in a cooking rut. Crisp rice, wispy thin cabbage, lots of fresh herbs, oily rich trout and a salty-sour-sweet dressing that tastes like a holiday from your usual dinners. It's a great way to use up leftover steamed rice and, if you're short on time, can even be made with shop-bought hot-smoked trout.

If you're cooking the rice from scratch, fill a medium-sized pot with water and bring it to a boil. Once boiling, stir in the rice and boil for precisely 8 minutes. Think of this like you're cooking pasta. Drain and allow to cool. Dry the cooked rice out by spreading it on a plate and placing in your fridge, uncovered, for at least 2 hours, or overnight.

To fry the rice, add the 2 cups (500 ml) of oil to a small pot and heat over a medium heat. Test if it's hot enough by dropping in a few kernels of rice – if they sizzle immediately, it's ready. Carefully add in half the rice and allow it to fry until crisp, about 8 minutes – it will sputter for the first few seconds, so stand back. When the rice is crisp, scoop it out using a skimmer or spoon, drain on paper towels and sprinkle with salt. Proceed with the rest of the rice, then toss it all in a bowl with the turmeric to coat the rice and set aside.

For the fish, heat a non-stick frying pan over a medium–high heat and add in the extra tablespoon of oil. While your pan is heating up, sprinkle the trout with salt. Cook the trout, skin-side down, for about 5–6 minutes, using a small heavy pan to weigh the fish down and crisp the skin. This should cook the fish all the way through so you don't have to flip it. Remove the fish from the pan and set it aside, skin-side up, while you prepare the rest of the salad.

To make the dressing, place the garlic, ginger and chilli (optional: reserve some chilli for garnish) in a mortar and pestle and crush until it forms a paste. Mix in the remaining dressing ingredients and stir to combine.

In a large mixing bowl, combine all the salad ingredients with the flaked fish (including its skin) and drizzle in the dressing. Give it all a good toss and serve the salad warm, cold or at room temperature. Garnish with the reserved chilli, if you like.

Fennel and pumpkin caponata with mozzarella

Makes: Enough to serve 4
Active time: 25 minutes
Inactive time: 40 minutes

Quarter of a large butternut
    pumpkin (squash) (or half
    a small honeynut pumpkin)
¼ cup (60 ml) extra-virgin
    olive oil, plus extra for
    roasting vegetables
1 medium fennel bulb
Half a brown onion, diced small
1 × 400 g (14 oz) tin cherry
    tomatoes, rinsed, or 250 g
    (9 oz) fresh cherry tomatoes
2 tablespoons pine nuts,
    toasted
2 tablespoons currants
1 tablespoon salted capers,
    rinsed
⅓ cup (50 g) pitted green
    olives (e.g. gordal or
    green Sicilian)
1½ tablespoons white
    (granulated) sugar
3 tablespoons white wine
    vinegar
1 stalk celery, diced small
1 ball (about 110 g/3¾ oz)
    fresh cow's or buffalo milk
    mozzarella (see note)
Fine sea salt

To serve
Good-quality extra-virgin
    olive oil
Flaked sea salt
Freshly cracked black pepper

I am very drawn to the Sicilian flavour profile of sweet, sour, salty and oily. Caponata is the perfect embodiment of this combination. This dish is best served at room temperature, with good crusty bread or focaccia to mop everything up.

Preheat your oven to 180°C (350°F) and line a baking tray with baking paper.

Peel and deseed the pumpkin and cut it into 3–4 cm (1¼–1½ inch) pieces. Toss the pumpkin with some of the extra olive oil and sprinkle with salt, then place it on the baking tray. Cut the fennel into eight wedges then toss with more of the extra olive oil and sprinkle with salt, then place on the same tray, next to the pumpkin. Roast for 30–40 minutes, until both are golden brown and tender.

Set a large sauté pan (with a lid) over a medium heat and add the ¼ cup (60 ml) of olive oil, the onion and a pinch of salt and cook until the onion is soft and sweet and beginning to brown. Add the tomatoes, pine nuts, currants, capers, olives, sugar and vinegar and cook together on a low heat for about 8 minutes. Turn off the heat.

When the pumpkin and fennel are ready, set the sauté pan with the tomato mix over a low heat and add the celery. Cook for 1 minute, then add the roasted pumpkin and fennel to the pan and stir to combine. Cook for a further minute, then turn off the heat and place the lid on the pan. Let it sit and steam together as it cools. Taste for seasoning and adjust with more salt and vinegar if needed.

Serve the caponata at room temperature with the torn mozzarella on top, finishing with a drizzle of good-quality olive oil, a sprinkle of flaked sea salt and a crack of pepper.

Note: Mozzarella is made with either cow's milk or buffalo milk. Cow's milk mozzarella, known as *fior di latte*, literally means "flower of milk", indicating its purity, and the name is used to describe both mozzarella and gelato. Mozzarella made with buffalo milk, known as *di latte di bufala*, has a creamier, more tangy flavour than the more traditional cow's milk mozzarella.

Seasonal adjustment: In summer, swap the pumpkin and fennel for a large purple eggplant (aubergine) for a more traditional caponata.

As with many Sicilian dishes, caponata has drawn its ingredients from across the Mediterranean. It is also a dish that traditionally travels, with the vegetables being bought fresh at port and the sailors preserving them with vinegar and sugar while at sea.

Fish crudo with caper and French shallot vinaigrette

This may feel like a 'cheffy' dish, and yes, it looks impressive, but the hard work is actually in the sourcing. If you have a fishmonger you trust (a great asset to the home cook), go and see them. Your safest bet is to buy a whole, good-looking fish (bright eyes, bright red gills, not slimy or smelling of the ocean) and ask the fishmonger to fillet and prepare it, leaving the fillets whole for you to slice at home. The fish is the star in any crudo dish, so keep this recipe up your sleeve for when you have access to a great fish market or fishmonger. I like an assortment of fish, but again, the freshness is the most important thing here – focus on that rather than the variety.

For the vinaigrette, combine all the ingredients and set aside. Do this just before serving, to avoid your chives turning brown from the acid in the dressing.

When ready to serve, thinly slice your fish and lay it out on a platter, or on individual plates. Sprinkle the fish with flaked sea salt and spoon the dressing over the slices. Finish with a garnish of chives and serve cold.

Note: "Sashimi grade" is unregulated, but typically has to do with freshness and best-handling practice. As you slice raw fish like this, it starts to change and oxidise – while there may be no change to the naked eye, it will start to absorb flavours from your fridge or its packaging, so always slice at home, just before serving.

Makes: Enough to serve 4
Active time: 15 minutes

Before you begin: Ask your fishmonger to prepare the fish for you in a way that makes it easy to slice for sashimi. They can cut out any blood lines or sinewy pieces (usually found near the tail) that aren't pleasant to eat when eating fish raw. Slice the fish yourself at home, just before serving. Make sure your knife is very sharp or you risk destroying the fish.

400 g (14 oz) assorted sashimi-grade fish (I like a mix of yellowfin tuna, snapper and wild kingfish, but use whatever your fishmonger suggests is best for eating raw, at that moment)
Flaked sea salt

Caper and French shallot vinaigrette
½ tablespoon salted capers, rinsed and chopped
½ tablespoon white wine vinegar
1 teaspoon lemon zest
1 tablespoon lemon juice
1½ tablespoons finely diced French shallot
3 tablespoons extra-virgin olive oil
2 tablespoons finely sliced chives, plus extra to garnish

We have elevated raw fish to the upper echelons of cookery, but the history of these dishes tells another story. Japanese sashimi, South American ceviche, Hawaiian poke, kinilaw from the Philippines, kokoda from the South Pacific and Italian crudo were all the ultimate in fast food – raw fish, sliced quickly, straight from the boat, to feed fishermen and their families alike. Its evolution has created the artform, but it's one that is firmly within reach of the home chef with a good fishmonger and a sharp knife!

The *great* extenders

"Great meals rarely start at points that all look like beginnings. They usually *pick up* where something else *leaves off*. This is how most of the best things are made – *imagine if the world had to begin from scratch each dawn*: a tree would *never grow*, nor would we get to see the etchings of gentle rings on a clamshell."

Tamar Adler, *An Everlasting Meal: Cooking with Economy and Grace*

Try as I might, I find I still get angry at a lot of things: a bad hair day, a late delivery, a stain that won't come out, a broken egg. Don't even get me started on the big things! The antidote to my internal fury is cooking. I live for cooking. It brings me joy and calmness; it resolves my inner turmoil in a way that nothing else does. It is where I work out my anxieties and fall in love over and over again.

And yet, sometimes, even I am angry or tired of it all. So much effort: shopping, cleaning, standing in the kitchen, and all just to feed myself. And then I'm angry that I am almost always hungry. *Do we really have to do this for ourselves several times a day??*, I ask myself in particularly dark moments. In those moments, something on bread is the solution.

If there's one item in the kitchen that I am happy to outsource, it's bread. Although I have tried making my own sourdough at home (with pleasing results), I would much rather spend my time thinking about what goes *on* the bread. It is the greatest of vessels to pile high with vegetables, fresh cheese and sometimes little fish or a slice of salumi. Buy a good loaf of bread, whatever that means to you. For me, a good sourdough, made by skilled hands, simply cannot be beaten, or go for ciabatta, baguette, or something with a good, chewy crust, and not too many large holes in the centre because, as gravity dictates, what is not held up, will fall.

Brush a piece of bread liberally on both sides with extra-virgin olive oil and fry in a pan, grill on your stove, or, if your outdoor grill is going, grill over charcoal. If it wasn't so wasteful, I would light a grill just to grill bread – it's by far my favourite way. Look for toasty colour on both sides, then scrape the cut-side of a garlic clove along one side of the toasted bread – a little goes a long way. Finish with a sprinkle of flaked sea salt. You could stop here, and most would be impressed, but continue to gild the lily for even greater results. See page 104 for a few ideas.

Crostini

Here are a few no-recipe recipes for some of my favourite crostini:

Crostini with roast pumpkin, pancetta (or thinly sliced bacon) and sage

Cut a small pumpkin (squash) in half, scoop out the seeds and brush the skin and flesh with olive oil and sprinkle with salt. Place it on a baking tray, cut-side up, and roast in a 180°C (350°F) oven until it's completely soft, about 40–60 minutes, depending on the pumpkin. Fry strips of pancetta in a pan until rendered and crisp. Fry the sage in the pork fat, until crisp, then remove it from the pan and fry the bread in the rendered fat, adding olive oil if needed. Scoop out the pumpkin and crush it lightly in a bowl with a drizzle of olive oil, lemon juice and salt to taste. Top the prepared crostino with the mashed pumpkin, crisp strips of pancetta, the fried sage and a drizzle of good-quality aged balsamic vinegar. Finish with freshly cracked black pepper.

Crostini with sweet-and-sour greens and ricotta

Blanch hearty greens like cavolo nero, silverbeet (Swiss chard), beet tops and even chicory (bitter greens) in boiling salted water. Drain and squeeze most of the water out, then roughly chop the greens. Sauté diced brown onion, minced garlic, diced celery and chopped sultanas in lots of olive oil until soft and sweet. Add your chopped greens to the pan and cover with a lid so everything steams together for a couple of minutes. Season with salt and red wine vinegar. Prepare your crostino and slather with seasoned ricotta. Top with the greens and some toasted pine nuts then, finish with a drizzle of good-quality olive oil.

Crostini with capsicum, capers and rocket

Char sweet red capsicums (peppers) on a hot grill or over an open gas flame. Place them in a bowl, cover with a plate and allow to steam and cool. Peel, deseed and cut the capsicums into strips. Season with salt, sherry vinegar or red wine vinegar and olive oil. Prepare your crostino and top with the dressed capsicum. Sprinkle with rinsed, salted capers and rocket (arugula) leaves that have been dressed with olive oil and salt.

Crostini with goat's curd, lentils, broad beans and mint

Boil lentils in salted water until tender and drain. Blanch podded broad beans in boiling water for 30 seconds and immediately plunge into ice water. Strip off the outer husks of the beans, then mix the beans with the lentils (the early-spring baby broad beans can be left unpeeled). Dress the lentil broad bean mix with red wine vinegar, olive oil, chopped mint, salt and black pepper. Prepare your crostino and top with creamy goat's curd. Spoon the lentil mix onto the toasted bread, and sprinkle with Parmigiano Reggiano and chopped chives.

Crostini with ricotta, bursting cherry tomatoes and anchovy

Preheat your oven to as high as it will go, about 230–250°C (450–480°F). Toss cherry tomatoes with olive oil, salt and fresh oregano on a baking tray and place in the oven. Cook until the tomatoes are bursting open and juicy, but not completely collapsed. Prepare your crostino and top with ricotta and a spoonful of the tomatoes, finishing with a good-quality anchovy fillet and a drizzle of good-quality olive oil.

Crostini with mozzarella and roasted lemon

When lemons are at their peak of the winter season (do not attempt this out of season), place thin slices of lemon on a baking tray lined with baking paper. Drizzle with olive oil, a sprinkle of salt and a light sprinkle of sugar. Roast the citrus rounds under a medium–hot grill (broiler) until they look softened, but not burnt. Prepare your crostino and top with slices of buffalo mozzarella, followed by the lemon slices and a drizzle of good-quality olive oil. Finish with a couple of basil leaves.

Crostini

Mayonnaise

It was a hot summer's night. I was living and working in the Napa Valley. My best friend David and I had gotten into a wonderful habit of making delicious meals late into the night, after we'd finished our shifts at the restaurant; it was part of our wind-down routine. We were still young enough to happily stay up late without consequence. There was something about going from a bustling restaurant service, with food running out of the kitchen at rapid pace, heart pounding, each minute presenting a new deadline, shouting and sweating, contrasted with the luxury of taking our time to make a meal, converse and appreciate the little things.

Luckily, David lived across the street from the restaurant; from clock off to glass of wine in hand and supper preparations underway, was about five minutes. David always had good bread around, good olive oil, eggs and bacon. Being the height of summer, also part of the scene on this particular night were a couple of juicy, ripe tomatoes and some crunchy lettuce. He set forth to make a sandwich that has given me one of the most delicious food memories I have to date. Thick-cut, black-pepper-crusted bacon, sizzled in a cast-iron pan to just the right balance of crisp and crunchy, juicy and chewy. Thick tomato slices seasoned with salt, ice-cold crunchy lettuce, garlic-rubbed toasted bread and a good lick of homemade mayonnaise on *both* slices of bread. No Michelin stars, no 50 Best lists, just a steamy night, eating that sandwich with my best friend and a glass of chilled red wine.

More often than not, what I need for a cheeky snack these days is mayonnaise. A mayonnaise is plain and simple. It's not aïoli – it's the neutrality that makes it so wildly useful. It adds richness and creaminess without the heaviness of dairy or robust flavour of punchy olive oil. It is essential in the construction of most sandwiches, and is the building block of many a dressing or dip. I don't turn my nose up at a good shop-bought mayonnaise either – I always keep some in the fridge. But for some things, like a good BLT, a delicious homemade version is worth the effort. It's also incredibly simple and a foundational kitchen skill that should be a part of everyone's repertoire.

A recipe for good mayonnaise

Add the egg, mustard, salt and vinegar to the bowl of a small food processor. Blend these together for 30 seconds until well combined.

With the machine running, slowly stream the oil through the opening in the lid of the food processor until all the oil is used up and a mayonnaise has formed. Store the mayonnaise in a clean glass jar in the fridge and use within a week.

Notes: The oil you use is important. Choose something of good quality with minimal flavour. I like using avocado oil, or even a very light olive oil, but taste around and see what you like.

The raw egg in homemade mayonnaise means it is not advised for pregnant women, babies and the immunocompromised (due to the elevated risk of salmonella). In any case, opt for super-fresh eggs from a trusted source.

By using the whole egg, there is much less chance the mayonnaise will split (the egg whites make for a much more stable emulsion because of their protein content). If, on the off chance, your mayonnaise does split, pour it into another bowl. Clean the bowl of the food processor and start again, using a single egg white as the base and slowly streaming in the split mayonnaise.

Makes: 1½ cups (355 g)

Kitchenalia: Food processor (alternatively, use a stick blender and the tall, slender jug that comes with it)

1 whole egg
2 teaspoons Dijon mustard
½ teaspoon fine sea salt
1 tablespoon white wine vinegar
1 cup (250 ml) neutral oil

Other uses for mayonnaise:

Sandwiches: Aside from adding creaminess and delicious flavour, a layer of mayonnaise prevents the other ingredients from making the bread soggy. Slather it onto both slices of the bread for best effect. I use mayonnaise in the Tarragon and celery chicken sandwich (see page 110), the Salad sandwich (see page 111) and the Pan bagnat (see page 116).

Egg salad: Mayonnaise mixed with chopped hard-boiled egg and a teaspoon of curry powder makes the most delicious egg salad. Sandwich this between two slices of buttery brioche, add a tangle of watercress leaves, and you have a pretty unbeatable breakfast or lunch.

Dressings: Green Goddess dressing is one of the more well-known creamy salad dressings. Mayonnaise blended with plenty of herbs, avocado and lemon juice. This is excellent drizzled on crunchy leaves, used as a dip for crudités or mixed through tinned tuna for a delicious tuna salad. Mayonnaise is also used in the sauce gribiche for the Leeks gribiche (see page 80).

Dips: A classic Marie Rose, or seafood dipping sauce, is mayonnaise mixed with tomato sauce (ketchup), Worcestershire sauce, lemon juice and seasoning. I like to add a little freshly-prepared horseradish to this, too. For 1¼ cups (300 g) of mayonnaise, mix in 3 tablespoons of tomato sauce, a few dashes each of tabasco and Worcestershire sauce, the juice of half a lemon, a crack of black pepper and 1–2 tablespoons of grated horseradish, if you like.

Tarragon and celery chicken sandwich

Makes: 4 sandwiches
Active time: 20 minutes

2 x 400–500 g (14 oz–1 lb 2 oz)
 poached chicken breasts
 (page 164)
Scant ½ cup (100 g) mayonnaise
 (page 109)
¼ cup (70 g) Greek-style plain
 yoghurt
2 stalks celery, diced small
 (preferably the inner-most
 yellowish stalks)
2 tablespoons chopped French
 tarragon
¼ cup (15 g) chopped chives,
 or thinly sliced spring onion
 (scallion)
1 tablespoon white wine vinegar
Scant ½ cup (55 g) toasted and
 chopped pecans or walnuts
Scant ½ cup (75 g) dried
 cranberries or sultanas
4 ciabatta-style sandwich buns,
 cut in half, or 8 slices soft
 wholegrain bread
Soft unsalted butter,
 to butter bread
8 leaves green oak or
 cos lettuce
Fine sea salt
Freshly cracked black pepper
 (*lots*)

A good chicken sandwich should be in everyone's repertoire. As old-fashioned as they may seem, they're still a favourite, perhaps due to the nostalgia they evoke. They make an excellent lunch and are perfect to wrap up for road trips and picnics.

Before you begin: You can poach your chicken breasts (see page 164) a day in advance to ensure they're nicely chilled before you make this recipe. You can also make your Mayonnaise (see page 109) a day ahead. Try swapping the chicken here for poached prawns and the tarragon for dill to make a delicious seafood version.

Cut the chicken into 1 cm (½ inch) dice. Place the chicken in a bowl and mix with the mayonnaise, yoghurt, celery, tarragon, chives, vinegar, nuts and dried fruit. Season with a pinch of salt and a good crack of pepper. Taste and adjust with salt as needed.

Spread each bun or slice of bread with the soft butter all the way to the edges. Top each bottom half with a quarter of the chicken and celery mix. Add a couple of lettuce leaves and close the sandwich with the top halves of the buns or slices of bread.

Slice in half and enjoy, or wrap with baking paper to eat later.

Salad sandwich

I ate my first "salad sandwich" in Australia. While I had never heard the term before, I recognised the flavours as I had been making versions of this meatless sandwich all my life: lots of crunchy vegetables, a few slices of cheese and a thick lick of mayonnaise to keep the bread from going soggy. I came to discover that the salad sandwich is an Australian relic, a staple of milk bars, lunch boxes and petrol stations around the country. Now, it's a little less ubiquitous, but no less loved. Tinned beetroot, carrots, alfalfa sprouts and buttered bread make up the classic version. Mine is a little more embellished – feel free to add or subtract as you want.

First, make your herb pesto by combining all the ingredients in the bowl of a food processor and processing until smooth. Check for seasoning and set aside.

Toast the cut sides of your bread and slather half a tablespoon of the mayonnaise on each bun. Start building your sandwich, first with the slices of cheese, then avocado, followed by the julienned carrot. At this stage, add a good spoonful of the herb pesto and a sprinkle of salt. Next, add the slices of beetroot, top that with the sprouts and pickle slices, then the apple slices. Finally, top it all with the cos lettuce leaves. Add a little more of the pesto and close the sandwich with the top halves of the buns.

Wrap the sandwich and leave it to sit, or slice in half and enjoy.

Note: It's a good idea to wrap the sandwich up tightly in baking paper or aluminium foil and let it sit for at least 10 minutes before eating (but longer is fine) to allow the bread to mould itself around the fillings and make it a little less messy to eat.

Makes: 2 sandwiches
Active time: 20 minutes

Kitchenalia: Food processor

Before you begin: You'll need a batch of homemade Mayonnaise (see page 109), which you can make a day ahead.

2 ciabatta-style sandwich buns, cut in half (or any bread with integrity)
2 tablespoons mayonnaise (page 109)
6–8 slices cheddar cheese
1 small ripe avocado, sliced
1 large carrot, peeled and julienned
4 small, cooked beetroot, thinly sliced (tinned or vacuum sealed)
1 cup (60 g) alfalfa sprouts
4 dill pickles, thinly sliced
Half a green apple, thinly sliced
8 cos lettuce leaves
Fine sea salt

Herb pesto
¼ cup (40 g) pepitas (pumpkin seeds)
½ cup (15 g) herbs, loosely packed (flat-leaf parsley, French tarragon, chervil, chives, rocket/arugula and/or watercress)
⅓ cup (80 ml) extra-virgin olive oil
Juice of half a lemon
1 small garlic clove
Pinch of fine sea salt

Salad sandwich

Tarragon and celery chicken sandwich

Sardine katsu sandwich with curry mayonnaise and lime

Makes: 2 sandwiches
Active time: 30 minutes

Quarter of a small red onion,
    thinly sliced
Zest and juice of 1 lime
½ teaspoon white
    (granulated) sugar
2 tablespoons Kewpie
    mayonnaise (alternatively,
    see page 109 to make
    your own)
½ teaspoon yellow curry
    powder
1 teaspoon soy sauce
¼ cup (35 g) plain
    (all-purpose) flour
2 eggs, beaten
1 cup (60 g) panko breadcrumbs
6 butterflied sardines,
    heads off, tails on
½ cup (125 ml) neutral oil
    for frying
4 slices soft white bread
    (preferably Japanese milk
    bread, shokupan, but any
    soft, white sandwich bread
    will work)
1 cup (75 g) finely shredded
    cabbage
Fine sea salt

Note: To get your sandwich to
hold together, you can do what the
Japanese do and wrap them tightly
in plastic wrap. Press each sandwich
under a heavy roasting pan or baking
dish for 10 minutes, flipping and
pressing for a further 5 minutes
on the other side. Unwrap, cut the
crusts off, cut in half and enjoy.
They'll look fantastic.

I think about this sandwich a lot – probably more than I should. Really
fresh sardines are hard to come by, but whenever I see them I make this
sandwich. The little fish are crumbed in the Japanese style, with panko
breadcrumbs, and sandwiched between soft and squishy white bread, with
a good smacking of curry-spiked Japanese mayo. This really is a winning
combination, arguably even for the sardine-averse among us.

Combine the onion with the lime zest and juice, the sugar and a pinch
of salt and leave it to sit.

In another small dish, combine the mayonnaise with the curry powder
and soy sauce and set aside.

Set up three shallow dishes for your frying station: the flour in the first,
eggs in the next and panko crumbs in the third, with an empty plate at
the end of the line. Season the sardines with salt and drag them through
the flour first, followed by the egg, and finally the breadcrumbs. Place the
crumbed sardines on the empty plate.

Heat a wide, cast-iron frying pan over a medium–high heat and add the
oil. When it's hot, fry two or three sardines at a time – they will only take
1–2 minutes per side, depending on their size. If they aren't browning in
that time, turn the heat up. Once the sardines are golden and crisp, place
them on a cooling rack set over a baking tray while you proceed with the
remaining sardines.

Lay out your four slices of bread and spread some of the curry mayonnaise
on each one. Add three sardines to each of the bottom slices and top them
with half the shredded cabbage and half the onions. Close the sandwiches
with the remaining bread slices (see note) and cut off the crusts using
a sharp knife. Cut each sandwich in half and serve immediately.

Pan bagnat

Makes: 2 sandwiches
Active time: 15 minutes

Before you begin: To speed up the making of this sandwich, use a good-quality, shop-bought mayonnaise and jarred, roasted red capsicum (peppers). You'll need to make your Tapenade (see page 34), but you can do that a day or two ahead (homemade trumps shop-bought in this case, unless you find yourself in France ...).

2 ciabatta bread rolls, preferably day-old
4 tablespoons mayonnaise (preferably homemade, page 109)
1 tablespoon Dijon mustard
2 tablespoons Tapenade (page 34)
2 x 95 g (3¼ oz) tins tuna in olive oil, drained
2 hard-boiled eggs
6 good-quality brown anchovy fillets (optional)
1 cup (30 g) basil leaves, loosely packed
1 cup (20 g) rocket (arugula) leaves
1 red capsicum (pepper), charred, peeled and sliced (jarred is fine)
1 tomato, sliced
2 teaspoons red wine vinegar
1 tablespoon extra-virgin olive oil
Flaked sea salt
Freshly cracked black pepper

A perfect summer-picnic sandwich that actually benefits from the voyage to the picnic ground. This is when all the ingredients will get to know each other, flavours melding while collectively soaking into the bread enveloping them. For that reason, it's ideally made a few hours, or even a day, ahead.

Preheat your oven to 180°C (350°F) degrees.

Slice open your bread rolls and toast them on a baking tray in the oven until golden. Slather both pieces of bread with the mayonnaise. Brush the bottom half of each roll with the mustard and the top with the tapenade.

Spoon the tuna onto the bottom piece of bread. Slice the hard-boiled egg and arrange the slices over the tuna. Lay three anchovies (if using) per sandwich over the egg, and top with the basil and rocket, followed by the red capsicum and tomato slices. Drizzle the vinegar and olive oil over the tomato and top with a sprinkle of salt and a good crack of pepper.

Place the top piece of bread on each sandwich, then wrap it tightly in baking paper. It is best after a couple of hours and at room temperature.

Note: Although French baguette is more authentic, I really like a chewy ciabatta roll for this sandwich. Use whatever bread you fancy.

Pan bagnat, named in the local Niçoise dialect, translates literally to "bathed bread". Another example of *cucina povera*, the locals used to make use of their day-old (or longer) bread. A little water to rehydrate, along with the traditional tomato and olive oil, would ensure that the bread was soft when the time came to eat. Flipping the sandwich every few hours as it sat became part of the ritual, ensuring that both sides of the bread got a good soaking from the tomato and olive oil. The sandwich evolved over time, adopting many flavours of the classic Niçoise salad, as it transformed into something that could travel – a sandwich for the local fishermen and other early-morning workers. While the sandwich has evolved, its place in the heart of Provençal culture has not ... this bathed bread is still "*le roi de la merenda*" – the king of the morning break.

"Some grandmothers from southern Italy use *anchovies* in place of *salt*, for these tiny fish *carry the flavour* of the sea and can be scooped out of nearby waters or bought at the markets at almost *no cost*."

Carol Field, *In Nonna's Kitchen: Recipes and Traditions from Italy's Grandmothers*

Gandhi marched across India for it, the Romans paid their soldiers with it (the root of the word salary lies in salt), the Vikings used it to keep their army strong (and alive); it's the only rock we eat, and we are rightly proud of it. To be deemed "worth your salt" or "salt of the earth" are both delightful compliments. Of course, there is nothing silent about the role salt plays in the kitchen – it is the ultimate amplifier.

But there are many other ways to bring this amplification into your kitchen: salty delights that come shackled with the mineral intricacy of the sea, the deep umami of salted and fermented soybeans, the sweet richness of cured ham and the herbaceous creaminess of highland pastures. These are the little soldiers of your store cupboard.

Like a great wine, a tin can be a time capsule, bringing the briny flavour of *that* fish, from *that* sea, into *your* kitchen. Along the Iberian Peninsula, the Spanish and Portuguese have turned these *conservas* into an artform: from razor clams to miniature cockles, tiny *chipirones* (squid) and glistening mussels. This is not just about the process of preserving, but also the ritual of eating, where a small tin of clams, a bowl of crisps and a glass of vermouth can make the most elegant of snacks.

The canning process is often delicate, designed to preserve not just the fillet but all its flavour. The fish or seafood is lightly steamed or fried before being committed to its bed fellow (*líquido de cobertura* in Spanish) – sometimes a natural brine, designed to mimic the sea from whence the creatures came or, in the case of tiny squid, their own ink. The more robust the seafood (think sardines, mussels and mackerel) the stronger the companion: from olive oil to escabeche, tomatoes and spices. The most prized of anchovies, traditionally coming from Collioure, where eastern Spain kisses France, are hand-packed and even labelled with their vintage.

There is a sustainable element to this, too. The fishing can be concentrated in the waters where the fish are plentiful and caught at the best time of year to protect their reproduction. The long shelf life (not requiring air freight) and easy traceability of preserved seafood also makes for a good choice in a world where we march with our wallets. This also allows us tastes of other seas when our own cannot provide. Fish should not be expected to swim in foreign oceans (I'm looking directly at you, poor, mistreated Atlantic salmon).

Salting, while largely concerned with transforming the product, is also about preserving a moment in time. Traditionally, this was a way to preserve the family pig, which had been fattened on the family scraps over spring and summer and slaughtered as the weather turned, to be hung in the rafters without the risk of spoiling: prosciutto from the leg, pancetta from the belly, guanciale from the cheek, and salumi from just about everywhere else! The idea was to stretch the pig over the year's meals – the cornerstone of a carefully stocked pantry.

The prosciutto industry in Parma was actually created in harmony with the production of parmesan cheese. The excess whey from the cheese-making fed the pigs, creating a delicious culinary cycle. The salt and protein in the whey lends prosciutto an acidity and sweetness that is unique to this Italian delicacy. (Pork slowly cooked in milk, or *maiale al latte*, is one of the great culinary classics and, when you understand this connection from within as well, it makes complete sense!).

While parmesan is a mainstay in almost everyone's kitchen, here, too, we see a world of difference between the powdery packaged grated version (to be avoided) and a 36-month-aged point of Parmigiano Reggiano cut from its wheel at your cheese monger.

Olives are also dry-salted or brined (and occasionally, albeit rarely, transformed by pure water or the sun) to remove their bitterness and create a ready source of snacks. The colour denotes the time of picking and, in turn, their ripeness, not their variety. It is true that some varieties lend themselves to early picking, while others are best left to mature. Among the greens, there are the large, buttery Castelvetrano, the tart, anise-y picholine and the famed gordal (meaning "the fat one" in Spanish). The Niçoise olive is a lovely little black olive, as is the small, mild Arbequina, and of course, there's the ubiquitous Kalamata. As common as the olive is, it is the one ingredient on this list of "good salty things" that we both still find a little mysterious. A magnificent olive can be one of the best things you will ever eat, and yet so many are flabby and sad. We're sure it wasn't always that way – a case of evolving tastes perhaps? The large commercial productions often cure their olives in an alkaline lye solution (time and cost-effective), which could be the problem. We're still tasting and debating!

While the silvery dance of the olive tree may be one of the most striking images of the Mediterranean, closer inspection will reveal festivals of caper bushes springing out of rock crevices with just as much regularity (and even more pizzazz). These little buds add colour, flavour and, when fried, can bring fabulous texture to your dish.

Of course, the Mediterranean doesn't have the monopoly on salty, umami deliciousness. The wonder of this elusive, and yet omnipresent, taste is that it's found in almost every cuisine the world over. Turning our regard eastwards, there's another pantry full of saline options, just played in a slightly different key – largely due to the fermentation they undergo.

Soy sauce is a fascinating staple that we tend to take for granted, it can be easy to forget that in parts of the world this remains an artisanal product. Perhaps thanks to those red-topped bottles. As the name suggests, it's traditionally made with soybeans, mixed with grains and naturally occurring mould cultures and left to ferment. Just as olive oils vary around the world, every soy sauce is different. Mass-produced, factory-made soy sauces give you salt, for sure, but little else. Small-batch, artisan-made soy sauces can give you smokiness, lightness and umami. It's an education in how millennia of tradition and the pursuit of taste have shaped cultures.

The fish sauces of Asia are also a wonderful addition to your kitchen. And then there are the fermented bean sauces and miso pastes – more fermented soybeans, this time inoculated with koji, that work well with both savoury and sweet flavours (like the sweetness inherent in corn or even chocolate).

These little culinary time capsules are a wonder in your pantry. Every bit as transportive as a good wine, they can take you from the seasides of Spain to the mountains of Japan. Let them transport you.

I turn to capers for saltiness, and consequently, find brined capers a little too pickle-y, rather than salty. Salted capers taste more of themselves to me.

If you are lucky enough to get your hands on a beautiful artisan soy sauce, treat it as you would a good wine vinegar (or wine, for that matter) – use it for tasting alone, or on special occasions as a last-minute addition to a dish, off the stove heat, to preserve its nuances.

My sardine pasta

Makes: Enough to serve 2
Active time: 25 minutes
Inactive time: 10 minutes

½ cup (55 g) dried sourdough
    breadcrumbs (or ½ cup/
    30 g panko breadcrumbs)
3 tablespoons extra-virgin
    olive oil, plus an extra
    4 tablespoons
½ cup (80 g) diced brown onion
    (about a quarter of an onion)
2 garlic cloves, minced
Pinch of chilli flakes (optional)
4 anchovy fillets, roughly
    chopped
2 tablespoons chopped fresh
    oregano (or 1 teaspoon
    dried oregano)
Scant ¼ cup (40 g) sultanas,
    chopped
2 tablespoons salted capers,
    rinsed
1 tablespoon tomato paste
    (concentrated purée)
1 x 400 g (14 oz) tin whole
    peeled San Marzano
    tomatoes, crushed
250 g (9 oz) dried spaghetti
1 x 120 g (4¼ oz) tin sardines
    in olive oil
Zest and juice of half a lemon
Freshly cracked black pepper
Fine sea salt

To finish
Parmigiano Reggiano,
    for grating

Sardines, like anchovies, can get a bad rap. The problem is that fresh sardines are only good when they are spectacularly fresh – still stiff in rigor. This is very hard to find. On the other hand, you can find excellent tinned sardines, quite different to the fresh ones. This is the best example of how small tins and salted things can create something utterly delicious.

To toast your breadcrumbs, heat a small sauté pan over a medium heat. Add the 3 tablespoons of olive oil, along with the breadcrumbs, and cook, tossing often, until golden brown all over. Scoop the golden breadcrumbs out of the pan and onto a plate to cool and become crunchy. Set aside.

Bring a large pot of salted water to a boil for your pasta (see note).

Place another large pot over a medium heat and add the extra 4 tablespoons of olive oil, together with the onion, garlic and a pinch of salt. Cook, stirring occasionally, until the onion starts to brown, about 10 minutes.

Add the chilli flakes (if using), anchovy fillets, oregano, sultanas, capers and tomato paste and fry for a further minute. Follow with the crushed tomatoes and stir to combine. Cook the sauce on a low heat while you boil your pasta.

Drop the spaghetti into the boiling water and cook until al dente.

While the pasta is cooking, split the sardine fillets and remove the backbone. Add the fillets to the sauce.

When the pasta is cooked, use tongs to lift it out of the water and drop it directly into the pot with the sauce. Add 2–3 ladlefuls of starchy pasta water. Stir vigorously to combine, using a wooden spoon or tongs, and cook over a medium heat for another minute or two to coat the pasta in the sauce. Finish with the lemon zest and juice, a drizzle of olive oil and a good crack of pepper.

Divide the pasta between two bowls and top with grated parmesan and the toasted breadcrumbs.

A ladle or two of pasta water is the magic ingredient in almost all pasta dishes. That starchy water has wizard-like properties: loosening the sauce, bringing a creaminess without cream and, perhaps most importantly, providing a bridge for the pasta to meet the sauce. Pulling out a mug of the pasta water before you drain your pasta is one of those culinary habits that will change your cooking forever. However, your new habit necessitates revisiting an old habit – the way you salt your pasta water. "As salty as the sea" is out: too much salt and you'll send the seasoning for the whole dish over the edge; not enough, and the pasta will be insipid. So, to clarify, when I say "pot of salted water" for cooking pasta, I'm imagining around 1½ tablespoons of salt per 500 g (1 lb 2 oz) of pasta in a pot with just enough water to cover your pasta by 2–3 cm (about 1 inch). Less water equals more starchiness, which is the goal with pasta water, so don't be too generous when you're filling your pot.

One-pot pasta with lentil sugo

Makes: Enough to serve 3–4
Active time: 25 minutes
Inactive time: 30 minutes

⅓ cup (80 ml) extra-virgin
    olive oil
Half a brown onion, diced
3 garlic cloves, minced
1 carrot, peeled and diced
1 stalk celery, finely diced
½ teaspoon dried oregano
1½ teaspoons fennel seeds
4 tablespoons tomato paste
    (concentrated purée)
½ cup (105 g) dried green
    French lentils (preferably
    du Puy)
4 cups (1 litre) water, plus extra
    as needed
250 g (9 oz) dried short pasta
    (casarecce or rigatoni)
Pinch of chilli flakes (optional)
Fine sea salt
Freshly cracked black pepper

To finish
Parmigiano Reggiano,
    for grating
Freshly cracked blacked pepper
Juice of half a lemon

If you've got a few mirepoix ingredients, chances are you've got the rest of these items in the pantry. Like a big warm hug that, despite a longer cooking time for the lentils, comes together very quickly.

Heat a large enamel-lined Dutch oven or heavy-based stock pot over a medium heat. Add the olive oil, onion, garlic, carrot and celery with a good pinch of salt and a good crack of pepper. Cook for about 15 minutes, until everything is soft, sweet and beginning to brown.

Add in the oregano, fennel seeds and tomato paste and cook for another minute. Add in the lentils and water and bring to a gentle simmer. Cover tightly with a lid and simmer for 40 minutes, or until the lentils are tender.

At this stage, add the pasta and simmer, leaving the lid ajar, and stirring every so often, until the pasta is tender but still al dente (the amount of time depends on the type of pasta you're using). If the pot looks dry and the pasta is not submerged in liquid, add another ½ cup (125 ml) water (or two) to keep things simmering. Don't add too much water towards the end of the cooking time – you want this mixture to be perfectly starchy and creamy, without being watery. Stir in the chilli flakes (if using).

Serve in bowls, with plenty of freshly grated parmesan, freshly cracked pepper and a squeeze of lemon juice.

Note: Regarding the pasta, this is one of those little exceptions to the rule. The pasta is cooked in a small amount of water, and is essentially starved of space thus, concentrating that exchange of starch and water. Unlike with a large pot at a rolling boil, cooking your pasta in close confines does require more attention, however. You'll need to give it a stir every now and then to ensure it doesn't stick. The result is worth the effort – this is pasta water to the power of ten!

The French call it *mirepoix*, the Italians *soffritto*, and the Spanish *sofrito*. In Norwegian, it's *de fire store* (meaning "the big four": leek, carrot, onion, celeriac), in German it's *suppengrün* (meaning "soup greens": leek, carrot, celeriac) and in Cajun or Creole cooking it's the "holy trinity" (onion, celery and capsicum/pepper). Whatever the name, in many culinary traditions this is the fundamental base for warming, and usually slow-cooked, dishes. The general ratio for a classic mirepoix is two parts onion, one part celery and one part carrot. The idea is to gently sweat (cook without colouring) these ingredients down to make a sweet, earthy base for your braise – this takes a surprisingly long time if you want to really gain the gustatory benefits on offer. Allow it that time, this is the building block for all that follows.

Bean and chorizo stew (fabada)

Makes: Enough to serve 6
Active time: 20 minutes
Inactive time: 12 hours

Kitchenalia: A large pot, blender
or stick blender (optional)

Before you begin: The beans
require an overnight (or 8 hour)
soak. If you don't have a pot large
enough to hold everything, divide
between two pots. Once much of the
water has evaporated, you should
be able to combine it all into one
large pot. This is a large recipe so
refrigerate or freeze any leftovers.

3 cups (500 g) dried white
    butter beans, or 2½ cups
    (500 g) dried cannellini beans
1 pork knuckle, fresh, uncured,
    unsmoked
12 cups (3 litres) water
1 brown onion, peeled and
    cut in half
1 head of garlic, cut in half
2 bay leaves
1 tablespoon Spanish smoked
    paprika (pimentón de La Vera)
Pinch of saffron strands
250 g (9 oz) slab bacon
    (unsliced streaky bacon),
    cut into large chunks
300 g (10½ oz) semi-dried
    Spanish-style chorizo,
    cut into 4 cm (1½ inch)
    lengths
200 g (7 oz) morcilla (Spanish
    blood sausage), cut into 4 cm
    (1½ inch) lengths
Fine sea salt
Freshly cracked black pepper

To serve
Crusty bread

I grew up on fabada. My great grandfather, on my mother's side, hailed from Asturias, the part of Spain where this dish comes from. When he arrived in Cuba, this dish came with him and was handed down to his daughter, Aida, my grandmother. Aida made this dish for her son and daughter, and later for her grandchildren. My grandmother was a wonderful cook, especially when she cooked with beans – hers were legendary. I think the thing that made them special was she blended or mashed some of the cooked beans and stirred that through the finished dish, thickening the liquid and turning the beans into an amalgamated stew. It's something I always do now.

Place the beans in a bowl and cover with 5–8 cm (2–3 inches) of cold water. Refrigerate overnight (or for 8 hours) to soak.

The following day, place the pork knuckle in a large stock pot and cover with the water. Bring to a simmer, cover the pot tightly and simmer for 30 minutes. Drain the beans of their soaking water and tip them into the pot with the pork. Add in all the remaining ingredients except for the chorizo and morcilla. Season with a few good pinches of salt and some cracked pepper.

Place the pot over a medium heat and bring it to a simmer, then reduce the heat to low and simmer gently for about 2–2½ hours, with the lid ajar, or until the beans and the pork knuckle are completely tender. Check the beans, giving them a stir every 30 minutes or so. If at any point the water falls below the top of the beans, add in an extra cup (250 ml).

When the beans and the pork knuckle are fork-tender, scoop 1–2 large ladlefuls of the beans and their liquid into a blender and blend until smooth (alternatively, do this in the pot using a stick blender, or in a bowl using a fork to mash the beans). Stir the blended beans into the fabada.

Remove the pork knuckle and place it on a plate. Shred the meat from the bone and add it back into the pot, along with the chorizo and morcilla.

Simmer everything together for another 15 minutes. To finish, remove and discard the onion halves and bay leaves. Squeeze the garlic cloves out of their skins and into the soup. Taste and adjust with salt and pepper.

Serve hot in bowls, with a good chunk of crusty bread.

Note: I wanted to write this recipe without the morcilla but, as Mom pointed out, it's not fabada without morcilla – it's the flavour of the spices in this sausage that give this dish its personality. Morcilla is a Spanish blood sausage made from pork. It is typically spiced with smoked paprika, onions, garlic and cloves, and thickened with rice to extend it further. Originating again from the principle of "waste not, want not", this sausage is made using the blood that's released from the pig during slaughter, becoming another ingredient to be appreciated. Although the idea may be unpleasant for some, as an omnivore myself, I like to try different parts of the animal, even if it's outside of my comfort zone. Luckily, I learned to love morcilla early on. You can leave it out if you can't find it, or don't want to use it – just don't tell Rosa!

Rigatoni with cime di rapa and sausage

The combination of cime di rapa and sausage tossed through pasta is an Italian classic. The slight bitterness of the greens works exceedingly well with the fatty pork, hence their lasting relationship. I like to add a touch of white wine and tomato passata (puréed tomatoes) for a little acidity and that beautiful red, oily tinge. If cime di rapa is not available where you are, cavolo nero or kale would make great substitutions.

Begin by prepping your cime di rapa. If the leaves are on the larger side, cut off and discard the bottom third of the stem, which can often be tough and fibrous (you can skip this step if the stems are nice and tender). Cut the rest into pieces around 3–4 cm (1¼–1½ inches) long and set aside.

Bring a large pot of salted water to a boil for your pasta.

Heat a large pan over a medium–high heat and add the olive oil. Crumble in the sausage meat and brown well.

Add in the garlic, tomato passata, chilli flakes (if using) and fennel seeds and sizzle for about 2 minutes. Pour in the white wine and simmer until the alcohol burns off, about 1 minute, then add in the cime di rapa. Put a lid on the pot and cook over a low heat for about 10 minutes, until the greens are very tender.

Cook the rigatoni in the boiling water until al dente. Reserve a mug of the pasta water before draining the pasta.

Add the cooked pasta and the reserved pasta water into the pot with the sausage and cimi di rapa and cook together over a medium heat until the sauce coats the pasta and is nice and thick. Add in the lemon zest and juice, parmesan and a good crack of pepper, then taste for seasoning.

Serve in bowls, finished with a drizzle of good-quality olive oil.

Serving suggestion: This dish would also be great with handmade gnocchetti in place of the dried rigatoni, using the Semolina pasta dough recipe (see page 141).

Makes: Enough to serve 2–3
Active time: 25 minutes
Inactive time: 20 minutes

1 bunch cime di rapa (about 4 cups once prepped)
2 tablespoons extra-virgin olive oil
4 pork and fennel sausages, meat removed from casings
2 garlic cloves, finely minced
⅓ cup (90 g) tomato passata (puréed tomatoes)
Pinch of chilli flakes (optional)
1½ teaspoons fennel seeds
⅓ cup (80 ml) dry white wine (preferably Italian)
250 g (9 oz) dried rigatoni
Zest and juice of half a lemon
½ cup (50 g) freshly grated Parmigiano Reggiano
Fine sea salt
Freshly cracked black pepper

To finish
Good-quality extra-virgin olive oil

Spaghetti alla Nerano

Makes: Enough to serve 4
Active time: 25 minutes
Inactive time: 10 minutes

Kitchenalia: Mandoline
    (alternatively, a very sharp
    knife to thinly slice)

6 small zucchinis (courgettes)
    (about 400–500 g/
    14 oz–1 lb 2 oz)
½ cup (125 ml) extra-virgin
    olive oil
400 g (14 oz) dried spaghetti
3 garlic cloves, minced
50 g (1¾ oz) unsalted butter,
    cubed
½ cup (50 g) freshly grated
    Parmigiano Reggiano
2 cups (60 g) basil leaves (about
    1 bunch), loosely packed, plus
    extra to garnish
Fine sea salt

To finish
Parmigiano Reggiano,
    for grating
Freshly cracked black pepper
Good-quality extra-virgin
    olive oil
1 lemon, cut into 4 wedges

Nerano is a small village on the Amalfi Coast of Italy. This dish is thought to have been created by a woman named Maria Grazia (in her restaurant there, which bears her name) and although the original recipe is not known, this is my best distillation. The original dish uses Provolone del Monaco, a local cheese that can be hard to find outside of the area. Parmigiano Reggiano isn't totally correct but it's still delicious. This is a perfect summer pasta and makes great use of a glut of zucchini (courgette).

Slice the zucchini into very thin rounds using a mandoline (or a very sharp knife).

Heat a large pan over a medium–high heat. Add the olive oil and when it's hot, add in a third of the zucchini slices. Fry until they are lightly golden, stirring occasionally. Use a skimmer or spoon to scoop them out onto a plate. Fry the remaining zucchini in another two batches and set aside.

Bring a large pot of salted water to a boil. Drop in your spaghetti and cook until al dente.

Pour out half the olive oil used to fry the zucchini and save it for another use. Return the pan to a medium heat and add the garlic, letting it sizzle until it becomes fragrant. Add in the fried zucchini and scoop a ladleful of the pasta water into the pan. Stir and crush the zucchini so that some pieces break down and some remain intact.

Reserve a mug of the pasta water before draining the pasta. Add the pasta to the zucchini pan and stir in half of the reserved water. Turn the heat to high. When the liquid is almost completely reduced, turn the heat down to low and add in the butter, parmesan and basil. Toss vigorously, using a wooden spoon or tongs, to combine and create a creamy sauce. Add more of the pasta water as needed. Taste the pasta for seasoning and adjust with salt.

Divide the pasta between four bowls and top with more grated parmesan, the extra basil leaves, pepper and a drizzle of good-quality olive oil. Serve with wedges of lemon.

This book was always meant to be a celebration of that which is humble, that which respects waste, that which is better at home than anywhere else. On reflection, it could happily just have been a book about the magical qualities of pasta water. As the salty water is bubbling around the pasta a beautiful exchange is occurring. The pasta is swelling, seasoning itself from the inside out as it absorbs its saline bath, meanwhile the water is amalgamating with the glutens and proteins that are making their escape from the pasta. The water becomes cloudy and slightly translucent as the three ingredients make love. All these pasta recipes make use of this alchemy, but this one in particular should convince you of its wonder.

Spaghetti with clams and tomato

Makes: Enough to serve 3
Active time: 30 minutes

Before you begin: Clean your clams by placing them in a bowl and covering them with cold water. Shake them around, then do this once more with another clean change of water.

2 kg (4 lb 8 oz) small vongole-
    type clams, cleaned
¼ cup (60 ml) white wine
¼ cup (60 ml) extra-virgin
    olive oil
3 garlic cloves, minced
1 teaspoon plain
    (all-purpose) flour
3 Roma tomatoes, or 1 large
    juicy heirloom tomato,
    crushed into large chunks
    using your hands
300 g (10½ oz) dried spaghetti
1 cup (20 g) picked flat-leaf
    parsley leaves (loosely
    packed), finely chopped
Fine sea salt
Freshly cracked black pepper

To finish
Good-quality extra-virgin
    olive oil
1 lemon, cut into 3 wedges

Note: Vongole are small clams with a white or light brown shell that is yellow on the inside (often with patches of purple). You can swap these for Australian pipis, but they range in size and can be quite large. Either one will work, but my preference is definitely for vongole.

The thing I have discovered from cooking this pasta in different countries is that the clam you use is the deciding factor in how delicious the finished dish will be. I call for *a lot* of clams to serve a couple of people because I like a lot of clams. The step of separating some from the shell and leaving some in the shell is optional, but I think it makes this pasta extra special as you get more clams per bite with less work at the table. Look for the small vongole-type clams and ensure they are alive and feel heavy for their size, a sign that they hold a lot of liquid. They should also be tightly closed.

Bring a large pot of salted water to a boil for your pasta.

Heat a medium-sized pot with a tight-fitting lid over a high heat. Add in the cleaned clams and the white wine and cover with the lid. Steam the clams open for about 3–4 minutes, giving the pot a shake every minute. Open the pot and have a look at the clams – if they've all opened, turn the heat off; if not, return the lid and cook for a further minute or two until most have opened. Remove and discard any clams that don't open.

Pour the clams and their liquid into a bowl and allow them to cool slightly. Pick half the clams out of the shells and discard the empty shells. Set the clams aside.

Return the empty clam pot to the stove over a medium heat. Add the olive oil and garlic and let it sizzle for a minute. Add in the flour and stir to combine. After a further minute, pour the clam liquid into the pot and add in the tomatoes. Taste and check for seasoning, adding a pinch of salt and a crack of pepper as needed. When the liquid has thickened slightly, return the pot to a high heat.

Drop your spaghetti into the boiling water and cook until al dente. Reserve a mug of the pasta water before draining your pasta.

Add the pasta and the reserved pasta water into the pot with the tomatoes and clam liquid and toss to combine. Once the sauce is coating the pasta nicely, add in all the clams and toss everything to combine.

Finally, toss through the parsley and divide the pasta between three bowls. Drizzle with good-quality olive oil and serve hot with the lemon wedges.

A much-loved Italian classic, *spaghetti alle vongole*, translating simply to "spaghetti with clams", is thought to have originated in Naples. Another dish we might consider *cucina povera*, it is interesting to note how little it has changed over time. The first recorded recipe, dating back to the 19th century, lists just five ingredients: pasta, olive oil, garlic, parsley and vongole. This version doesn't have too many more!

Casarecce with prawns, mint and pistachio

This pasta will only be as delicious as the quality of the prawns you use. Although I've not specified it as an ingredient, feel free to top the dish with a dusting of grated Parmigiano Reggiano – I won't judge!

Bring a large pot of salted water to a boil for your pasta.

Once you've gathered and prepared your ingredients, drop your pasta into the water and cook until al dente. It should take about 12–13 minutes (if you use a different shape of pasta, then adjust the cooking time to suit).

Season your prawn meat with a good pinch of salt and set aside.

Heat a pan over a medium heat and add the olive oil, garlic, tomatoes and chilli. Add in a pinch of salt and sizzle for 2–3 minutes.

Add in the lemon zest and juice, along with the orange juice. Bring to a simmer, then add in the prawns. Simmer until the prawns turn pink, then immediately turn the heat off to avoid over cooking them.

Once the pasta is cooked, drain it, reserving a mug of the starchy pasta water. Return the prawn pan to a high heat, and add in the pasta and the reserved pasta water. Bring to a vigorous simmer and cook until the sauce is coating the pasta and looks glossy.

To finish, add in the butter and the chopped herbs and toss together. Taste for seasoning and adjust with salt.

Divide the pasta between two bowls and serve hot, topped with the toasted pistachios.

Note: While it may not be typical to serve parmesan on seafood pastas, cheese and anchovies are such good friends that this can't be a hard-and-fast rule. Do whatever makes it more delicious for you, I say.

Makes: Enough to serve 2
Active time: 30 minutes

250 g (9 oz) dried casarecce
250 g (9 oz) peeled green king or tiger prawn meat, chopped into large chunks (about 12–15 whole raw prawns)
¼ cup (60 ml) extra-virgin olive oil
4 garlic cloves, minced
1¾ cup (250 g) cherry tomatoes, halved
1–2 red birdseye chillies, thinly sliced
Zest and juice of 1 lemon
Juice of 1 orange
25 g (1 oz) unsalted butter, cubed
2 tablespoons flat-leaf parsley, finely chopped
2 tablespoons mint, finely chopped
2 tablespoons chives, finely chopped
Fine sea salt

To finish
¼ cup (30 g) toasted pistachios, crushed in a mortar and pestle

Almost everyone has their ideal level of *al dente* ("to the tooth" – a little bite). I'm quite sure your al dente is different to mine, which is in turn different to your nonna's, or the Italian chef down the road – this is *as it should be*. That said, no matter where you find the bite in your pasta, you're going to need to taste your way there. Each and every dried pasta has its own cooking time (not just by shape, but also by brand) so you will need to be vigilant. The first clue is found on the packet – most will provide a rough guide for al dente by which you can set a timer and taste from there. The more pasta you cook, the more intuitive this becomes – if I had a dollar for every time I checked my timer, only to see it counting down the last three seconds! Slightly more ambiguous, but also helpful, is the perfume of the pasta – it changes ... and when it does, it's often ready.

Roasted garlic and sage pastina

Makes: Enough to serve 2–3
Active time: 15 minutes
Inactive time: 1 hour

1 head of garlic
1 tablespoon extra-virgin
  olive oil
3 cups (750 ml) good-quality
  chicken stock
1 parmesan rind
1 cup (170 g) dried tubettini
  (alternatively, orzo or stelline)
10 sage leaves, plus extra for
  optional garnish (see note)
¼ cup (25 g) freshly grated
  Parmigiano Reggiano,
  plus extra to garnish
1 egg
25 g (1 oz) unsalted butter,
  cubed
Juice of quarter of a lemon
Fine sea salt
Freshly cracked black pepper

This will cure whatever is ailing you, even if it's just hunger. My version of the classic Italian chicken soup is thickened with an egg and fortified with sage and roasted garlic to make something that is both nourishing and mouth-watering.

Preheat your oven to 180°C (350°F).

Cut the very top off the head of garlic. Tear off a large sheet of aluminium foil and place the garlic, cut-side up, on the foil. Pour the olive oil over the garlic and sprinkle with a pinch of salt. Wrap it up tightly, place it on a baking tray and bake for 1 hour. Remove from the oven, open the foil up and allow the garlic to cool. The cloves should be nice and soft.

In a large saucepan, bring the chicken stock and the parmesan rind to a boil. Add a good pinch of salt if the stock is unseasoned, then add in the pasta and the sage leaves. Let it boil until the pasta is al dente, about 6–8 minutes. Stir in the grated parmesan and squeeze the roasted garlic cloves out of their skins directly into the pot, whisking well to combine. Remove and discard the parmesan rind and turn the heat off.

Crack the egg into a bowl and give it a good whisk. Slowly add two ladlefuls of the hot pasta and broth into the egg, while continuously stirring. Pour this back into the pot and stir to combine. Turn the heat back on to its lowest setting and stir continuously. You want the egg to thicken the mixture but not scramble. This will only take about 30–60 seconds. Turn the heat off. Stir in the butter and add a good crack of pepper. Taste for seasoning and adjust with salt. Finally, stir in the lemon juice and sprinkle with fried sage leaves (see note), if you like.

Divide between the bowls and top with extra grated parmesan.

Note: To dress up your finished dish, fry a handful of sage leaves to sprinkle over the pastina. Heat $\frac{1}{4}$ cup (60 ml) of neutral oil in a small pot over a medium–high heat until hot. Add 6–8 sage leaves at a time, frying for a few seconds, until crisp. Use a skimmer or spoon to remove the leaves from the oil and drain on paper towel. Sprinkle with flaked sea salt.

The nonna ratio

Although making fresh pasta in Italy – even daily – is commonplace, for most of us, it needs a bit more planning to factor this into our routine. It's something I like to do on my weekend when I have a bit more time on my hands. I relish the process.

Time aside, the big question is: which recipe to use? It seems there as many recipes for pasta dough as there are for pasta dishes. At its simplest, pasta, like bread, can be made from just flour and water (commonly seen in the southern regions of Italy). However, often, it's made with a richer mixture, using a combination of flour and eggs.

From these simple beginnings, we complicate things. I am as guilty as the next person. We change the ratio of eggs to flour, we add all the yolks and leave out the whites entirely, we add olive oil and salt – I've even seen milk used as an addition! All in search of that perfect balance of extensibility (the ability of the dough to stretch) and chewiness. If I am going to make pasta at home – a worthy but time-consuming endeavour – I want it to be enjoyable. I don't want to waste egg whites, I don't want to feel like I'm getting a full-body workout, I don't want a layer of white flour to cover every inch of my kitchen when I'm done. I just want to take it slow and keep it simple. I also want it to be delicious.

Using the golden ratio you see in the Simple egg pasta dough recipe (see opposite page) – the "nonna ratio" as I like to call it – you will find that pasta is a *joy* to make. This is because there is no waste and the dough is wet enough to make the kneading easy. *But*, there is a compromise to be had. The dough has just a little more moisture than you want, making it difficult to cut without lots of added flour, which then sits as a gummy coating on the pasta after it's cooked.

The key to using this ratio is to let the pasta sheets dry slightly before attempting to cut or fill them. Traditionally, this was achieved with the aid of a *mattarello* – the very long and thin rolling pin especially designed for rolling sheets of pasta by hand across a timber bench. Rolling by hand allows the pasta sheet to dry slowly as you roll it, the moisture subtly being absorbed by the rolling pin and the bench. By the time you finish, the sheet is ready to be cut without the need for additional flour.

If you are using a pasta machine, its metal rollers will make the job quick, but that's just the problem; thick discs of dough quickly roll down to thin sheets, and without any wooden surface or rolling pin to absorb the excess moisture, you'll find yourself resorting to handfuls of flour to keep the sheets from sticking to each other and the bench.

It's taken me a long time to realise that the simple compromise is to roll your pasta into sheets and then let the sheets dry slightly by hanging them on a pasta drying rack, the back of a chair, over a broom handle or even on a clothes hanger. About 10–15 minutes should do the trick; you don't want to dry it for too long, or your dough might crack or become brittle. Of course, you can dry the pasta after cutting it as well, which will only help to achieve optimal chew. This may seem obvious to many, but it wasn't to me. It's a subtle detail that I think makes a world of difference.

Simple egg pasta dough

Place the flour in a mound on your clean, dry benchtop. Make a little well in the mound, add the salt and drop the whisked egg into the centre.

Use a fork to very slowly and carefully begin to incorporate flour from the sides of the well in with the egg, without allowing the walls to collapse.

Once you have a thick, eggy mass, use a bench scraper to fold the remaining flour into the centre and begin to knead the dough, picking up any scraggy bits as you go. Bring the dough together then wrap in a damp tea towel, or cover with an overturned mixing bowl, and allow the dough to rest for 15 minutes.

Once rested, knead the dough for as long as it takes for it to become completely uniform in smoothness – you want it to spring back to the touch. This takes longer than you think, about 10 minutes – as soon as you think it's never going to become smooth, that's usually right when it does!

Wrap the dough again and leave it on your bench to rest for at least an hour (if any longer, it should go in the fridge). You can make this dough up to 24 hours in advance and keep it tightly wrapped in the fridge – just let it come to room temperature before you roll it out.

Roll the dough through your pasta machine, or by hand on a wooden board, to your desired thickness, only using the tiniest amount of 00 flour, as needed.

Allow the sheets to dry by hanging them on a pasta drying rack, or similar, for 10–15 minutes before cutting or shaping. Use coarse semolina or rice flour to dust the sheets before cutting them into shapes (see over page).

Serving suggestion: This pasta dough is excellent for the Tagliatelle Bolognese (see page 144).

Pasta kitchenalia:

Machines and tools can certainly make life easier and speed things up, but don't let it put you off if they aren't part of your kitchen kit. There are many nonnas out there using rolling pins and a knife, or even a pizza cutter, to feed their families – you'll just need to stick to the simpler (but still delicious) pasta shapes.

That said, these are my most-loved tools that help make regular pasta making that little bit easier:

· Pasta machine
· Pasta drying rack
· Bevelled-edge pasta wheel
· Gnocchi board and dowel
· Fine-mist spray water bottle for filled pasta

Makes: 1 serving of pasta (see notes)
Active time: 40 minutes (plus time to shape pasta)
Inactive time: 1 hour 30 minutes

Kitchenalia: Bench scraper, pasta machine, pasta drying rack (all optional). Depending on your desired shape, you may want a bevelled-edge pasta wheel, gnocchi board and dowel or fine-mist spray water bottle.

100 g (scant 1 cup) 00 flour, plus extra for dusting
Pinch of fine sea salt
1 extra-large egg (about 60 g/ 2¼ oz), cracked and whisked in a small bowl
Coarse semolina or rice flour, for rolling

Notes: Simply multiply the ingredients by the amount of people you are serving.

For a chewier and more yellow pasta, replace all of the 00 flour, or a percentage of the total weight, with semola rimacinata flour. For more on this flour, see note on page 141.

When rolling your dough to the desired thickness, keep in mind that pasta will swell and become thicker as it boils. I find you usually want it to be slightly thinner than you think when rolling it out. If you're unsure, set up a small pot of boiling water as you're rolling and test a piece out before rolling the rest of the dough.

Tips for different shapes:

TO MAKE PAPPARDELLE, TAGLIATELLE OR TAGLIOLINI: Roll the pasta sheets to your desired length. Sprinkle the sheets with rice flour or coarse semolina (which can be dusted off easily before the pasta is cooked) and stack them on top of each other. Fold and roll the short side of the pasta until you reach the centre and do the same with the other end. You'll have something that looks like a scroll. Cut the pasta into your desired width and separate the strands. Dust off the flour or semolina and hang up the strands to dry for at least 15 minutes before boiling.

TO MAKE RAVIOLI: A misting spray bottle filled with water is a necessary tool if making filled pasta at home. Once the pasta sheets have dried out for a few minutes, lay one sheet on your bench. Place tablespoons of your prepared ravioli filling in a row 3–4 cm (1¼–1½ inches) apart on the top half of the sheet. Finely spray the pasta sheet with water then fold it over and seal the edges to create little pillows of pasta, being careful to push out any trapped air pockets. Cut in between each square of the ravioli using a knife or a bevelled-edge pasta wheel.

When your ravioli is filled and cut, lay them out on trays that are well dusted with rice flour or coarse semolina, which can be dusted off easily before boiling. Keep the ravioli covered with a slightly damp tea towel after shaping, but try not to refrigerate them unless you're making them a few hours ahead. They are best freshly made. If you absolutely must make the ravioli a day ahead, or a few hours ahead, I find it best to parboil the freshly made ravioli for a minute or two in boiling salted water before allowing them to cool and then storing them in the fridge. You can then boil them again to finish when you're ready to serve.

TO MAKE FARFALLE: Cut your pasta sheets into little rectangles 4–5 cm (1½–2 inches) in length and 3–4 cm (1¼–1½ inches) in width. For a zigzag edge, use a bevelled-edge pasta wheel to cut the sides, then pinch the centre of the rectangle to create a bow-tie or butterfly shape. Allow to dry for about 20–30 minutes before boiling.

TO MAKE GARGANELLI: This requires a gnocchi board and dowel, which usually come together as a set. Cut your pasta sheets into 4 cm (1½ inch) squares. Roll the square around the dowel, joining two opposing corners of the square and forming a penne-like shape. Roll the pasta on the dowel across the board to create little ridges. Ease the pasta off the dowel and allow to dry for about 20–30 minutes before boiling.

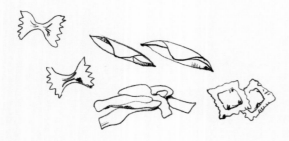

Semolina pasta dough

Another simple pasta dough recipe that uses only flour, water and a touch of olive oil is a fresh semolina pasta dough. Typical of southern Italy, this pasta dough is easy and fun to work with. You can make a number of different shapes, like pici, gnocchetti, busiate – all of which go well with thick, tomato-based sauces.

In a mixing bowl, combine the flour, water, olive oil and salt. Use a spoon or fork to stir together. When you get a shaggy dough, tip it out onto a bench and knead for 2–3 minutes.

Wrap the dough in a damp tea towel and allow to rest for 15 minutes before resuming kneading for a further 5–7 minutes. You want the dough to be smooth and to spring back to the touch. Wrap in a tea towel again and leave at room temperature for at least an hour.

Once rested, your pasta is ready to be rolled into your desired shape.

Tips for different shapes:

TO MAKE PICI: Roll out your pasta dough into a rough square about 5 mm (¼ inch) thick. Cut the dough in half and then cut each half into strands about 4–5 mm (¼ inch) in width. Keep half the dough under a damp tea towel while you shape the first half. Using your hands, roll each strand on the bench to form a long, thin snake 2–3 mm (about ⅛ inch) thick. Do the same with the second half of the dough. Place the finished pici on a semolina-dusted tray and cover with a slightly damp tea towel to keep it from drying out.

TO MAKE BUSIATE: Roll your pasta dough into a rough square. It needs to be very thin, about 1–2 mm (¹⁄₁₆ inch) thick. Cut the dough in half and then cut each half into strands 4–5 mm (about ¼ inch) in width. Keep half the dough under a damp tea towel while you shape the first half. Using a specially made rod (known as a *ferretto* in southern Italy), or a regular bamboo skewer, start from the base of each strand. Keeping your skewer at a 45-degree angle from the pasta strand, push the pasta onto the skewer, rolling the skewer up the length of the pasta to form a corkscrew shape. Ease it off the skewer and repeat with the rest of the strands. Allow the busiate to dry for about 20–30 minutes on a semolina-dusted bench.

TO MAKE GNOCCHETTI: Roll out your pasta dough into a rough square about 5 mm (¼ inch) thick. Cut the square into 1.5 cm x 5 mm (½ x ¼ inch) small rectangles. Work with a few at a time, keeping the rest under a damp tea towel. Use either the back of a fork, the back of a cheese grater or a gnocchi board to roll the gnocchetti. Take the longer side of the rectangle and use your thumb to simultaneously press and roll the pasta along the fork, grater or board to curl and get ridges all the way around. Those ridges are important for capturing and holding the sauce.

Makes: 1 serving of pasta
(see notes on page 139)
Active time: 10 minutes
(plus time to shape pasta)
Inactive time: 1 hour 15 minutes

Kitchenalia: Pasta machine, pasta drying rack (optional). Depending on the shape you are making, you may need bamboo skewers or a *ferretto* (the *ferretto* is a delightful, if slightly indulgent, piece of kitchenalia; it is traditionally brass and is used to make long, tubular pasta shapes) or a gnocchi board and dowel.

100 g (scant ½ cup) semola rimacinata (see note)
50 ml (2½ tablespoons) warm water
1 teaspoon extra-virgin olive oil
Pinch of fine sea salt

Note: Semolina is ground from a species of wheat called durum. It is extremely high in gluten, which is what gives pasta its excellent chew. Semola rimacinata is finely ground semolina. While coarse semolina may be white, and is often ground much larger, more like polenta, semola rimacinata (also known as semola di grano duro) is remilled, making it ideal for pasta or durum wheat breads. In Australia, it's available at selected grocers and is a great addition to your pantry if making your own pasta becomes a regular ritual.

Serving suggestion: This pasta dough recipe is great for the Pici with smoky, spicy tomato sauce (see page 149).

Simple egg pasta dough, Tagliatelle Bolognese

Tagliatelle Bolognese

Makes: Enough to serve 4–6
Active time: 1 hour 10 minutes
Inactive time: 4 hours

1 kg (2 lb 4 oz) minced (ground) beef, pork and/or veal (a third of each is ideal, but half pork and half beef or veal is also great)
2 tablespoons extra-virgin olive oil
2 tablespoons unsalted butter
2 large carrots, peeled and finely diced
1 large brown onion, finely diced
2 stalks celery, finely diced
3 garlic cloves, minced
2 tablespoons tomato paste (concentrated purée)
2 bay leaves
1 branch rosemary
2 cups (500 ml) whole milk
¼ cup (60 ml) white or red wine
4 cups (1 litre) chicken or beef stock
1 x 700 g (1 lb 9 oz) jar tomato passata (puréed tomatoes), or 2 x 400 g (14 oz) tins whole peeled San Marzano tomatoes, crushed with your hands
¼ cup (50 g) dried mushrooms (preferably porcini)
1 parmesan rind (optional)
2 teaspoons fish sauce (optional, but adds great umami flavour)
500 g (1 lb 2 oz) dried tagliatelle (or fresh pasta for 6, cut into tagliatelle)
Fine sea salt
Freshly cracked black pepper

To finish
Good-quality extra-virgin olive oil
Freshly cracked black pepper
Parmigiano Reggiano

A classic Bolognese – this is my gold standard. The sauce is umami-rich, using both milk and tomato. If you're serving less than 4–6 people, save the extra Bolognese sauce in the freezer for a rainy day – you'll be thrilled when that rainy day comes around.

Before you begin: For the fresh pasta, you'll need to prepare the Simple egg pasta dough recipe (see page 139). Multiply the ingredients by 6 and cut the dough into tagliatelle (see page 140). Alternatively, use 500 g (1 lb 2 oz) dried tagliatelle or pappardelle. To speed things up, chop the soffritto ingredients (carrot, onion, celery and garlic) by pulsing them in a food processor, one ingredient at a time.

Heat a large enamel-lined Dutch oven or heavy-based pan over a high heat. Salt the minced meat and brown it in batches in the olive oil and butter. This is best done by not breaking up the meat but instead browning it in large pieces and flipping them. Remove and continue with the remaining meat.

Remove the last batch of meat, reduce the heat to low and add in the soffritto (carrot, onion, celery, garlic) with a good pinch of salt. Cook the soffritto low and slow for 30–40 minutes.

Add in the tomato paste, bay leaves and rosemary and a few cracks of pepper. Stir to combine and cook for a minute or two. Add the meat back in, along with the milk. Increase to a medium heat and simmer until the milk has almost completely evaporated.

Add in the wine, and let it simmer to cook out the alcohol, about 1 minute. Finally, add in the stock, tomato passata or tomatoes, dried mushrooms and parmesan rind (if using). Simmer over a low heat for 2 hours, partially covered. When it's finished cooking, add in the fish sauce (if using) and taste for seasoning, adjusting with salt and pepper. Remove from the heat and set aside.

Bring a large pot of salted water to a boil and drop in the tagliatelle. Cook until al dente (only about 2 minutes for fresh pasta, longer for dried pasta).

Return the Bolognese to a medium heat and add 2–3 ladlefuls of the pasta water before draining your pasta. Add the cooked pasta to the Bolognese. Stir vigorously, using a wooden spoon or tongs to combine. Once the sauce has thickened and is coating the pasta, spoon it into bowls.

Finish with a drizzle of good-quality olive oil, a good crack of pepper and finally, as much grated parmesan as your heart desires.

Note: My go-to tinned tomato, the San Marzano, only comes whole and peeled. I like to use my hands to crush them over the pan before letting them tumble in to ensure they're well crushed, but if you don't fancy getting your hands dirty, simply add the tin of whole tomatoes to the pan and use your wooden spoon to break them down as they cook.

Cavolo nero and anchovy risotto

Makes: Enough to serve 3
Active time: 45 minutes

Kitchenalia: Blender
(alternatively, use
a stick blender)

4 cups (about 1 bunch) cavolo
nero, leaves stripped from
the stems
2 tablespoons extra-virgin
olive oil, plus an extra
3 tablespoons
6 good-quality anchovy fillets
2 garlic cloves, peeled
1 brown onion, diced
2 teaspoons chopped rosemary
4 cups (1 litre) good-quality
beef stock
1 cup (220 g) Carnaroli
or Arborio rice
¼ cup (25 g) freshly grated
Parmigiano Reggiano
Fine sea salt

To finish
¼ cup (40 g) stracciatella
cheese
Good-quality extra-virgin
olive oil
Strips of lemon zest

The striking bright green colour of this dish is like the promise of spring on a winter's day, only made better by the silky texture and umami-rich flavour that follows. Risotto is dependent on good-quality rice and cooking it *just* enough to be tender throughout, but not sloppy. The flavour, however, is completely dependent on the stock you use. If you haven't made your own beef stock, get some from a local butcher – you want something rich and gelatinous, otherwise the flavours fall flat.

Bring a large pot of salted water to a boil. Add the cavolo nero leaves and blanch for 2–3 minutes, until tender. Remove the greens from the water, reserving the blanching water. Blend the greens, a ladleful of the reserved water, the 2 tablespoons of olive oil, the anchovies and garlic until totally smooth. Set aside.

Heat a pot over a medium heat and add the extra 3 tablespoons of olive oil, the onion and a pinch of salt and sweat until soft and sweet, about 10–15 minutes. Add the rosemary and sizzle for 30 seconds.

In separate pot, heat the beef stock until it's simmering.

Add the rice to the softened onions and toss to coat. Increase the heat to medium–high. Begin adding in the hot beef stock one to two ladlefuls at a time, while continuously stirring, until the rice is very nearly al dente. If you need more liquid, add in the reserved cavolo nero blanching water, one ladleful at a time.

When the rice is almost finished, stir in the cavolo nero purée and continue cooking until the right consistency is reached – it should be loose, but not gloopy or soupy. Stir in the grated parmesan and taste for seasoning.

Serve in bowls, topped with a spoonful of the stracciatella. To finish, add a drizzle of good-quality olive oil and garnish with strips of lemon zest. Serve immediately – risotto doesn't like to sit around.

Note: "Stracciatella" refers to three quite disparate foods in Italian: an egg-drop soup, a milk-based gelato with small flints of chocolate through it, and, as we're using here, a soft cheese. All are somewhat inspired by the other – *straccia* meaning "to tear" or "to shred". You may know it better as the delicious filling that oozes from a burrata when you cut it open.

Rice was introduced to Sicily and Spain by the Arabs in the 14th century, slowly making its way further north into Italy where it became a (rather lucrative) staple crop. As the Spanish oversaw the region at the time, it is here that we see the confluence of saffron and risotto, leading to the creation of the classic risotto alla Milanese. Risotto rice must be plump, short-to medium-grain, with a high starch content. The Mediterranean climate was best adapted for short-to medium-grain rice, and their dishes were influenced accordingly. There are three key varieties for risotto rice, some easier to find than others: Carnaroli (wonderfully starchy and holds its integrity), the rarer Vialone Nano (grown in the Veneto region, also with high starch), and Arborio (not as starchy, but the most widely available). As you want your risotto to be creamy, it's very important to not rinse the rice before cooking.

Pici with smoky, spicy tomato sauce

Pici is one of my favourite pasta shapes and it's such fun to make – an excellent one to get children involved with. This recipe is inspired by a dish called *pasta al fumo* from Cortona, Italy. The original dish included smoked pancetta in a creamy tomato sauce, giving it a smoky flavour, hence the name. Smoked pancetta can be tricky to find, and bacon is not the same, so to mimic this smokiness while also adding some heat (which I love) I've added tinned chipotles in adobo – not authentic, but utterly delicious. Reduce the quantity if you don't like heat.

Bring a large pot of salted water to a boil for your pasta.

To make the sauce, begin by adding the tomatoes, tomato paste and chipotle chillies in adobo to a blender and purée until smooth. Set aside.

Heat a wide pot over a medium heat and add the butter, garlic and rosemary leaves. Sizzle this for about 2 minutes, lowering the heat if the garlic starts to brown. Add in the tomato and chilli purée with a pinch of salt and bring to a simmer. Simmer over a low heat for 5 minutes. Add in the cream, stir to combine and reduce to the lowest possible heat.

Add the pasta to the boiling water and cook until al dente (fresh semolina pasta will only take 2 minutes; dried pasta will take longer, depending on the shape). Drain the pasta, reserving a mug of the pasta water. Add the drained pasta and reserved pasta water to the sauce and turn the heat up to high. Shake and mix the pasta vigorously using a wooden spoon or tongs. When the sauce is thick and coating the pasta, add in the parmesan and toss once more.

Divide between bowls and top with the extra grated parmesan.

Makes: Enough to serve 4
Active time: 45 minutes
Inactive time: 1 hour

Kitchenalia: Blender

Before you begin: Make your pasta dough following the Semolina pasta dough recipe (see page 141). Multiply the ingredients by 4, and roll the dough into pici (see page 141). Alternatively, if you're simply needing to get dinner on the table, use 500 g (1 lb 2 oz) dried spaghettoni.

1 x 400 g (14 oz) tin whole peeled San Marzano tomatoes, crushed
2 tablespoons tomato paste (concentrated purée)
1–2 chipotle chillies in adobo (see note)
40 g (1½ oz) unsalted butter
4 garlic cloves, minced
1 sprig rosemary, leaves picked
½ cup (125 ml) single (pure) cream
1 semolina pasta dough recipe, rolled into pici shapes (page 141)
¼ cup (25 g) freshly grated Parmigiano Reggiano, plus extra to garnish
Fine sea salt

Note: Chipotle chillies in adobo come tinned. Once you've opened your tin and removed the chillies that you need for this recipe, decant and freeze the remaining chipotles for next time.

Semolina pasta dough, Polenta with sweet-spiced lamb ragù

Polenta with sweet-spiced lamb ragù

Makes: Enough to serve 6
Active time: 35 minutes
Inactive time: 2 hours 30 minutes

Ragù

1 kg (2 lb 4 oz) boneless lamb
  shoulder, cut into 5–6 cm
  (2–2½ inch) pieces
¼ cup (35 g) plain
  (all-purpose) flour
¼ cup (60 ml) extra-virgin
  olive oil
1 brown onion, diced small
1 carrot, diced small
1 stalk celery, diced small
6 garlic cloves, minced
1 red capsicum (pepper),
  split in half, seeds removed
1 teaspoon fennel seeds
Pinch of chilli flakes
2 tablespoons tomato paste
  (concentrated purée)
2 sprigs rosemary, leaves
  picked
2 tablespoons chopped
  oregano
1 cinnamon quill
2 star anise
1 bay leaf
1 cup (250 ml) red wine
2 cups (500 g) tomato passata
  (puréed tomatoes)
2 cups (500 ml) chicken stock
Fine sea salt

To serve

1½ cups (285 g) dried polenta,
  prepared soft (see opposite)
Parmigiano Reggiano,
  for grating
Good-quality extra-virgin
  olive oil
Freshly cracked black pepper

Sweet spices in a ragù are typical of northern Italian cooking, and they are surprisingly perfect with meats like lamb, beef and game. The star anise and cinnamon lend sweetness and depth, while the tomato, red wine and rosemary bring this back to more recognisable territory. Don't let the long ingredients list put you off – once everything is in the pot, this ragù is pretty hands off.

Place an enamel-lined Dutch oven or a large heavy-based ovenproof pan with a tight-fitting lid over a high heat.

While your pan is heating, salt the lamb pieces. When the pan is hot, toss the lamb pieces in the flour, add the olive oil to the hot pan and immediately add in the lamb – as many pieces as will fit in one even layer; you will likely need to do this in two batches. Brown the meat on all sides then remove it from the pan and continue with the remaining lamb.

Leave all the fat from the lamb in the pan, turn the heat down to medium and add the onion, carrot, celery, garlic, capsicum halves and a good pinch of salt. Sweat until the diced vegetables are soft, sweet and beginning to brown, about 15 minutes.

Add in the fennel seeds, chilli flakes, tomato paste, rosemary, oregano, cinnamon quill, star anise and bay leaf, and cook everything together for a minute. Deglaze with the red wine, running your wooden spoon along the base of the pan to incorporate any of the umami-rich meat caught on the bottom. Finally, add in the tomato passata, chicken stock and browned lamb and bring to a simmer.

Preheat your oven to 160°C (315°F). When the lamb is simmering, cover the pan with the lid and transfer it to the oven for 2–2½ hours, or until the meat is meltingly tender.

Remove from the oven. Remove and discard the capsicum halves, rosemary stalks, cinnamon quill, star anise and bay leaf – they've done their job.

Divide the hot polenta between the bowls and spoon the braised lamb over the top. Add a sprinkle of parmesan, a drizzle of good-quality olive oil and a good crack of pepper.

Note: I prefer to put long braises like this in the oven, as opposed to cooking them on the stove top, as I find the cooking is more even, so you minimise the risk of burning the bottom. I also like to have it out of the way!

Soft polenta

Bring a large, heavy-based pot of water to a simmer.

Slowly add the dried polenta into the simmering water while whisking. Immediately reduce to a very low heat and swap your whisk for a wooden spoon. Leave your polenta to cook over a low heat, with the lid ajar.

Cook for 45 minutes, giving it a stir every 10 minutes or so, and adding ½ cup (125 ml) water when the mixture appears more like thick, wet sand than porridge.

To finish, mix through the butter, a few heavy pinches of salt (to taste) and the parmesan.

Makes: Enough to serve 6
Active time: 50 minutes

6 cups (1.5 litres) water
1½ cups (285 g) dried polenta (not the instant variety)
50 g (1¾ oz) unsalted butter, cubed
½ cup (50 g) freshly grated Parmigiano Reggiano
Fine sea salt

It's no surprise when trying to make a meal stretch, we turn to grains to help us through. Historically, they've been cheaper than fresh fruit, vegetables, meat and fish due to their ability to be stored dry, and thus almost indefinitely. A little culinary insurance policy against unforeseen risk, having a secure store of grain made people feel safe. Depending on where you are in the world, this may still be the case. In our modern western world this is less true, but as much as some people try to banish grains from their diets, I only see our fascination with pasta, rice and beans growing. This is a great thing.

The *main event*

At home in three restaurants

After all the years spent working in professional kitchens, I find cooking at home a luxury. I have time to gather ingredients, maybe a glass of wine in hand while I prep, my music of choice playing, and most importantly, I'm able to sit down and enjoy it with someone I love. I do not take it for granted.

There is something else, though, something I hadn't necessarily anticipated. Some dishes taste better at home. Not a little bit better, a lot better. Of course, I am free of constraints – of timing, of how many hands each dish will need to pass through, of considering what time it will need at the hearth, and how many burners I already have in play. But cooking at home, I am also without the luxuries that come with cooking in professional kitchens: daily access to those just-harvested vegetables and the freshest market fish, or a choice between a raging wood-fired oven and an open hearth. It's been incredible to return to my home kitchen and rediscover these flavours, and hone the skills required to coax them out.

Paradoxically, I was dining in a restaurant in Nice when the penny dropped. La Merenda is an absolute celebration of simplicity and conviviality; the walls are as crammed with wonderful bright artworks as the tiny tables are packed with the sun-kissed produce of southern France. The chef, Dominique Le Stanc, is a two-Michelin-starred chef who left behind his stars in favour of taking over this tiny twenty-seat jewel.

With tables so close they had to be pulled out to squeeze you in, there was nothing private about our conversation, and yet there was an incredible feeling of intimacy. I think it was found in that shared menu. A small chalkboard passed from table to table with only a couple of options for each course, essentially meaning we were a room full of people eating the same food: pissaladière, veal tongue with gribiche, beef daube with panisse, green pasta with pistou, a fresh rocket (arugula) salad with olives and tomatoes. A breath of French air after all the rich food of our holiday. And to finish, strawberries soaked in rosé and a tarte au citron. It wasn't just that it was delicious, it was that we felt like we were home – like someone had pulled together stools to make the table big enough for two more. Plates were ungarnished, unadorned and confident. Only someone cooking the food they grew up with can cook this way.

The incredible shared intimacy was new to me, but the traditions behind this kind of cooking weren't. Over the years I spent in the kitchen at Chez Panisse – to my mind, the greatest restaurant in the world – I had cooked food that was very refined, yet, at its core, the cooking was rooted in tradition and focused on flavour.

When Chez Panisse was opened fifty-plus years ago by Alice Waters and her friends, it was meant to be a place where they could gather and discuss the topics of the day as they prepared and ate wonderful food. The restaurant's food has evolved since then, and over its long life it has become a pillar of American cuisine – a symbol of hope for the future of sustainable farming and restaurant relations, and an incubator of amazing chefs and service talent. It was there, in the kitchen of Chez Panisse, that I learned the joy of a menu that changes with the ingredients to hand. The menu changed every single day. In that kitchen you needed to pay attention, be thoughtful and taste at every step.

Unlike typical restaurants – where menus may change seasonally, but the *mise en place* will roll from one day to the next, only ever getting a top-up of freshness – changing the menu daily is much more like home cooking. You could taste that difference. Over my four years at Chez Panisse, there were only a handful of dishes that appeared with some regularity: the cheese and garlic soufflé, the bouillabaisse, the tomato carpaccio, the pissaladière. These were the dishes I was able to tinker with, to really understand how small changes affected the finished dish. You can see how my experiences of these two restaurants have now come together in a humble dish of pastry and stewed onions on page 72.

Another hand-written chalkboard, another daily changing menu, another restaurant that feels as cobbled together as a home with the addition of new children, but this one in Sydney. Sean's on Bondi Beach has grown, shifted and changed to fit a space that was not built for its current purpose: handmade shelving, pokey hallways and a kitchen that looks like it would be more at home in a home than in a restaurant.

It has a feeling I immediately recognised from Chez Panisse. Sean Moran is not just a chef, but an artist, and all the little details are personal: oyster shells for salt cellars, mussel and scallop shells adorning light fixtures, local artists' paintings hanging on the walls from floor to ceiling, against a light-blue backdrop – the colour of the sky on a bright Sydney day.

Sean's famous roasted chicken with farm vegetables; pipis with corn chowder; a plate of vegetables from his farm, with a sesame-crusted soft-boiled egg and herb dressing; tagliatelle with rocket, parmesan and chilli oil. It's all the food you want to eat, all of the time.

These are restaurants that would love to throw off the shackles of their restaurantness, and yet, even if they did, I'm quite sure they would serve you the same meal. Elevated home cooking. This is it. This is what made me fall in love with restaurants in the first place, and this is what made me realise the incredible possibilities at home.

"Probably one of the most *private* things in the world is an egg until it is *broken*."

M.F.K. Fisher, *How to Cook a Wolf*

If you want to know what a person is like, ask them to cook you an egg. Do they ask you how you like them, or do they fall back on their favourite technique? Are they precise and gentle, or do they like a flash in the pan? (You can be both, by the way.) Are they slowly scrambled, quickly fried, carefully boiled? Are the eggs broken into an omelette to have with a glass of wine, or hidden among the greens in a frittata? It's a Freudian field day!

I have a place in my heart for all kinds of egg cookery, and rotate through them often, *but* if I could only eat one type of egg for the rest of my life, it would have to be fried. For greater visibility into my character, that egg needs a crisp, lacy white (no uncooked albumen please) and a rich, runny yolk. For this, I used to take them over-easy, but the risks were many. If I broke the yolk on that flip, the whole thing was ruined – not just the egg, but the whole day. There's no worse omen than a failed egg cook. I had to find a better way …

The perfect fried eggs, I discovered, need the right tools. I now have a little non-stick frying pan that is only big enough to cook two eggs at a time. It has an accompanying glass lid that fits snugly. It has only ever cooked eggs – I'm not sure why, but the moment you open the door to cooking other things in the pan, it all starts to disintegrate. Nothing metal ever touches the pan, just a rubber spatula to gently move my eggs around, and I never put it in the dishwasher, only giving it a gentle hand wash.

What a chicken doesn't tell you about character, it makes up for in care. A whole roast chicken means someone loves you, a symbol of family, affection and conviviality. Indeed, chickens have been used the world over to nurture the sick back to health, and the sad back to happiness. They are a culinary wonder; small enough that you can easily work with the whole animal in your home, and a treat of varied tastes and textures, of hard-working muscles and lazy ones. To be able to offer so much contrast in one meal is incredible.

And yet, for all the symbolism, we tend to mistreat the chicken. It's one of the most intensively bred and commercially reared of all the farmyard animals. Not only are the birds themselves unrecognisable from their rather recent barnyard ancestors, but in favouring the breast over the rest, we've given up the unique wonder of a whole bird. We've removed them literally, and figuratively, from their nature.

There is such beauty in buying a whole chicken. For starters, you get much better value for money – a whole chicken is always *at least* two meals: a family roast, followed by a delicious soup made from the carcass. And, if you're feeding less than four, you have even more options: roast the chicken breasts on the bone one night, separate the legs for dinner another, and then use the carcass to make a broth for soup. That's *three*!

An organic bird is my minimum standard, but I also try to buy from a small local farm – I think this is the necessary way forward. Don't fret if you can't find a good fresh one; a frozen healthy chicken, from a trustworthy place, is better than a fresh battery-farmed bird any day of the week. Once you've seen the conditions these battery birds are farmed and processed in, you will *not* want to serve them to your friends, your family, or to yourself. A healthy bird, raised on a healthy diet, with care and using regenerative farming methods, is a joy to cook and serve. That is how to show your love.

The perfect fried egg:
I put my pan over a high heat and let it get really hot. I drizzle in a couple of teaspoons of olive oil and swirl it around the pan – you want the whole pan licked by the oil. I quickly crack two eggs into the pan and, almost in the same movement, put the lid on. You should hear some vigorous sizzling and splattering under the lid. This is where a glass lid comes in handy; through the steam, I can see when the white of the egg has blinded the yolk, turning it opaque. If you can't see, know this takes about 2 minutes. I immediately lift the lid off and slide the eggs onto the plate. For this reason, it's important to have all bread toasted or garnishes cooked before frying the eggs – it all happens so quickly. I always season with flaked sea salt and freshly cracked black pepper, and usually some sort of hot sauce.

Fried eggs with corn and cabbage kimchi:
Strip the kernels from an ear of corn. Place a sauté pan over a high heat and add a pat of butter. When the butter is foamy, add the corn kernels and a pinch of salt. Allow the kernels to get nicely browned and start jumping from the pan. Add a heaped tablespoon of chopped cabbage kimchi and fry for another couple of seconds. Scoop this onto a plate and fry the eggs as described above. Place the eggs onto the corn and grate fresh Parmigiano Reggiano over the plate. If you have chives, a generous scattering of those would be delicious. Eat immediately.

The simplest of stocks:

To the bones of your roast chicken, add half an onion, a celery stalk, a carrot, a bay leaf and a few of those tiny little garlic cloves that remain on the head that you can't be bothered to peel. Cover with water and simmer for a couple of hours, at which point you are left with liquid gold. (If the cupboard is bare, but the bones are good, your stock can simply be the chicken and water!)

This stock can be seasoned with soy sauce and star anise for a noodle soup; or use it to cook soaked dried beans for added depth of flavour. You could even continue using it as a stock for poaching chicken, freezing it after every use to preserve a "mother stock" basically for eternity (just bring to a rolling boil for a couple of minutes before each use). It will only get better and better!

Yoghurt and za'atar marinated thighs:

Toss boneless, skinless chicken thighs with $\frac{1}{4}$ cup (70 g) of Greek-style plain yoghurt, a tablespoonful of tomato paste (concentrated purée), the juice of a lemon, a few crushed cloves of garlic and a teaspoon of za'atar for an excellent marinade before grilling. Boneless chicken with acidic marinade, like lemon and yoghurt, should only be marinated for up to 10 hours, as it can start to break down too much and become cottony on the palate.

Now, the sticking point. We can't ignore the modern convenience of chicken parts, but among those little plastic trays – denuded, deboned, deskinned – there is not much to inspire. It's just not what makes me excited to get into the kitchen! However, I appreciate that for feeding a family, they are convenient. Here are my favourite ways to cook chicken parts:

Boneless, skinless chicken thigh lends itself to methods that add a protective layer, such as flour or crumbs, a thick marinade, or those that involve a quick dice and sauté. They can also be minced or finely chopped for a meatball.

Boneless, skinless chicken breasts: The shape of the whole breast – one thick end and one thin end – makes it particularly difficult to cook well. You either want to cook this cut in a very moist way, to keep it juicy and ensure even cooking (steaming or gentle poaching is best), or cook it hard and fast. To do this, you need to thin it out. Butterfly or cut the breast into slices and bash with a mallet. This is perfect for paillard (see page 179), which you could then grill for less than a minute or, much like the boneless, skinless thighs, you can coat in flour or breadcrumbs and pan-fry to keep in the moisture.

Bone-in, skin-on chicken pieces (including wings): These are my favourites; meat cooked on the bone is simply more delicious. The bone adds flavour, both slowing down the cooking and insulating the meat, helping to retain moisture – and once the heat is in there, the bone keeps it there longer (the reason why resting is so much more relevant to pieces of meat cooked on the bone). The skin does similar things, slowly basting the meat with its rendered fat, while protecting the meat from direct heat. It also tastes delicious! Chicken wings have the best meat-to-skin ratio on the bird, and for that reason, they are my absolute favourite. They are also (happily) the most economical cut. Bone-in, skin-on cuts are the most forgiving and can be grilled, roasted, deep-fried or braised.

Golden roasted wings: My favourite way to eat chicken wings is inspired by the memory of roasting wings for chicken stocks in restaurants, always sneaking a wing or two before they went into the pot. Set your oven to 200°C (400°F). Toss your wings with a little olive oil, salt and black pepper and spread them out on a baking tray so they're not touching each other. Cook until golden brown all over, about 20–25 minutes. Allow to cool slightly before eating with your hands. These would be excellent dipped into the Buttermilk herb dressing (see page 79) or brushed with a good barbecue sauce, something I wish I'd had when I was stealing them from the tray.

Zucchini frittata for one

Makes: Enough to serve 1
Active time: 12 minutes

1 large zucchini (courgette)
2 teaspoons extra-virgin
    olive oil
3 eggs
½ tablespoon unsalted butter
25 g (1 oz) soft goat's cheese
1 tablespoon chopped chives
Flaked sea salt
Freshly cracked black pepper

Serving suggestion: Toasted bread,
a rocket (arugula) salad (see page 71
for a simple vinaigrette recipe)
and/or a few slices of wild smoked
salmon would all be excellent
additions here.

Seasonal adjustment: In the
cooler months, swap the zucchini for
spinach or wilted, chopped greens
like silverbeet (Swiss chard), noting
that they will need slightly less
cooking time than zucchini.

A simple and delicious frittata should be within everyone's reach. It takes
minutes to prepare, and is a saviour in lean times.

Grate the zucchini on the large holes of a box grater. Heat a small non-stick
frying pan over a medium heat and add the olive oil and zucchini. Sprinkle
with a pinch of salt and spread the zucchini out, leaving it untouched to
sizzle until you start to see browning at the edges.

Give it a stir and repeat until the zucchini is well caramelised and looking
quite dry, about 5–7 minutes.

Spoon the cooked zucchini onto a dish. Splash the pan with a bit of cold
water and wipe it clean. Return the pan to the stove over a low heat.

Turn your oven grill (broiler) on to a high heat.

Crack the eggs into a small bowl and whisk vigorously using a fork until
well mixed and add in the zucchini, whisking again to distribute.

Add the butter to the pan and swirl it around before pouring in the eggs.
Using a rubber spatula, scrape around the edges of the egg, pulling it to
the centre while lifting and tilting the pan to allow the liquid egg to fill the
gap and make contact with the pan. Do this a few times until there is still
liquid egg on top of the frittata, but the base has firmed up.

Place the pan under the grill for a few seconds, until the top is cooked.
Remove from the grill, crumble over the goat's cheese and place a lid on
the pan for 1 minute to help melt the cheese before sliding the frittata
onto your plate. Sprinkle with the chives and finish with a little flaked sea
salt and a crack of pepper.

Poaching the perfect chicken breast

Makes: Enough to serve 4
Active time: 10 minutes
Inactive time: 1 hour

Kitchenalia: Internal meat
    thermometer

2 x 400 g (14 oz) chicken
    breasts, boneless and skinless
2 garlic cloves
1 teaspoon fennel seeds
1 bay leaf
2 teaspoons fine sea salt
Freshly cracked black pepper,
    to taste

Note: You really do need a
thermometer to do this accurately,
but if you don't have one, you can
rely on your senses: 65°C (150°F) is
the temperature when water is just
starting to steam; if it's simmering
(small bubbles popping at the
surface), it's gone well above this
temperature. You don't want to see
anything moving around in the pot
– it should be quite still with an ever-
so-gentle whisp of steam coming off
the top. Hold it at this temperature
until the chicken breast is firm, but
not tough, to the touch.

A poached chicken breast is an excellent thing to have on hand for recipes like the Poached chicken and freekeh salad with tarragon and lemon vinaigrette (see page 168) or the Tarragon and celery chicken sandwich (see page 110). Although I'll admit that the chicken breast is not my favourite cut, it is possible to cook in such a way that it becomes a juicy and flavourful part of your meal.

Add your chicken breasts into a pot with all the remaining ingredients and fill with enough cold water to just cover.

Place over a medium–low heat and slowly bring the water up to a temperature of 65–70°C (150–160°F) (use your thermometer, or see note). At this point, turn the heat down to its lowest setting and try to hold it at this temperature until the internal temperature of the meat (at its thickest point) is 65°C (150°F). For a 400 g (14 oz) chicken breast this will take about 40–45 minutes – smaller breasts will take less time. Flip the chicken around once or twice during this time, to ensure even cooking.

Once the meat reaches temperature, remove from the poaching liquid and allow to cool. Strain the poaching liquid and use as a light stock, keeping in mind that it's seasoned (it's wonderful to cook your pasta in – try it with the Roasted garlic and sage pastina on page 136), or discard it.

Whole poached chicken with ginger-spring onion dressing and rice

I love the circular beauty of this dish: nothing wasted, everything valued; this, is home cooking. It's a dish classically known as "Hainanese chicken" or "chicken rice", and its origins are in southern China, but many cultures in South-East Asia have their own versions. At its most basic, a whole chicken is poached in water that's seasoned with spring onions and ginger. The accompanying rice is cooked in the resulting chicken fat and broth, and served with a simple condiment of sautéed ginger, spring onion and soy sauce. It's pure and simple, and I crave it so often that I had to figure out how to make it at home.

Rinse your chicken under cold running water (being mindful not to splash water everywhere and to sanitise the area once you've finished rinsing).

Place the chicken in a pot and add enough water to cover the chicken by 2 cm (¾ inch). This is just to judge how much water you need in the pot. Remove the chicken and set it aside.

Take your 4 cm (1½ inch) piece of ginger and cut it into four slices. Add it to the water, along with 6 spring onions. Bring it up to a boil. Once boiling, slowly lower your chicken into the water and turn the heat down to medium–low. Skim and discard any brown or greyish foam that may rise to the top. Allow the chicken to simmer gently and slowly for 40–60 minutes, depending on the size of the bird. You can tell if it's done by removing the chicken from the water and piercing a small knife in between the chicken breast and the thigh: if the juices run clear, it's done; if they run pink or cloudy, let it simmer for another 10 minutes.

Set up a large bowl of ice water next to your chicken pot. When the chicken is cooked, lift it out of the broth using tongs and a large spoon or spider (being careful not to tear the skin), then lower it into the ice water, breast-side down. This is to firm the skin around the meat, providing a nice texture. (If you don't have ice, simply lift the chicken out of the broth and leave it on a tray or plate to cool – the texture of the skin won't be the same, but it will still be delicious.)

While the chicken cools, cook your rice (you can do this in a rice cooker or in a pot). Add the rice to an empty pot. Using a ladle, skim as much chicken fat from the top of the broth as possible and add it to the rice. Add enough broth to cover the rice by about 2 cm (¾ inch) (tip: If you were to place the tip of your index finger on the rice, this is around the same length from the rice to the first joint of your finger). Bring the rice to a boil, give it a quick stir, then cover tightly and turn the heat down to the lowest heat for 17 minutes. When the timer is up, turn the heat off and allow the rice to rest for 5 minutes before fluffing with a fork and serving.

While the rice cooks, make your ginger-spring onion condiment. Thinly slice the remaining spring onion – you should have about ¼ cup (20 g). Heat a small saucepan over a medium–low heat and add the oil. Heat the oil until it begins to shimmer, then sizzle the spring onion and the extra 3 tablespoons minced ginger for about 30 seconds and turn the heat off. Pour into a small serving dish, and add the soy sauce and stir to combine.

Makes: Enough to serve 4
Active time: 25 minutes
Inactive time: 1 hour 20 minutes

1 x 1.5–2 kg (3 lb 5 oz–4 lb 8 oz) whole organic chicken
4 cm (1½ inch) piece of ginger, plus an extra 3 tablespoons finely minced ginger
1 bunch spring onions (scallions), light green and white parts only
1 cup (200 g) jasmine rice, rinsed in 6 changes of cold water
¼ cup (60 ml) neutral oil
¼ cup (60 ml) light soy sauce

⟶

To serve, you can either cut the chicken into pieces on the bone or, for ease of eating, cut the meat off the bone by first removing the breast meat and slicing it, and then slicing the leg meat.

Serve the hot broth in small cups or bowls (you may have a bit extra, which is excellent to freeze or to keep in the fridge and use within a few days). Serve the chicken on top of a heaping spoonful of the hot rice, along with the condiment to spoon over the whole dish.

The traditional Hainanese chicken rice is derived from a Hainan specialty, Wenchang chicken, and is cooked by "white cutting", where the chicken is immersed in near-boiling water. The dish moved with the many migrants who headed south to make Singapore their home. It was so loved in Singapore that it took on a personality of its own in the city's many bustling street markets. Traditionally, this chicken preparation involves a few added steps, like dropping the chicken into boiling water and then into an ice bath to tighten the skin. The wonder is not just in the delicious chicken rice, but also the texture of the chicken.

Poached chicken and freekeh salad with tarragon and lemon vinaigrette

Makes: Enough to serve 4
Active time: 20 minutes
Inactive time: 1 hour 30 minutes

Kitchenalia: Mandoline
(alternatively, a very sharp
knife to thinly slice)

Before you begin: You'll need
poached chicken breasts (see page
164) for this recipe, which you can
do up to a day ahead.

½ cup (100 g) dried freekeh
(or farro)
½ cup (80 g) raw almonds
2 × 400 g (14 oz) poached
chicken breasts (page 164),
shredded
1 small fennel bulb, thinly
shaved on a mandoline
(or with a very sharp knife)

Dressing
1 garlic clove
2 tablespoons lemon juice
(from about half a lemon)
1 teaspoon Dijon mustard
4 tablespoons extra-virgin
olive oil
1 tablespoon chopped French
tarragon
1 tablespoon chopped mint
Fine sea salt
Freshly cracked black pepper

To finish
1 bunch rocket (arugula) leaves,
to garnish
1 ripe avocado

This is a favourite grain salad that I make often. Grain salads are excellent picnic food as they hold up so well over time. To make this vegetarian, skip the chicken and use steamed asparagus and/or sugar snap peas instead.

Cook the freekeh or farro according to the package instructions and leave it to cool.

Preheat your oven to 175°C (345°F). Toss the almonds onto a small baking tray and toast them in the oven for 12 minutes. Remove the almonds from the oven and allow to cool, then roughly chop them – you want nice textural contrast here, so definitely not too fine. Set aside.

To make the dressing, grate the garlic clove into a small bowl and add in the remaining ingredients with a pinch of salt and a crack of pepper. Stir to combine and set aside.

In a large mixing bowl, combine the almonds, shredded chicken, freekeh and fennel. Toss with most of the vinaigrette, along with a pinch of salt.

Spoon the salad into bowls, or onto a serving platter, and top with the rocket and avocado. Finish with a drizzle of the remaining dressing.

Chicken noodle soup with star anise, fish sauce and herbs

Makes: Enough to serve 2
Active time: 30 minutes
Inactive time: 10 minutes

2 tablespoons neutral oil
5 garlic cloves, thinly sliced
2½ cups (625 ml) good-quality
    chicken stock
2 star anise
80 g (2¾ oz) vermicelli rice
    noodles
1 bok choy, split in half
2 teaspoons light soy sauce
2 teaspoons fish sauce

To finish
1 handful basil leaves
1 handful coriander
    (cilantro) leaves
Quarter of a white or red onion
    (or one small French shallot),
    thinly sliced in rounds
Sambal oelek (optional)
1 lime, halved

Serving suggestion: The Crunchy chilli oil (see page 88) or the Ginger and chilli jam (see page 194) would both make for perfect alternatives to the sambal oelek.

The benefit of poaching a whole chicken is not just the delicious chicken, but the resulting broth. This is the perfect use for that broth but can also work with the simple stock you make from your leftover Spatchcocked roast chicken (see page 174). Be sure to pull off any remaining pieces of meat from the carcass to add to this soup, or add in some sautéed mushrooms or fried tofu. If you don't want to make your own stock, buy a good-quality one from a small producer or butcher. This dish tastes like it's been simmering for hours but actually comes together in minutes.

In a large enamel-lined Dutch oven or a heavy-based pot over a medium heat, add the oil and sizzle the garlic until golden. Use a skimmer or slotted spoon to scoop the garlic chips out and set aside. Add in the chicken stock and star anise and bring to a low simmer. Simmer for about 10 minutes.

Meanwhile, place your vermicelli into a heatproof bowl and bring a full kettle of water to the boil. Pour the boiling water over the vermicelli and allow them to sit for 3 minutes before draining and rinsing the noodles in cold water. Divide between two serving bowls.

Add the bok choy to the broth and simmer for another minute. Remove and discard the star anise and stir in any extra vegetables or leftover shredded chicken you may have (see introduction above).

Season the broth with the soy sauce and fish sauce. Taste the soup and adjust the seasoning with more of each as it needs.

Ladle the broth, vegetables and chicken (if using) over the noodles. Top with the basil and coriander, raw onion slices, the reserved garlic chips and a spoonful of the sambal oelek (if using). Serve with the lime halves.

Lentils and rice with jammy eggs and yoghurt

Makes: Enough to serve 4
Active time: 45 minutes
Inactive time: 25 minutes

1 cup (210 g) dried green
   French lentils (preferably
   du Puy)
4 brown onions
¼ cup (60 ml) neutral oil
3 garlic cloves, minced, plus an
   extra whole clove, peeled
2 teaspoons yellow curry
   powder (I like Keen's!)
1 cup (200 g) basmati rice,
   rinsed in cold water
4 eggs
Heaped ½ cup (160 g)
   Greek-style plain yoghurt
Fine sea salt

To finish
Chilli flakes, to garnish
1 lime, cut into 4 wedges

Note: On frying versus caramelising: when I say "fry", I mean at a high heat, so the onions become browned but are still slightly crunchy. It's important to heat your oil before adding the onions to the pan when frying (same goes for when you're looking to brown or sear an ingredient, for example meat or fish). Caramelising is done at a lower heat and takes much longer – the onions become soft and sweet and evenly golden brown all over. When you're sautéing or caramelising, it's not necessary to heat your cooking oil first, so simply add your ingredients to your pan along with the oil.

This dish combines a few ideas from my youth and a classic dish from the Levant, called mujaddara. In Cuba, rice cooked together with beans is commonplace, as is yellow curried rice – a favourite among Caribbean cultures. By replacing the beans with lentils, you get a quicker cook, and by adding a few extra flourishes like the fried onions, a jammy egg and yoghurt sauce, you have a dish worthy of dinner-time.

Place the lentils in a small pot and cover with 4 cm (1½ inches) water. Add a pinch of salt and bring to a simmer. Cook the lentils until tender, about 20–30 minutes, then set aside to cool. Once cooled, strain and reserve the cooking liquid, keeping the lentils and liquid separate. Measure the liquid and add enough water to make 3 cups in total.

Thinly slice three of the onions and dice the remaining one. Heat a large, heavy-bottomed pot over a high heat and add the oil. Fry the sliced onions until they are a deep golden brown. You are frying here, not caramelising, so keep the heat on high and stir frequently (see note). Drain the cooked onions on paper towels and sprinkle with salt. Set aside.

In the same pot, cook the diced onion and minced garlic over a medium heat until soft and sweet. Once softened, add the curry powder and sizzle for about 20 seconds.

Add the rice and stir to coat in the oil and garlic. Add the lentils and the 3 cups of reserved cooking liquid with a teaspoon of salt. Stir and bring to a boil. Stir again, scraping the bottom of the pan, then cover with a tight-fitting lid. Lower the heat to its lowest setting and cook for 17 minutes. Turn the heat off and leave covered for 5 minutes before opening.

While the rice is cooking, bring a small pot of water to the boil. Slowly lower the eggs (straight from the fridge) into the boiling water and set a timer for 7 minutes. Once cooked, drain and run cold water over the eggs to cool, then peel and set aside.

In a small bowl, combine the yoghurt and the extra clove of garlic, grated on a microplane. Add a pinch of salt and stir to combine.

Fluff the rice just before serving. Divide the lentils and rice between bowls, or serve it straight out of the pot. Top with the halved boiled eggs, a spoonful of yoghurt and the fried onions. Sprinkle with the chilli flakes and serve with wedges of lime.

The idea of terroir is wildly romantic – that a wine, cheese or even lentils can transport you across continents. In the case of the geographically protected *lentilles vertes du Puy*, that place is the volcanic belt of France, in the Auvergne. Volcanic soils are highly regarded for their ability to produce beautiful wines – how wonderful to find a place that's willing to invest that much care into their lentils! But it's not all about the soil. The growing region is nestled among mountains at an altitude of between 600 and 1,200 metres. The warm summer winds must climb those mountains first, releasing their humidity before descending on the valley of maturing lentils with only warm, dry air. This halts the lentils' growth, keeping the skin fine, while limiting the development of the compound that creates a floury texture in other lentils.

Spatchcocked roast chicken on crouton

Makes: Enough to serve 4
Active time: 15 minutes
Inactive time: 3 hours

Before you begin: Season your bird and leave it uncovered in your fridge up to a day in advance, or for a minimum of 1 hour. This will help to dry out the skin, so it goes crisp when cooked. Bring the chicken to room temperature before cooking. It's great to get a head start by making your stock after spatchcocking the chicken, either the day before roasting the bird, or a few hours before.

1 x 1.6 kg (3 lb 8 oz) whole
  organic chicken
2 teaspoons thyme leaves
2 tablespoons unsalted butter,
  at room temperature
Zest of 1 lemon
2 tablespoons extra-virgin
  olive oil
2 thick slices of sourdough
¼ cup (60 ml) chicken stock
  (see note on opposite page)
Juice of half a lemon
Fine sea salt
Freshly cracked black pepper

For my money, a butterflied bird ("butterflied", "spatchcocked", "flat-roasted" – a cacophony of names for the same technique!) is the best way to roast a chicken (or turkey) at home. It cooks faster, helping to stop it from drying out, and more evenly, resulting in a juicy breast and well-cooked drumsticks. You can ask your butcher to butterfly it for you, just be sure to ask to keep the backbone and wing "forearm" so you can use them to make the stock. This flattened bird is baked on thick slices of bread, which you may find to be the real star of the dish after they've absorbed all the drippings of the chicken as it cooks.

To spatchcock the chicken, place the bird breast-down on a chopping board and using either kitchen shears or a sharp, heavy knife, cut along either side of the backbone to remove it. Flip the chicken over and, breast-side up, push on the breast to break the breastbone and make it flatter.

Season the chicken with salt up to a day ahead (the longer, the better). Leave it in the fridge, breast-side up and uncovered, so the skin can dry out. Pull it out to come to room temperature an hour before you intend to start cooking.

When ready to cook the chicken, preheat your oven to 200°C (400°F).

Mix the thyme with the butter and lemon zest. Gently wiggle your fingers under the skin of the chicken breast and push the butter in, spreading it out as best you can across the whole breast without tearing the skin.

Heat a frying pan over a medium–high heat and add the olive oil. Fry the bread on each side until golden brown, adding more olive oil if necessary. Place the bread in your roasting pan and splash with the chicken stock. Place the chicken, breast-side up, on the bread.

Roast your chicken in the oven for 40–50 minutes, depending on the size of the bird, until it is cooked through. An easy way to check if it's cooked is by gently lifting it up and looking at the underside of the breast. If the bones are fully browned with no pink or red remaining, it's done. Pull your chicken out, but leave your oven on.

Allow the chicken to rest in the pan for at least 20 minutes, still sitting on the bread. Move the chicken to your chopping board, then pour off any juices that have accumulated in the pan into a dish and set aside. Return the bread in the pan to the oven for 5–7 minutes to crisp up.

Carve your chicken by first removing the legs and splitting them into thigh and drumstick pieces at the joint. Carve the breasts off the bone and cut each one in half. Cut the slices of sourdough in half.

Serve the chicken on a platter with the juicy, crisp, custardy bread. To finish, add the lemon juice to the reserved pan drippings, stir well and pour over the entire dish. Finish with a crack of pepper.

Note: It's great to get into the habit of liberating your poultry from its plastic bag before storing it in the fridge. Place on a plate to catch any juices and give it a sprinkle of salt. You'll be getting a jump start on a crisp skin by allowing the dry air in the fridge to start drawing out the moisture (this also works with a pork roast and its crackling).

Chicken stock note: Just after you've removed the backbone of the chicken, throw it into a pot with half an onion, a stalk of celery and a carrot, both chopped into large chunks, and cover with cold water by at least 4 cm (1½ inches). Simmer for 1–2 hours, strain and use as the stock called for in the recipe.

To extend the meal: Save all the bones after carving, and any bits of meat that may have fallen off the bone, along with your reserved backbone from the stock, and toss in a pot. Cover with cold water by 4 cm (1½ inches) and add half an onion, a carrot and a celery stalk (both chopped into large chunks), a bay leaf and a teaspoon of black peppercorns. Bring to a simmer. Skim off any foamy bits that come to the surface and simmer for 2 hours before straining. You'll have a delicious chicken stock that you can keep in the fridge for up to a week, freeze for several months, or use immediately to make a pot of soup, such as the Chicken noodle soup with star anise, fish sauce and herbs (see page 170).

Spatchcocked roast chicken on crouton

Chicken paillard with sage, garlic and brown butter

An instant classic. *Paillard* is a lovely French word that simply means "flattened". It's a great technique for chicken breast, which can be difficult to cook properly; the (gentle) bashing will tenderise the meat, while the uniform thickness ensures the meat cooks evenly, removing one of the great chagrins of this cut. For this small effort you'll be rewarded with a succulent, golden chicken breast ... add crisp fried capers and sage leaves, brown butter and lemon juice and this becomes a recipe for pure happiness.

Butterfly the chicken breast (see note) and place it in-between two sheets of baking paper. Use a rolling pin to bash the chicken until it's 3–4 mm (about ⅛ inch) thick. Remove the paper and season the chicken with salt and pepper on both sides. Tip the flour onto a plate or tray and dredge the chicken in the flour.

Set a wide, flat frying pan over a high heat and add the olive oil. When the pan is hot, add the chicken and cook for 1–2 minutes per side, until slightly golden. Remove the chicken from the pan and reduce the heat to medium.

Add in the butter and garlic cloves. When the butter has browned, add in the capers and sage and fry for 30 seconds. Next, add in the lemon zest and juice, along with the chicken stock. Simmer the pan sauce until it has reduced by half, then add the chicken back in, coating it in the sauce and cooking for a further minute just to heat it through. Serve immediately.

Makes: Enough to serve 2–3
Active time: 25 minutes

2 x 200 g (14 oz) chicken breasts, boneless and skinless
½ cup (75 g) plain (all-purpose) flour
2 tablespoons extra-virgin olive oil
50 g (1¾ oz) unsalted butter
8 garlic cloves, unpeeled and smashed
2 tablespoons capers in brine, rinsed
Half a bunch of sage, leaves picked (about 20–30 leaves)
Zest and juice of half a lemon
100 ml (3½ fl oz) chicken stock
Fine sea salt
Freshly cracked black pepper

Note: To butterfly a chicken breast, lay it in on a chopping board with the thicker end pointing away from you. Press down onto the chicken with the palm of your hand while you use your other hand to cut through the length of the chicken breast using a chef's knife, aiming to get as close to the centre as possible. Do this slowly and carefully. As you cut, use the hand that's pressing down on the breast to lift the top piece of breast away from the bottom. Cut all the way through to the other end, leaving you with two thin slices of chicken breast.

Serving suggestion: Serve this dish with the Potato purée (see page 232) or Soft polenta (see page 153).

Chicken thighs with spiced ghee and yoghurt

Makes: Enough to serve 4
Active time: 30 minutes
Inactive time: 2 hours

Before you begin: The chicken requires half an hour to marinate but can be left marinating for up to 10 hours, so plan accordingly.

1 kg (2 lb 4 oz) chicken thighs, bone in, skin on
¼ cup (70 g) Greek-style plain yoghurt, plus an extra ½ cup (130 g)
3 cm (1¼ inch) piece of ginger, grated on a microplane
4 garlic cloves, grated on a microplane
1 brown onion, peeled and cut into 8 wedges
½ cup (100 g) ghee (see note)
2 long green chillies, split in half
1 teaspoon brown mustard seeds
30 curry leaves
1 teaspoon cumin seeds
1 cinnamon quill
½ teaspoon ground turmeric
Fine sea salt
Freshly cracked black pepper

To serve
Steamed basmati rice (see serving suggestion)
A few sprigs coriander (cilantro)
1 lemon or lime, cut into 4 wedges

I've had my fair share of unimpressive chicken tray bakes over the years, mostly made by me. Until this one. Marinating the chicken in yoghurt, ginger and garlic gives this dish a depth of flavour, and the spiced ghee, which gets drizzled over everything at the end, can't be beaten. This treatment requires bone-in, skin-on chicken thighs, or full chicken marylands (drumstick plus thigh) would also work well.

Season your chicken thighs with salt and pepper. In a large bowl, combine the ¼ cup (70 g) of yoghurt with the grated ginger and garlic. Place the chicken in the bowl and use clean hands to rub the marinade all over the chicken, ensuring the chicken is nicely coated. Cover and refrigerate for at least 30 minutes, but up to 10 hours. Remove the marinated chicken from the fridge 30 minutes before baking.

Preheat your oven to 200°C (400°F).

Toss the onion wedges on a large baking-paper-lined tray and nestle the chicken thighs (skin-side up) among them. Everything should be in one even layer with a little breathing space, so use two trays if needed. Heat half the ghee in a small pot and, once melted, drizzle it over everything, then sprinkle with a good pinch of salt and a crack of pepper. Bake for 35–40 minutes until the chicken is deeply golden on top.

While the chicken is baking, steam the rice (see below).

Remove the tray from the oven and cover it loosely with a sheet of aluminium foil. Set aside to let the chicken rest.

Heat the remaining half of the ghee in the same pot. Once hot, add the chillies and mustard seeds. When the mustard seeds start popping, add in the curry leaves and allow them to sizzle. Next, add in the cumin seeds, cinnamon quill and turmeric and cook over a low heat for 30 seconds, then turn the heat off. Leave everything to sit and infuse for 15 minutes.

To serve, uncover the tray and drizzle the spiced butter over everything. Serve with steamed rice, the extra yoghurt, fresh coriander and lemon or lime wedges.

Note: Ghee is like a clarified butter, only its cooking is taken slightly further. This allows the milk solids to caramelise before the butter is strained, lending ghee its characteristic nuttiness. It can be bought ready prepared but to make your own, place butter in a pot and simmer until all the liquid has evaporated and the butter just begins to brown. Quickly strain it through a fine mesh sieve and store it in the fridge to use as needed. As you have now removed all the milk solids, it will keep indefinitely.

Serving suggestion: To cook basmati rice, rinse 1½ cups (300 g) rice under cold running water until the water runs clear. Place the rice in a small pot with a tight-fitting lid with 2¼ cups (560 ml) water (1.5 times the volume of water to rice). Bring to a boil over a high heat, stir once with a fork then place a lid on the pot and turn it down to the lowest heat. Cook for 17 minutes, then turn off the heat completely and allow it to rest for 5 minutes before fluffing with a fork and serving.

"Pounding *fragrant* things – particularly *garlic, basil, parsley* – is a tremendous *antidote* to depression. But it applies also to *juniper berries, coriander seeds* and the grilled fruits of the *chilli pepper.* Pounding these things produces an alteration in one's being – from sighing with fatigue to inhaling with *pleasure.* The *cheering effects of herbs* and alliums cannot be too often reiterated."

Patience Gray, *Honey from a Weed*

Herbs are a particular love of mine. To be honest, I'm not sure I could cook if I didn't have an assortment of fresh herbs at my disposal. This reliance means either spending a small fortune on herbs each week or growing them myself. My "garden" is currently limited to numerous pots, but each one is spilling over with fragrant herbs: parsley, French tarragon, thyme, basil, chives and the wonder that is lemon verbena! Simple to grow, and definitely more cost-effective.

Take an extra minute when you're unpacking your market bag or groceries to wrap your herbs (except for basil) in a damp tea towel before popping them to bed in the fridge – this will make them last at least twice as long, especially if you dampen the tea towel every few days. In early summer, when the basil is young and tender, it should be treated like a bunch of fresh flowers – trim the stem end and keep in a vase or glass on your bench.

Don't let the lack of a garden stop you from buying a delightful variety of herbs – when they start to look sad and you haven't found a place to use them, you can chop them all up, place them in a jar and submerge them in olive oil. Keep this in your fridge. Add lemon juice or vinegar and chopped French shallots just before using: spoon over your morning fried eggs, serve with a piece of grilled fish, or drizzle over boiled vegetables like fennel and potatoes.

Soft herbs: *Fleeting but essential*

PARSLEY: Not just for colour, but because it imparts a subtle verdant nuttiness. I prefer flat-leaf parsley, but curly parsley has a place and is widely used around the world. I go through a lot of parsley because it's so wonderful raw or cooked – a bunch doesn't last long in my kitchen!

Salsa verde butter, two ways (page 186), Blue-eye cod with clams, garlic and parsley en cazuela (page 205), Spaghetti with clams and tomato (page 132)

BASIL: The flavour of summer. Basil hates the fridge, so you must use it quickly. As the seasons shift from spring to summer, the basil becomes woodier and is less receptive to being kept in a glass jar on your bench, wilting within a day or two no matter what you do. Basil is one that I simply must grow myself; you don't always need a whole bunch, so this allows me to snip a few leaves here and there, and still keep it alive for a few weeks.

Pan bagnat (page 116), Spaghetti alla Nerano (page 130), Grilled asparagus with pine nut salsa (page 246)

DILL: My preferred herb for fish. Dill is wonderful both fresh and cooked. Best in spring, but available year-round.

Smoked trout rillettes (page 35), Greens, feta and ricotta pie (page 53), Salsa verde butter steamed coral trout (page 187)

CHIVES: Chives have established a firm spot in my kitchen. As with basil, I like to grow them myself because I don't always need a whole bunch. Chives are part of the allium family and have a mild onion flavour; they are excellent when an onion, even a spring onion (scallion), would be overpowering.

Crisp leaves with peas and buttermilk herb dressing (page 79), Leeks gribiche (page 80), Fish crudo with caper and French shallot vinaigrette (page 99)

TARRAGON: I could write a love letter to tarragon (okay, I did – see page 248). My favourite springtime herb. I always look for French tarragon, which is thinner and milder in flavour than the Russian or sawtooth variety. Tarragon has a slight liquorice flavour, which pairs wonderfully with everything chicken.

Tarragon and celery chicken sandwich (page 110), Poached chicken and freekeh salad with tarragon and lemon vinaigrette (page 168), Long-cooked peas with tarragon and verjus (page 248)

Smoky eggplant with garlic, harissa, mint and feta, with yoghurt flatbreads (page 44), Fennel, mandarin and olive salad (page 74), Crispy rice and trout salad with fish sauce dressing (page 94)

MINT: A herb that grows in abundance. If you plant mint in your garden, you will soon find it growing everywhere, so keep it contained. I prefer round mint over spearmint in my cooking, but use what you have access to.

Beer-steamed clams with corn, miso and chilli (page 206), Grilled eggplant with salsa verde, pomegranate and chèvre (page 84), Salad sandwich (page 111)

CHERVIL: Similar in flavour to tarragon, but milder. I've used this a lot in restaurants for its beautiful lively and light appearance, but I tend to use it less at home because it's harder to find, and it yellows and wilts quickly.

Hard herbs: Perennial favourites

Pissaladière (page 72), Beef daube with panisse (page 221), Caramelised fennel gratin (page 245)

THYME: Fresh thyme is widely available, and is wonderful both cooked and raw. It's perfect atop a pissaladière or simmered into soups and stocks. Anything French-leaning loves a bit of thyme. Lemon thyme, as you might expect, has a wonderful light lemon flavour, and it is beautiful tossed onto a roast chicken or over a plate of olive-oil-doused anchovies.

ROSEMARY: Rosemary is hearty and works well with meatier dishes – try it in a marinade for grilled steak, or in a Bolognese or lamb ragù braise. Surprisingly, it also works with more delicate vegetables; perhaps chopped finely and sautéed with olive oil, garlic and blanched green beans or broad beans. That said, I would never use raw rosemary on anything, as its flavour can be extremely overpowering. Instead, I like it fried in oil or simmered in a pot to infuse its wonderful flavour into a dish. Rosemary is also one of those herbs that is equally good in desserts and sweet dishes, imparting a subtle herbal earthiness.

Tagliatelle Bolognese (page 144), Polenta with sweet-spiced lamb ragù (page 152), Blood orange, rosemary and olive oil cake with citrus compote (page 257)

OREGANO: Fresh oregano has been finding its way into my kitchen for years. It lasts a long time and I think it's great friends with tomatoes, potatoes, capsicums (peppers) and basically anything summertime. This is one herb that I find quite interchangeable with its dried companion.

My sardine pasta (page 122), Sheet pan pizza (page 190), Long-cooked green beans (page 240)

MARJORAM: A beguiling herb that is hard to get right. Too much of it can overpower and become soapy or too floral in flavour. *But* when you use *just* the right amount, it's incredible. You can dry out any leftovers to use in place of the fresh herb. Interestingly, this is one herb that softens in flavour with drying.

One of my favourite summer salads is raw, sliced tomatoes sprinkled with salt, a drizzle of olive oil and few small leaves of marjoram.

SAGE: My autumnal flavour companion: fantastic with pumpkin, beautiful with eggs, essential in heartier braises and stews. This herb's particular skill is to become crisp and almost crackly in hot butter – like the curry leaves below – meaning these leaves impart both texture *and* flavour to your dish. Nature is so clever!

CURRY LEAVES: Not belonging to the traditional western lexicon of herbs, fresh curry leaves are something I now can't live without. Native to India, this herb has nothing to do with curry powder, but instead has a flavour of its own. In my opinion it tastes like buttered popcorn, so naturally it goes well with anything savoury relating to butter or ghee, whether it be poultry, seafood or vegetables. Curry leaves were new to me when I arrived in Australia, but I'm so happy I can now find them readily at any good greengrocer. The leaves last a long time in the fridge, but sadly lose a lot of their punch when dried, so try and use them fresh. They tend to come in large bunches so it's great to plan for a few curry leaf recipes at a time, having dishes up your sleeve ready for any leftover leaves. Welcome to the family, curry leaf!

Roasted garlic and sage pastina (page 136), Crostini with roast pumpkin, pancetta and sage (page 104), Chicken paillard with sage, garlic and brown butter (page 179)

Pumpkin, curry leaf and coconut soup (page 64), Chicken thighs with spiced ghee and yoghurt (page 180), Whole roasted flounder with curry leaf brown butter (page 202), Roasted cabbage with charred chilli and curry leaf butter (page 242)

Salsa verde butter, two ways

A salsa verde butter is a wonderful staple in your kitchen – not as complex as a Café de Paris butter, nor as much an affront to the tastebuds – it's delicious with chicken and vegetables like asparagus, green beans and potatoes. Both these dishes feel sophisticated, without being complicated. While I've added a specific herb to each preparation here, the butter is entirely lovely with parsley alone (just ensure you have upped the quantity, so you have the total amount of herbs in parsley). You can always make this with any herbs you have that are about to turn, and can easily double the recipe – wrap the finished butter with baking paper in a sausage shape (for ease of cutting off a pat when needed) and keep it in the freezer.

Makes: Enough to serve 4
Active time: 15 minutes
Inactive time: 40 minutes

Kitchenalia: Food processor

8 small chicken thighs, bone in, skin on
85 g (3 oz) soft unsalted butter
2 tablespoons extra-virgin olive oil
2 garlic cloves, peeled
½ cup (10 g) flat-leaf parsley leaves
¼ cup (7 g) French tarragon leaves
2 tablespoons salted capers, rinsed
Zest of 1 lemon
Fine sea salt
Freshly cracked black pepper

To serve
1 lemon, cut into 4 wedges

Salsa verde butter roasted chicken thighs

Tomato to basil, salt to an egg, butter to anchovy, and tarragon to chicken – there are fireworks when these two get together. Here, the butter is smoothed under the skin, while a hard roast ensures crisp skin and juicy chicken. I like this served with white steamed, buttery rice, but you can't go wrong with roasted potatoes or steamed asparagus … or steamed potatoes and roasted asparagus, for that matter!

Season your chicken thighs with salt and pepper on both sides. Place on a baking-paper-lined baking tray so they're not touching (you may need two trays). Let them come to room temperature while you make the salsa verde butter.

Place the butter, olive oil, garlic, parsley, tarragon, capers and lemon zest in the bowl of a food processor with a pinch of salt and blend until well combined. Stop and scrape the sides of the bowl every so often to ensure it blends evenly.

Preheat your oven to 210°C (410°F).

To place the butter under the skin of the chicken thighs, you need to first loosen it, creating a little pocket. Wiggle your index finger under one edge of the skin until it's free from the meat but still attached around the edges. Divide the butter into eight portions and slide one under the skin of each chicken thigh.

Bake the chicken thighs for 35–40 minutes, or until the skin is crisp and well browned. Allow the chicken to rest for 5 minutes before serving time. Drizzle the melted butter from the tray over the chicken and serve with the lemon wedges.

Salsa verde butter steamed coral trout

The fish is slathered in a salsa verde butter, resplendent with dill – as tarragon is to chicken, dill is to fish – before being wrapped in aluminium foil and baked. This allows the fish to steam, resulting in a gelatinous, unctuous texture, and flesh that is cooked just enough to come off the bone. I love this served with steamed white rice – the rice mixes with the herby butter so well, creating the perfect balance.

Wipe your fish with a dry cloth or paper towel to ensure it's clean and free of any errant scales. Make three deep cuts down to the spine along each side of the fish and season with salt and pepper. Set the fish aside to come to room temperature, at least 20 minutes.

Place the butter, olive oil, garlic, parsley, dill, capers and lemon zest in the bowl of a food processor with a pinch of salt and blend until well combined.

Preheat your oven to 180°C (350°F).

Place the fish onto a large sheet of baking paper. Slather the entire fish with the butter, including inside the belly. Place two large sheets of foil on your bench so they overlap in the middle. Place the baking paper and fish on top of the foil and wrap it up tightly. Use a third piece of foil to wrap it up once more, with the seam-side up.

Bake the fish for 45 minutes then take a peek inside the foil parcel. Use a small paring knife to help you judge if the fish is done: insert the tip into the thickest part of the fish, all the way to the bone; hold it there for a few seconds, then place the tip of the knife on the inside of your wrist. If it feels warm, the fish is done; otherwise rewrap it and cook for a further 5–10 minutes. Allow the fish to rest for 10 minutes before serving, being mindful of the bones. Spoon the butter over the fish and serve with lemon wedges.

Makes: Enough to serve 4
Active time: 20 minutes
Inactive time: 1 hour 10 minutes

Kitchenalia: Food processor

1 x 2 kg (4 lb 8 oz) whole coral trout, cleaned
85 g (3 oz) soft unsalted butter
2 tablespoons extra-virgin olive oil
2 garlic cloves, peeled
½ cup (10 g) flat-leaf parsley leaves
¼ cup (7 g) dill leaves
2 tablespoons salted capers, rinsed
Zest of 1 lemon
Fine sea salt
Freshly cracked black pepper

To serve
1 lemon, cut into 4 wedges

Note: As with chicken and pork, it's great to get into the habit of liberating your fish from its plastic bag before storing it in the fridge. Place the fish on a plate, laying it on paper towel to absorb any excess moisture, and always skin-side up. Removing the fish from plastic will help to draw out some of its moisture, which is especially important in dishes where you're after a crisp skin.

Salsa verde butter roasted chicken thighs

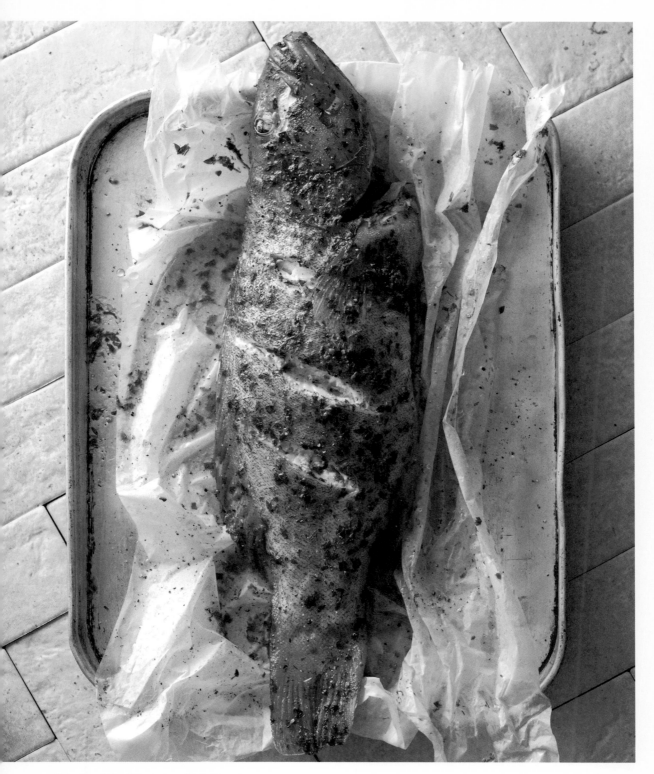

Salsa verde butter steamed coral trout

Sheet pan pizza

Makes: Enough to serve 4–6
Active time: 1 hour 15 minutes
Inactive time: 5 hours

Kitchenalia: Two baking pans
about 23 x 33 cm (9 x 13
inches), stand mixer fitted
with the dough hook

Before you begin: My topping
recipes are for one pizza of each
kind, but you can make two pizzas
of the same variety, simply double
the quantities of your toppings.

Dough
350 ml (12 fl oz) warm water
½ teaspoon instant dry yeast
540 g (1 lb 3 oz) baker's flour,
plus extra for dusting (plain/
all-purpose flour works fine,
but baker's is preferred for
chewier dough)
1 teaspoon honey
2 teaspoons fine sea salt
Extra-virgin olive oil, for coating
and greasing

Salami and tomato pizza
3 tablespoons extra-virgin olive
oil, plus extra for drizzling
2 garlic cloves, minced
1 x 400 g (14 oz) tin whole
peeled San Marzano
tomatoes
2 tablespoons tomato paste
(concentrated purée)
1 cup (125 g) low-moisture
mozzarella (also known as
fior di latte), shredded
¼ cup (7 g) oregano leaves,
plus extra to garnish
1 cup (100 g) tasty cheese,
shredded
50 g (1¾ oz) sliced salami
Dried chilli flakes, for finishing
(optional)
Parmigiano Reggiano,
for grating
Fine sea salt

This pizza takes its cues from the much-loved Detroit-style pizza, which is
also rectangular, with a light, fluffy dough and excellent crisp, cheesy sides.
Rumoured to have been invented by the serendipitous use of a cast-iron
tray that once held car parts, the pan is about more than aesthetics; the
high edges mean the cheese can nestle all the way up to the edge of the pan,
caramelising and forming that spider's web of flavour.

Traditionally, it is made with Brick Cheese, a smear-ripened (washed-rind),
cow's milk cheese from Wisconsin that is produced in a similar way to
cheddar – it is the subsequent smear-ripening and maturing that develops
its flavour profile from gentle mozzarella notes to more pungent Taleggio or
Limburger accents. This recipe uses a combination of mozzarella and tasty
cheese, but you could happily experiment by replacing the mozzarella with
more pungent washed-rind cheeses; alternatively, a crumbly sharp cheddar
works well. As for the dough, we're leaning on the poolish method (see note
on opposite page) and the whole process from start to finish takes around
6 hours, so plan accordingly.

To make the dough:

Combine 200 ml (7 fl oz) of the warm water with the yeast in the bowl of
your stand mixer and stir to dissolve. Add in 200 g (7 oz) of the flour and
mix to combine. Cover with a damp tea towel and leave in a warm spot in
your kitchen. After 1½ hours, it should be bubbly on the surface.

Next, add in the remaining 150 ml (5 fl oz) warm water and 340 g (12 oz)
of flour, along with the honey and salt. Mix on a low speed for about
8 minutes.

Grab a bowl big enough to allow the dough to double in size and grease
its sides with olive oil. When the dough is finished mixing, dump it into this
bowl. Drizzle a little olive oil on the surface of the dough to prevent it from
drying out, and cover again with a damp tea towel. Set the bowl in a warm
spot in your kitchen. If your kitchen is cold, as mine often is, turn your oven
into a makeshift proving oven by heating it at 50°C (120°F) for 3–4 minutes,
then turning it off and placing the covered dough inside. The dough will
take around 2 hours to rise but keep your eye on it – this time can vary.

Prepare your two baking pans by greasing them with the olive oil and
laying a sheet of baking paper on the base of each (the oil will help the
baking paper to stick and not slide all over the place, which would make it
hard to stretch the dough). It's okay if the paper comes up the sides; you
just don't want a lot of excess paper, which can burn while the pizzas bake.

When the dough has doubled in size, knock it back by pushing it down to
deflate it a little, and dump it onto a floured surface. Divide the dough in
half. Shape each half into a ball (use extra flour if needed) and leave on
your bench, covered with a damp tea towel, for about 15 minutes. After
this time, use a rolling pin to roll your dough into rough rectangles and lift
them into your pans (the dough won't reach the edges of the pans yet).
Cover with a damp tea towel and leave for another 15 minutes.

Use your hands to stretch the dough into the corners of the pan, pulling it all the way to the edges. Make sure the centre and the edges are about the same thickness – pull from the centre if you need to. Rub the olive oil over the entire surface of the dough, then cover it again with a damp tea towel, allowing it to proof at room temperature for about 1½–2 hours; when it's ready, it will look puffed and light.

You are going to bake these directly on the floor of the oven to get a crisp base, so adjust the shelves before turning on your oven. Towards the end of the proofing time, heat your oven to 250°C (480°F), or as high as it will go. Note: If your oven isn't wide enough to bake the pizzas side by side on its floor, start one on the floor and one on a shelf, swapping them halfway through baking. Bake your pizza bases, without toppings, for 20 minutes, then remove them from the oven and proceed with the toppings.

For the tomato and salami pizza:

Start by making the pizza sauce, which is a simple marinara. Heat the olive oil in a small saucepan over a medium heat and sauté the garlic for a minute. Open the tin of tomatoes and crush them with your hands before tipping into the pan along with a pinch of salt. Simmer for about 10 minutes, then set aside to cool. (If you're only making one tomato and salami pizza, this will be slightly too much sauce, but you can freeze the excess for your next pizza night, or even toss it with pasta.)

When your dough is par-baked, spread the tomato paste over the entire surface of the dough and sprinkle with the mozzarella. Spoon your tomato sauce over the mozzarella, again spreading it all the way to the edges. Follow with the oregano and tasty cheese, sprinkling the cheese heavily on the edges. Season with a pinch of salt and add the slices of salami. Finish with a drizzle of olive oil over the whole pizza. Bake on the floor of the oven for 25–30 minutes, until crisp and deeply browned.

To serve, sprinkle the pizza with dried chilli flakes (optional), the extra oregano leaves and grated parmesan, then cut into squares.

For the mushroom, rosemary and caramelised onion pizza:

Start by making your caramelised onions. Add the olive oil and onions to a wide sauté pan with a pinch of salt and set over a medium heat. Sweat them down and, when they start browning, add the water. Continue cooking for about 15 minutes, adding a bit of water every time the pan gets too dry. Stir in the vinegar, and set aside to cool.

When your dough is par-baked, spread the sour cream over the dough, all the way to the edges. Top with the caramelised onions, then the mozzarella, followed by the mushrooms, garlic, rosemary and, finally, the tasty cheese. Sprinkle everything with salt and drizzle the whole pizza with olive oil. Bake on the floor of the oven for 25–30 minutes, until crisp and deeply browned.

To serve, grate parmesan over the pizza and cut into squares.

Mushroom, rosemary and caramelised onion pizza

2 tablespoons extra-virgin olive oil, plus extra for drizzling
1 brown onion, thinly sliced
2 tablespoons water, plus extra as needed
2 teaspoons red or white wine vinegar
2 heaped tablespoons sour cream (or crème fraîche)
1 cup (125 g) low-moisture mozzarella (also known as *fior di latte*), shredded
1 cup (90 g) thinly sliced shiitake mushrooms (or any mushroom)
3 garlic cloves, minced
2 tablespoons rosemary leaves
1 cup (100 g) tasty cheese, shredded
Parmigiano Reggiano, for grating
Fine sea salt

Note: I've avoided the need for an overnight proof by using the poolish method. This pre-fermentation (think sourdough starter, without all the outlandish demands of a sourdough starter) will give your dough a wonderful deep flavour. The rise doesn't have time to draw on wild yeasts like sourdough (you add the yeast), but it does require making a small batch of heavily hydrated dough first, allowing it a solo proof before adding the rest of the flour and water. The Italians use a similar pre-ferment known as *biga*, literally translating to "chariot", as in the vehicle to pull the flavour forward. This little cheat creates a flavoursome dough that can be mixed and eaten on the same day.

Mushroom, rosemary and caramelised onion pizza

Salami and tomato pizza

Prawns with ginger and chilli jam

Makes: Enough to serve 4
Active time: 30 minutes
Inactive time: 40 minutes

Kitchenalia: Food processor

Before you begin: A food processor makes quick work of chopping the chilli, French shallot, ginger and garlic. Be sure to add each ingredient separately, so they chop evenly.

12 extra-large prawns, peeled and deveined, heads and tail left on

Ginger and chilli jam
½ cup (75 g) diced red chilli (deseeded), about 3 long red chillies
Scant ¼ cup (30 g) minced French shallot, about 1 large shallot
½ teaspoon Korean red chilli flakes (optional)
1 tablespoon minced garlic (about 3–5 cloves)
1½ tablespoons (20 g) minced ginger
Generous ⅓ cup (90 ml) neutral oil
1½ tablespoons Shaoxing wine
½ tablespoon light soy sauce
1 tablespoon white (granulated) sugar
½ tablespoon fish sauce

To serve
1 lime, cut into 4 wedges

While this is a recipe for prawns, I think the sweet, umami-rich jam is really the star. Beyond the grilled prawns, this jam is excellent with lobster, fish and chicken, or greens such as wilted bok choy.

For the ginger and chilli jam, combine the chilli, shallot, chilli flakes (if using), garlic and ginger in a small pot and add the oil. Sizzle this over a low heat for 15–20 minutes, until most of the water in the aromatics has evaporated and they are just beginning to brown. Stir often, ensuring you scrape the bottom of the pan. Some bits will stick and caramelise, which is fine; just make sure they don't burn. Carefully (it will spit!) add in the Shaoxing wine, soy sauce, sugar and fish sauce and simmer for 5 minutes, until the mixture appears jammy and has thickened. Set aside.

Place a rack in the top-third of your oven and preheat to 220°C (425°F). If your oven has a grill (broiler) option, use that here to cook the prawns on a high heat.

Line a baking tray with baking paper and lay the prawns on the tray. Spoon a couple of teaspoons of the ginger and chilli jam over each prawn and bake in the oven for 5 minutes, flipping them over halfway through cooking. Note: if using your grill, you may need to adjust the cooking time slightly – you're looking for the prawns to turn a nice pink colour.

Remove the prawns from the oven and serve with wedges of lime and perhaps a small ramekin of the ginger and chilli jam on the side.

Note: I've written this recipe to be cooked using your oven but these prawns would be excellent cooked on an outdoor charcoal grill. Just brush the prawns with a small amount of neutral oil and grill for 2 minutes per side. Spoon the ginger and chilli jam over the cooked prawns.

Serving suggestions: The ginger and chilli jam recipe can be doubled and excess kept in a glass jar in your fridge for several weeks, or frozen indefinitely. The jam is a great addition to the Noodles with pork mince and black vinegar, chilli and soy dressing (see page 67) and the Chicken noodle soup with star anise, fish sauce and herbs (see page 170).

Rainbow trout with red wine and borlotti beans

Makes: Enough to serve 2
Active time: 25 minutes

Before you begin: You'll need cooked borlotti beans for this dish (see opposite page) but feel free to swap them for a 400 g (14 oz) tin of cooked borlotti beans. The tinned beans will just need to be rinsed with water, then combined with ¼ cup (60 ml) water or chicken stock.

2 x 150–180 g (5½–6¼ oz) rainbow trout fillets, boneless, skin on (see notes)
1 tablespoon extra-virgin olive oil, plus extra for brushing
½ teaspoon finely chopped rosemary
3 garlic cloves, minced
¼ cup (40 g) quartered cherry tomatoes
400 g (14 oz) cooked borlotti beans, with their liquid (see opposite page), or 1 x 400 g (14 oz) tin (see above)
½ cup (125 ml) red wine
Fine sea salt
Freshly cracked black pepper

To finish
Good-quality extra-virgin olive oil
Lightly-fried rosemary (see notes) or flat-leaf parsley

You may not have considered cooking fish with red wine, but trout lends itself exceptionally well to this accompaniment.

Thoroughly dry the skin of the trout using paper towel and season it with salt and pepper. Set the fish aside and let it come to room temperature.

In a small saucepan set over a medium heat, add 1 tablespoon of the olive oil. Add in the rosemary, garlic and cherry tomatoes with a pinch of salt. After about 1 minute, add in the borlotti beans, with their liquid and the red wine, and simmer for about 6–7 minutes. This can be left to simmer while you cook the fish.

Preheat a cast-iron grill or flat cast-iron pan over a medium–high heat.

Brush the skin of the trout liberally with olive oil and, when the pan is really hot, add the fish, skin-side down. Gently press down on the fillets for the first minute, using your spatula, to help them stay in contact with the pan and not bow upwards in the middle. Cook the fillets for 4–5 minutes on the one side until they look almost completely cooked but are still slightly undercooked on top (see notes). Carefully lift the fillets out of the pan and place them onto warm plates.

Check the beans for seasoning and adjust with salt as needed. Spoon the beans over the fish, drizzle with olive oil and finish with fried rosemary or flat-leaf parsley. Serve hot.

Notes: All recipes calling for rainbow trout in this book will work with wild salmon if you're lucky to have access to that where you live. I do not like ocean-farmed Atlantic salmon for the devastating effects it has on the environment, so I cannot endorse using it.

I slightly undercook the fish so it doesn't fall apart when you try to lift it out of the pan, but also because it will continue to cook on the plate, especially when you spoon the hot borlotti beans over it.

To lightly fry rosemary, heat ¼ cup (60 ml) of neutral oil in a small pot over a medium–high heat until hot. Add a handful of rosemary leaves and fry for a few seconds, until just crisp. Use a skimmer or spoon to remove the fried rosemary from the oil and drain on paper towel.

Cooked dried borlotti beans

If you're using dried beans, soak them overnight (or for at least 8 hours) covered by about 5 cm (2 inches) of cold water in your fridge. If using fresh beans, you can skip this step.

Drain the beans and add them to a pot. Cover with 6–7 cm (2½–2¾ inches) of cold water and add in the bicarbonate of soda, along with the onion, celery, carrot, bay leaf, salt and olive oil. If you're using fresh beans, leave out the bicarbonate of soda.

Bring the pot to a low simmer and cook slowly, with the lid left slightly ajar, for 1½–2 hours. Fresh beans will take closer to 40 minutes, just keep checking them. If at any point the water level is no longer covering the beans and they haven't finished cooking, add ½ cup (125 ml) water and continue cooking until the beans are tender and creamy, but not falling apart.

Remove and discard the onion, celery, carrot and bay leaf, but keep the liquid the beans have been cooking in.

The beans are now ready to use. Allow any leftover beans to cool in their liquid (draining cooked beans while they're still hot causes them to explode) and store them in your fridge for a few days, or in your freezer indefinitely. Be sure to always store cooked beans in their liquid, only draining them just before using.

Makes: 800 g (1 lb 12 oz) cooked borlotti beans
Active time: 5 minutes
Inactive time: 10 hours

Before you begin: If you're using dried beans, they'll need to be soaked for at least 8 hours. This recipe makes more than is required for the Rainbow trout dish, but cooked beans are great to have in your fridge or freezer to add to soups (with their broth) or salads.

1 cup (200 g) dried borlotti beans (or fresh, if you're lucky!)
Pinch of bicarbonate of soda (baking soda)
Half a small brown onion
1 stalk celery, cut into 3 pieces
1 carrot, cut into 2 pieces
1 bay leaf
1 teaspoon fine sea salt
3 tablespoons extra-virgin olive oil

Note: I add a pinch of bicarbonate of soda (baking soda) to dried beans when they cook, to help soften their skins. It also makes them cook faster. A pinch is a tiny amount, never more than $\frac{1}{4}$ teaspoon – add too much and the beans can turn to mush.

Serving suggestion: Use leftover beans to make the Cavolo nero and farinata soup (see page 61).

Rainbow trout with red wine and borlotti beans

Mackerel polpette

Little "meatballs" of mackerel, spiked with the Sicilian flavours of mint, currants and toasted pine nuts. A perfect aperitivo snack for four people to share, or a delicious main for two.

Before you begin: Try to buy whole mackerel and ask your fishmonger to fillet and skin it for you – this way you can check its eyes to ensure it's fresh – clear eyes equals fresh fish. You can substitute the mackerel for fresh sardine fillets here and can get a head start by rolling your polpette up to a day ahead.

Makes: Enough to serve 2–4
Active time: 40 minutes

Kitchenalia: Food processor
  (optional)

2 tablespoons extra-virgin
  olive oil, plus an extra
  ½ cup (125 ml)
2 garlic cloves, minced
Half a brown onion, diced
170–200 g (6–7 oz) blue
  mackerel fillets, pinboned
  and skin removed
½ cup (30 g) breadcrumbs,
  soaked in 3 tablespoons water
2 tablespoons chopped
  flat-leaf parsley
1 tablespoon chopped mint
1 egg
1 tablespoon freshly grated
  Parmigiano Reggiano
½ cup (75 g) plain
  (all-purpose) flour
Fine sea salt
Freshly cracked black pepper

Tomato sauce
3 garlic cloves, minced
2 tablespoons extra-virgin
  olive oil
⅔ cup (150 g) tomato passata
  (puréed tomatoes)
¼ cup (60 ml) dry white wine
  (preferably Italian), or water
Pinch of chilli flakes
Scant ¼ cup (30 g) currants,
  soaked in hot water
Fine sea salt

To finish
¼ cup (40 g) pine nuts, toasted
Zest and juice of half a lemon
Extra-virgin olive oil

Place a saucepan over a medium–low heat. Add the 2 tablespoons of olive oil, the garlic and the diced onion with a pinch of salt. Sauté until soft and beginning to brown, about 10–15 minutes, then cool to room temperature.

Ensure the mackerel fillets are free from any bones and roughly chop them. Add the mackerel to a food processor with a good pinch of salt and a crack of pepper. Add in the cooked onion and garlic, along with the soaked breadcrumbs, parsley, mint, egg and parmesan. Process until everything is well combined and a paste has formed. Alternatively, mince the ingredients finely with a sharp knife and then mix them in a bowl.

Place the flour in a shallow dish. Shape the fish mixture into about a dozen little meatballs, tossing them immediately into the flour. Roll the balls through the flour to coat well, then place on a clean plate and chill in your fridge until you're ready to cook. This can be done a day ahead.

To make your tomato sauce, sauté the garlic in the olive oil in a saucepan over medium heat. After about 30 seconds, add in the tomato passata, white wine and chilli flakes with a pinch of salt. Drain the currants and add them to the pan. Simmer for about 5 minutes and taste for seasoning, adjusting with salt. Turn the sauce down to a low heat and let it simmer while you brown your meatballs.

Heat a wide frying pan over a medium heat and add the ½ cup (125 ml) of olive oil. When the oil is hot, add in the mackerel meatballs (do this in batches if need be, so as not to crowd the pan). Once they have browned all over, use tongs to lift them out and drop them into the saucepan with the tomato sauce. Give it all a gentle stir and simmer for 2–3 minutes.

To serve, place the mackerel polpette on a platter. Spoon the tomato sauce over them and finish with the toasted pine nuts, lemon zest and juice and a generous drizzle of good-quality olive oil.

Serving suggestion: To make a complete meal, serve the meatballs over Soft polenta (see page 153) or on top of Sautéed garlicky greens (see page 232).

Polpette ("meatballs") is another dish in our collection of *cucina povera*, and is simply minced meat or fish (of many and varied animals, with many and varied herbs and spices) formed into a ball. It is one of the oldest and most delicious solutions to the cuts and textures that might otherwise not appeal. From the Persian *kofta* to Greek *keftedes*, the Italian *polpette* to Slavic *bitki*, the humble meatball offers the chance to travel, your destination dependant on its companions within and the sauce without.

Whole roasted flounder with curry leaf brown butter

Makes: Enough to serve 2
Active time: 10 minutes
Inactive time: 30 minutes

Before you begin: Place your fish on a baking tray, white-belly-side up, and allow it to come to room temperature before cooking.

1 x 800 g (1 lb 12 oz) whole flounder, or 2 x 400 g (14 oz) whole flounder, cleaned
1 tablespoon extra-virgin olive oil
60 g (2¼ oz) unsalted butter
4 stems curry leaf (each with about 12–14 leaves), leaves picked
1½ tablespoons rice wine vinegar
Flaked sea salt

Serving suggestion: Serve this with the Sautéed garlicky greens (see page 232).

So few ingredients, but a completely stunning result. Curry leaves are worth seeking out if you have a good greengrocer nearby. Their nutty, popcorn-like flavour works incredibly well in tandem with brown butter and fish.

Brush the flounder with the olive oil and sprinkle it with salt.

Place a rack in the top-third of your oven and set your grill (broiler) to a high heat. Alternatively, if your oven doesn't have a grill option, preheat your oven to as high as possible, about 230–250°C (450–480°F).

Place the fish under the grill (or in your oven) for 5 minutes then flip it and cook for a further 4 minutes on the dark-skin side. Bring the fish out of the oven and allow it to rest for 5 minutes on the tray. If using two small fish, cook them for 3 minutes each side.

While the fish cooks, heat a small saucepan over a high heat. Add the butter and allow it to brown (see note). Add half the curry leaves to the brown butter and let them sputter and sizzle. When they stop sizzling (seconds later!), scoop them out and set aside. Take the butter off the heat.

When the fish is resting, heat the butter again and add the remaining curry leaves. Let them sputter and sizzle again, but leave them in for slightly longer this time, until the leaves start to turn brown. Scoop out and discard these leaves too. Turn the heat off, add in the vinegar (which will bubble up!) and a pinch of salt and stir to combine.

To fillet your flounder, first place the fish on your serving platter. If it's a larger fish, split the top fillet down the centre using a fish spatula or spoon and push the fillets off the bone. For smaller fish (pictured), use a fish spatula or spoon to push the side off the bone, keeping it whole, coming in from the top and bottom of the fish. Lift the spine bone from the fish, discarding it, along with the head, tail and any other bones you encounter along the way. Place the top fillets or side back onto the fish.

To serve, spoon the curry leaf brown butter over the fish and finish with the reserved fried curry leaves and a sprinkle of salt. Serve hot.

Note: A voyage to brown butter: set over heat, butter will first melt, freeing the liquid that is trapped within the fat. As that liquid simmers, it will bubble up and become steam. The bubbles will be even in size, and the bubbling will sound gentle. When that liquid has almost evaporated, the sound will change and there will be more sizzling as the bubbles become uneven in size and start to foam. When all the liquid is gone, that foam – and the milk solids beneath – will start to caramelise. The butter will go silent; there is no more liquid to evaporate, so it becomes still. *Now* is when you really need to pay attention; it can go from nutty and golden to burnt very quickly. When the liquid smells deliciously nutty and turns an amber shade of gold, it's perfect. Remove the brown butter from the heat immediately, or add liquid, such as lemon juice, vinegar or water, to stop it from cooking further.

Blue-eye cod with clams, garlic and parsley en cazuela

This ultra-simple fish dish is all about the cooking vessel and the gentle, slow cook. I cook this on my stove in a cazuela. This ancient cooking pot conducts heat evenly and delicately, which is perfect to cook the meaty cod slowly and gently, while still steaming open the clams. The sauce, thickened with a bit of flour, is made in the pot as the fish cooks. You could also use the base of a tagine or another terracotta dish, or even an enamel-lined Dutch oven if you're very careful with the heat – but if you have a cazuela, or always wondered what you might cook in one, this is the dish to try.

Cut your fish into four evenly sized pieces. Season it with salt and dust with the 2 tablespoons of flour. Set aside.

Wash your clams in cold water and set them aside.

Heat your cazuela over a low–medium heat and add the olive oil. When it is hot, turn down the heat and add in the fish, skin-side down. Cook for about 5 minutes on this very low heat, gently shaking the pot every few minutes to ensure the fish isn't sticking.

Add the garlic and the remaining 1 teaspoon of flour into the oil. Use a spoon to stir this around the fish without breaking the fish up. Let it sizzle for about 1 minute.

Add the clams and white wine and bring to a simmer, then flip the fish over and cook for about 10 minutes. Again, shake the pot every couple of minutes to ensure the fish isn't sticking. The fish is fully cooked when it feels firm to the touch – give it a few minutes longer if you think it needs it.

To serve, flip the fish back over so it's skin-side down and shake the pan again (discard any clams that haven't opened). Add in the parsley, shake to mix it through and taste for seasoning. Serve straight from the cazuela.

Notes: Blue-eye cod is easily found in Australia, but you can replace this with another type of cod or any other meaty white, flaky fish depending on what's available where you are. Vongole are the small clams with a shell that's brownish on the outside and yellow on the inside.

Serving suggestions: Serve this with the Sautéed garlicky greens (see page 232) and a slice of crusty bread to mop up the sauce. The Long-cooked green beans (see page 240) or the Ghee roasted potatoes (see page 239) result in an equally delightful meal.

Makes: Enough to serve 3–4
Active time: 25 minutes

400 g (14 oz) blue-eye cod fillet (or the best available cod), boneless, skin on
2 tablespoons plain (all-purpose) flour, plus an extra 1 teaspoon
500 g (1 lb 2 oz) vongole clams (see notes)
¼ cup (60 ml) extra-virgin olive oil
5 garlic cloves, thinly sliced on a mandoline (or with a very sharp knife)
½ cup (125 ml) white wine
¼ cup (10 g) finely chopped flat-leaf parsley
Fine sea salt

As "tagine" is to a tagine, "cazuela" is to a cazuela – as with so many of these vessels, their name is so instrumental to the dish that the two have become synonymous. A term derived from the Spanish for "cooking pot", the shallow earthenware cazuela is often glazed, and thus less porous than its ancient cousins (if yours isn't glazed on the outside, beware of any residual moisture before cooking, which may expand and crack the pot). While the clay takes longer to heat than a metal pot, once it does, it retains heat for long and steady cooking. Like all the best kinds of cookware, terracotta pots seem to retain a little of the soul of the dishes that came before. It's part of their magic.

Beer-steamed clams with corn, miso and chilli

Makes: Enough to serve 2–3
Active time: 35 minutes

1 kg (2 lb 4 oz) small clams or pipis (I like a lot!)
2 tablespoons extra-virgin olive oil
25 g (1 oz) unsalted butter, plus an extra 40 g (1½ oz)
Half a brown onion, diced
1 stalk celery, diced small
Half a large leek, thinly sliced and washed
2 ears corn, kernels cut off the cob, and milk scraped from the cob (see note)
2 teaspoons white miso
½ cup (125 ml) beer (something light and erring towards sweet and dry, not bitter)
Juice of 1 lime
Fine sea salt

To finish
Mixed soft herbs (flat-leaf parsley, coriander/cilantro, basil, French tarragon, chervil and/or chives cut into batons) to garnish
1 long green or red chilli, thinly sliced
Extra-virgin olive oil, for drizzling
Freshly cracked black pepper

To serve
Crusty bread

This summery dish will become one of your favourites. Serve it with good crusty bread to dip into the buttery sauce.

Wash your clams with cold water and keep them cold until you're ready to cook.

Heat a large sauté pan over a medium heat and add the olive oil and the 25 g (1 oz) of butter. When the butter has melted, add the onion, celery and leek with a pinch of salt. Cook until soft but with no colour, about 10 minutes.

Add the corn and the milk from the cob (see note) and continue to cook on low for another 10 minutes with a pinch more salt. Add the miso towards the end and stir to combine.

Turn the heat up to high, add the clams, pour the beer over the top and immediately cover with a lid to steam the clams open.

Once the clams have opened (discard any that haven't), stir in the extra butter and squeeze the lime juice over the clams.

Place the clams in a serving bowl and top with the mixed herbs, sliced chilli, a crack of pepper and a drizzle of olive oil. Serve with slices of toasted, crusty bread on the side.

Note: Once you've cut the kernels off the cob, use the back of your knife to scrape the milky white liquid from the cob. This "milk" is super sweet and worth the added step.

Bistec empanizado con mojo
Crumbed Cuban steak with garlic mojo

Makes: Enough to serve 2
Active time: 30 minutes

2 x 135 g (4¾ oz) thin beef
 steaks (see below)
½ cup (75 g) plain
 (all-purpose) flour
2 eggs, beaten
1 cup (60 g) breadcrumbs
 (not panko or sourdough,
 just regular ol' breadcrumbs –
 see note)
Neutral oil, for frying
Fine sea salt

Mojo
2 garlic cloves, peeled
½ teaspoon ground cumin
¼ teaspoon freshly cracked
 black pepper
½ teaspoon dried oregano
½ tablespoon fresh oregano,
 chopped
Juice of half an orange
Juice of 1 lime
1 tablespoon extra-virgin
 olive oil
Fine sea salt

To finish
Black beans (see serving
 suggestion)
Quarter of a white onion,
 thinly sliced
Steamed white rice
1 lime, cut into wedges

Ask your butcher for steaks for
schnitzel, or you can bash a couple
of fillet steaks between two sheets
of baking paper to get a final
thickness of around 5 mm (¼ inch).
These steaks are so thin you actually
want to slow down the cooking of
the meat to give the breadcrumbs
time to brown, which is why you
cook them straight from the fridge.
The meat will be cooked through –
you don't want it pink, but you
also don't want shoe leather!

Mojo runs in my veins. This all-purpose garlicky marinade/sauce/dressing
is ubiquitous in every Cuban household. Served with an empanizado
(somewhat like a schnitzel), this meal was on heavy rotation when I was
growing up. While I don't remember my mom ever serving mojo with
bistec, I'm doing it here because I love it so much. Mojo is heavy on the
garlic, but that's the point. You can easily make this for four people, just
double the recipe and keep the first two fried steaks warm in the oven while
you cook the others. I wouldn't try this for more unless you want to feel like
a short-order cook!

Season the steaks with salt on both sides and set aside.

Set up a crumbing station with three shallow dishes: the flour in the first,
followed by the eggs in the second and the breadcrumbs the third.

One at a time, drag each steak through the flour, then the egg (ensuring
all dry spots are covered) and lastly, coat with the breadcrumbs. When the
steaks are fully coated, without any bald spots, place them on a plate in
the fridge until you're ready to cook.

To make the mojo, crush the garlic cloves in a mortar and pestle with
a pinch of salt until you have a smooth paste. Add in the remaining mojo
ingredients and stir to combine. Set aside.

When you're ready to fry your steaks, preheat your oven to 60°C (140°F).
Heat a wide sauté pan over a high heat and add a 1 cm (½ inch) depth of
neutral oil. To test when your oil is hot enough, dip the handle of a wooden
spoon into the oil – if small bubbles appear, you're ready to fry. Lay your
steak in (straight from the fridge) one at a time and cook until golden on
each side – this should only take about 2 minutes per side. Place the fried
steak on a rack sitting on a baking tray (to keep them crisp) in the warm
oven while you fry the remaining steak.

Drizzle the mojo over the hot crumbed steaks, and eat with Cuban-style
black beans (see below), white onion slices and white rice for a truly
authentic Cuban meal. Serve with lime wedges.

Note: When it comes to breadcrumbs, panko and sourdough serve a very specific
textural purpose when they are fried and spooned atop pasta or salads, for
example. However, in this case, the finely grated breadcrumbs you find in bags at
supermarkets is what my mom would have used. The fine crumbs' smaller surface
area provides a more even and consistent coating.

Serving suggestion: To make Cuban-style black beans, soak 2 cups (400 g)
of dried black beans in cold water overnight. Drain the beans and simmer with
a quarter of a green capsicum (pepper) over a low heat, covered by at least 4 cm
(1½ inches) water, until tender, about 1½ hours. Scoop a ladleful of beans with their
liquid into a blender. Add a peeled and quartered brown onion and a quartered,
deseeded red capsicum. Purée into a fine pulp and stir back through the simmering
beans. Discard the green capsicum. Simmer the beans until thickened, about
30 minutes. Season with salt, a tablespoon or two of apple cider vinegar,
a ¼ cup (60 ml) of olive oil and a few pinches of white (granulated) sugar.

Pancetta-wrapped pork neck roast

Makes: Enough to serve 6
Active time: 35 minutes
Inactive time: 2 hours

Kitchenalia: Butcher's string,
    internal meat thermometer

Before you begin: The pork
requires seasoning 1 hour
before cooking.

1 x 1.25 kg (2 lb 12 oz) pork
    neck roast
1 tablespoon chopped rosemary
2 tablespoons chopped sage
3 garlic cloves, minced
2 teaspoons fennel seeds
Zest of 1 lemon
1 tablespoon extra-virgin olive
    oil, plus an extra 3 tablespoons
12–15 thin slices round pancetta
    (double this if you're using
    flat pancetta – see notes)
¼ cup (60 ml) white wine
Juice of half a lemon
Fine sea salt
Freshly cracked black pepper

Notes: Rolled pancetta tends to
have more moisture and a fresher
flavour, while flat pancetta is drier,
with a more pronounced fermented
flavour – which I love, but it's not
for everything. The flat version also
usually comes with skin on top,
which you'll need to cut off before
dicing. To make use of this normally
discarded ingredient, sauté it with
olive oil to add a little extra flavour
to your cooking onions, or sweat
with mirepoix for soups and braises.

With roasts like this, an internal
meat thermometer is really the only
way to know when it's perfectly
cooked. However, you can use
the old-school trick of inserting a
stainless-steel skewer into the centre
of the meat, leaving it there for a few
seconds then pressing it onto your
wrist – if it feels warm to the touch,
it's ready.

I remember the first time a fellow chef said we were going to cook pork neck as a roast, rather than braised or minced for sausage. I thought to myself, *won't it be as tough as nails?* How naive I was! The result was juicy, succulent, filled with sweet porky flavour and tender. I love moments like this in the kitchen; they stick with you forever. Look for a pork neck that is uniform in shape and size – the best piece for roasting this way.

Remove your pork from the fridge 1 hour before cooking and season it with salt and pepper. Leave it at room temperature.

Preheat your oven to 165°C (320°F).

In a small bowl, combine the rosemary, sage, garlic, fennel seeds, lemon zest and the 1 tablespoon of olive oil. Rub this mixture over the pork, coating it well.

To wrap and tie the pork roast, cut five pieces of butcher's string around 30 cm (12 inches) in length and one piece around 50 cm (20 inches). Working on a small, flat tray with the short end facing you, lay the longer piece of string vertically from bottom to top. Then, lay the five shorter pieces horizontally across the longer piece, spacing them about 4 cm (1½ inches) apart. Check and ensure the string is spaced correctly to wrap around the pork. Next, lay six slices of pancetta horizontally over the string, spreading them out to cover as much surface area as possible, while still staying along the vertical piece of string. Lay your pork roast on top on the pancetta, with the short end facing you. Cover the top of the roast with the remaining pancetta slices. Lift and tie the two ends of the long piece of string together first, being sure to pull it tightly. Then, tie the remaining five pieces of string tightly around that. Admire your work.

Heat an oven-safe pan over a medium–high heat. Ensure the pan is wide enough to hold the pork. When the pan is hot, add the extra 3 tablespoons of olive oil and brown the pork on all sides. Transfer the pan to the oven and cook until the meat reaches an internal temperature of between 65–70°C (150–160°F); use your thermometer (see notes). This will take about 35–40 minutes.

Remove the roast from the oven, cover loosely with foil and let it rest on a plate or board for at least 15 minutes before slicing.

While the pork is resting, put your roasting pan over a low heat and deglaze with the white wine. Use a spatula or wooden spoon to loosen all the delicious umami bits that are stuck to the bottom while cooking the alcohol out of the wine. Season the pan juices with the lemon juice and a crack of pepper.

Slice the pork and serve it drizzled with the pan juices.

Serving suggestions: For a complete meal, serve this with the Potato purée (see page 232) or the Maple and miso sweet potato purée (see page 233), and greens that are in season, perhaps the Sweet-and-sour cabbage (see page 249), the Sautéed garlicky greens (see page 232), the Long-cooked green beans (see page 240) or the Zucchini alla scapece (see page 234).

Lemongrass grilled pork belly with cucumber and peanut salad

Makes: Enough to serve 4–6
Active time: 35 minutes
Inactive time: 2–8 hours

Kitchenalia: Blender, outdoor grill or indoor grill pan

Pork belly

800 g (1 lb 12 oz) pork belly, cut into 1.5 cm (⅝ inch) thick slices
1 tablespoon fish sauce
2 tablespoons dark soy sauce
2 tablespoons brown sugar
4 garlic cloves, peeled
1 small French shallot, peeled and halved
2 stalks lemongrass, tough outer husk removed and tender, yellow heart cut into thin slices

Cucumber salad

2 continental (English) cucumbers
¼ cup (60 ml) fish sauce
¼ cup (60 ml) lime juice (juice of about 2–3 limes)
1 tablespoon brown sugar or coconut sugar
1–2 red birdseye chillies, sliced
1 small garlic clove, grated on a microplane
2 tablespoons neutral oil
½ cup (25 g) chopped coriander (cilantro)
½ cup (25 g) chopped mint
2 French shallots, thinly sliced
Heaped ¼ cup (40 g) toasted peanuts, lightly crushed in a mortar and pestle

Fight the urge to turn your grill heat up too high here – a dark soy marinade containing sugar will burn if you cook it too quickly. With the right heat, you'll have a juicy, succulent, smoky grilled pork belly with vibrant Vietnamese flavours.

Before you begin: The pork requires at least 1 hour to marinate, but ideally 8 hours. If you're using a charcoal grill (which will make this most delicious), you'll need to get it going an hour or so before you want to start cooking.

To prepare the pork marinade, blend the fish sauce, soy sauce, brown sugar, garlic cloves, shallots and lemongrass to a pulp. Mix this with the pork belly slices and refrigerate overnight (8 hours), or for at least 1 hour. Be sure to pull your pork out of the fridge and allow it to come to room temperature 1 hour before cooking.

To prepare the cucumber salad, halve the cucumbers lengthways and scoop out (and discard) the seeds. Cut the cucumber halves in half again and then into 3–4 cm (1¼–1½ inch) lengths and place in a bowl. In a separate small mixing bowl, or in a jar with a lid, combine the fish sauce, lime juice, sugar, chilli, garlic and oil and stir or shake to combine and dissolve the sugar. Pour this onto the cucumbers and toss together. Just before serving, add in the herbs, shallots and toasted peanuts. Toss again to combine.

Preheat your outdoor grill or heat a grill pan over a high heat on your stove.

Grill your pork belly for 2–3 minutes per side, until the pork is nicely charred and cooked through, but not blackened. Allow the pork to rest for about 5 minutes, before serving with the cucumber salad.

Serving suggestion: Serve this dish with steamed coconut rice for a complete meal. Rinse 2 cups (400 g) of jasmine rice until the water runs clear. Soak the rice in cold water for 15 minutes. Drain and place the rice in a pot with 1 x 400 g (14 oz) tin of coconut milk and ½ cup (125 ml) water, plus a teaspoon of fine sea salt. Stir to combine and bring to a gentle simmer. Place a tight-fitting lid on the pot and turn the heat down to the lowest setting. Cook for 14 minutes exactly. Turn the heat off and leave the pot to sit, untouched, for 10–15 minutes. Remove the lid, fluff the rice with a fork and serve with the pork belly.

Sausages with red-wine-braised lentils and fennel salad with mustard dressing

Braising lentils in chicken stock, red wine and something meaty, like sausages, creates an incredible depth of flavour. It will taste like you've been simmering these for hours, when really the whole thing comes together in about an hour.

In a medium, enamel-lined Dutch oven or heavy-based braising pan set over a medium–high heat, add the olive oil and brown the sausages on two sides, then remove them from the pan and set aside.

Reduce the heat to low and add in the onion, garlic, celery and carrot with a pinch of salt. Sweat gently and slowly until the vegetables are soft and sweet, at least 10 minutes.

Add in the tomato paste and sizzle for a few seconds, stirring. Add in the lentils, stock, rosemary, fennel seeds and bay leaf and bring to a gentle simmer. Simmer for about 40–50 minutes, until the lentils are tender.

Add in the red wine, then return the sausages to the pan and simmer for a further 10 minutes. Taste the lentils – if they are still slightly firm in the middle, simmer for an additional 5 minutes, adding a splash of water as needed so they don't get too dry. Taste again and adjust the seasoning with salt and pepper.

While the sausages are cooking, shave the fennel very thinly on a mandoline (or with a very sharp knife) and place in a mixing bowl. In a separate bowl, whisk together the mustard, crème fraîche, vinegar and lemon juice, then season with salt and pepper. Toss the dressing and the parsley through the fennel. Taste and adjust the seasoning as needed.

To serve, spoon the lentils and sausages onto plates. Top with the fennel salad and finish with a drizzle of good-quality olive oil.

Serving suggestion: One small, peeled and julienned raw celeriac in place of the fennel makes for an excellent substitute in this salad.

Makes: Enough to serve 4
Active time: 35 minutes
Inactive time: 1 hour 10 minutes

Kitchenalia: Mandoline
 (alternatively, a very sharp
 knife to thinly slice)

3 tablespoons extra-virgin
 olive oil
4–6 pork and fennel sausage,
 or Italian pork sausages
1 brown onion, diced
3 garlic cloves, minced
2 stalks celery, diced
1 carrot, peeled and chopped
1 tablespoon tomato paste
 (concentrated purée)
1 cup (210 g) dried green
 French lentils
 (preferably du Puy)
4 cups (1 litre) chicken stock
 (or water)
1 sprig rosemary
1 teaspoon fennel seeds
1 bay leaf
½ cup (125 ml) red wine
Fine sea salt
Freshly cracked black pepper

Fennel salad
2 fennel bulbs
1 tablespoon wholegrain
 mustard
2 tablespoons crème fraîche
1 tablespoon white wine vinegar
1 tablespoon lemon juice
½ cup (10 g) flat-leaf parsley
 leaves
Fine sea salt
Freshly cracked black pepper

To finish
Good-quality extra-virgin
 olive oil

Turkish lamb meatballs with rice pilaf and yoghurt

Makes: Enough to serve 4
Active time: 35 minutes
Inactive time: 10 minutes

Meatballs
¼ cup (15 g) breadcrumbs
    (panko or dried, not
    sourdough)
¼ cup (60 ml) whole milk
500 g (1 lb 2 oz) minced
    (ground) lamb
1 teaspoon ground cumin
1 teaspoon ground coriander
1 teaspoon crushed caraway
    seeds
1 teaspoon fine sea salt
A good crack of black pepper
2 eggs, lightly beaten
Half a brown onion, grated
    on the large holes of
    a box grater
2 garlic cloves, grated on
    a microplane
2 tablespoons extra-virgin
    olive oil, for frying

Tomato sauce
1⅔ cups (420 g) tomato passata
    (puréed tomatoes)
2 large garlic cloves, grated
    on a microplane
100 g (3½ oz) unsalted butter
1 tablespoon tomato paste
    (concentrated purée)
1 teaspoon smoked paprika

Yoghurt sauce
Heaped ½ cup (150 g)
    Greek-style plain yoghurt
2 garlic cloves, grated on
    a microplane
Juice of half a lemon
1 teaspoon dried mint

To serve
Rice pilaf (see serving
    suggestion)
4 pita breads (optional)

This recipe is inspired by Turkish Iskender kebabs, which are traditionally served with sheep's milk butter, hot tomato sauce and yoghurt. It's deeply satisfying and wonderfully easy to put together.

Before you begin: You can mix and form the meatballs up to a day in advance to get a head start.

For the meatballs, soak the breadcrumbs in the milk in a mixing bowl. Add in the remaining meatball ingredients except for the olive oil. Use your (clean) hands to mix and bring the ingredients together – don't overmix or the meatballs will become tough. Form the mixture into 15–20 balls and place them onto a tray or plate, then leave in the fridge until you're ready to cook. This can be done up to a day in advance.

Prepare the rice pilaf (see below).

Combine all the tomato sauce ingredients in a bowl and set aside.

Combine all the yoghurt ingredients in a separate bowl and set aside.

Heat a wide sauté pan over a medium–high heat. Add the olive oil and brown the meatballs on all sides. Pour the tomato sauce over the meatballs and cover with a lid, leaving it slightly ajar. Turn the heat down and cook at a low simmer for 8–10 minutes. Check the sauce for seasoning.

Place the meatballs onto a serving platter, or serve straight out of the pan, spooning the yoghurt over the top. Serve the meatballs hot with the rice pilaf (see below) and pita breads, if you like.

Serving suggestion: To make rice pilaf for 4 people, take 1½ cups (300 g) of basmati rice and rinse it well in several changes of cold water. Drain and set aside. Dice and sauté 1 small onion in 30 g (1 oz) of unsalted butter over a medium heat. After 5 minutes, add in the rice and a good pinch of salt and stir to coat the rice in the butter. Add in 2¼ cups (560 ml) of chicken stock or water and bring to a boil. Stir once, using a fork, then cover with a tight-fitting lid and reduce to the lowest-possible heat for 17 minutes. Turn off the heat and allow to rest for 5 minutes before removing the lid. Fluff with a fork before serving.

Sweet-and-sour cumin lamb shoulder with garlic yoghurt

Makes: Enough for 6
Active time: 1 hour 30 minutes
Inactive time: 10 hours

Before you begin: The lamb needs to be seasoned for a minimum of 4 hours before roasting, but preferably overnight, so plan accordingly. Remove the lamb from the fridge and bring it to room temperature 2 hours before you want to start cooking.

1 x 1.8–2 kg (4–4 lb 8 oz) lamb
    shoulder, bone in
1 brown onion
2 carrots, peeled
2 stalks celery
4 garlic cloves, peeled
2 tablespoons tomato paste
    (concentrated purée)
1⅔ cups (420 ml) water
Fine sea salt

Garlic yoghurt
1 cup (260 g) Greek-style
    plain yoghurt
¼ cup (15 g) chopped mint
1 large garlic clove, grated
    on a microplane
1 teaspoon lemon zest
1 tablespoon lemon juice
½ teaspoon white
    (granulated) sugar
½ teaspoon fine sea salt

Glaze
1 tablespoon dark soy sauce
¼ cup (60 ml) sherry vinegar
¼ cup (60 g) brown sugar

Spice crust
1 tablespoon cumin seeds
1 tablespoon coriander seeds

Lamb cooked until tender, brushed with a richly coloured sweet-and-sour glaze, and crusted in spices. The combination of yoghurt with these spices is a real thrill. This recipe offers a gear shift from the more gentle, classic aromatics that you often see with slow-cooked lamb, but with the same deliciously unctuous rewards.

Season your lamb liberally with salt and leave it in the fridge, covered, overnight (or for at least 4 hours). Ensure the lamb is at room temperature before cooking.

For the garlic yoghurt, add all the ingredients to a small bowl and stir to combine. Chill until you're ready to serve the lamb. This can be made up to 6 hours ahead.

When ready to cook, preheat your oven to 200°C (400°F).

Cut the onion, carrot and celery into rough, large pieces and place them in a roasting pan, along with the garlic cloves. Place the lamb on top, and roast, uncovered, for 40 minutes.

Stir the tomato paste into the water. Add the tomato water to the roasting pan, then cover the pan tightly with a layer of baking paper followed by a layer of aluminium foil.

Reduce the oven temperature to 150°C (300°F) and cook the lamb shoulder for 3½ hours. While the lamb cooks, combine the glaze ingredients in a small pot and bring it to a simmer over a medium heat. Simmer until thick, sticky and resembling molasses. Set aside until you are ready to use. After 3½ hours, uncover the pan and brush the lamb with the sticky glaze, reserving any excess. Increase the oven temperature to 175°C (345°F) and cook, uncovered, for a further 20–30 minutes, until the lamb is dark, sticky and nicely glazed. Remove the lamb from the oven and carefully lift it out of the pan. Set it aside on a plate.

Toast the cumin and coriander seeds in a small, dry sauté pan over a medium heat until fragrant. Lightly crush the toasted spices in a mortar and pestle until just crushed (you don't want a powder). Sprinkle the spices over the lamb and allow it to rest in a warm place for 15 minutes.

Strain the braising liquid into the small pot with any remaining glaze (discard the vegetables). Skim and discard the fat from the top of the braising liquid and simmer until thickened and slightly salty.

Serve the lamb with the thickened braising liquid and the garlic yoghurt.

Serving suggestions: Serve this dish with simple wedges of roasted pumpkin, the Carrots in butter, dill and black pepper (see page 232), the Shaved cabbage with pine nuts, currants and vinaigrette (see page 93) or the Long-cooked green beans (see page 240).

Beef daube with panisse

I'll never forget the perfection of the daube at La Merenda restaurant, in Nice. This typical Provençal beef stew uses ingredients from the region – rosemary, red wine and a pop of citrus – along with the usual mirepoix vegetables. The restaurant served the stew with fat fingers of panisse, another local specialty, which were crisp and chewy on the outside and custardy on the inside. I can still taste it if I close my eyes, transporting me back to that colourful Niçoise dining room. This stew is also excellent served atop buttered pappardelle, if making the panisse is a step too far.

Before you begin: The beef needs to be seasoned and marinated overnight (8 hours) so plan accordingly (a longer marinating time is fine). The panisse batter can also be made a day ahead (see over page).

Cut your beef into large 6–7 cm (2½–2¾ inch) square chunks. Season the beef with salt and submerge it in the red wine before refrigerating, covered, for a minimum of 8 hours.

When ready to cook, preheat your oven to 150°C (300°F).

Heat a large enamel-lined Dutch oven or a heavy-based pot with a lid over a high heat and add the olive oil. Brown the beef in the oil in several batches so you don't overcrowd the pan, which would cause the beef to stew. Once the pieces have browned on all sides, remove them from the pot and set aside on a plate. Reserve the marinade.

Turn the heat down to medium. Add in the onions with a pinch of salt and sweat until they are soft and sweet and starting to caramelise. Stir in the flour and cook for about 30 seconds.

Add in the reserved marinade and let that simmer for about 1 minute. Add the browned beef back in, along with the carrots, celery, garlic, bouquet garni, orange zest, stock, and a few cracks of pepper. Bring to a simmer, cover with a lid and transfer to the oven. Leave the beef daube to cook for 3–3½ hours, until the beef is meltingly tender.

Makes: Enough to serve 6
Active time: 1 hour
Inactive time: 11 hours
30 minutes

Kitchenalia: Entrée plates with a small rim about 18–22 cm (7–8½ inches) across, butcher's string (optional)

2 kg (4 lb 8 oz) beef chuck (or other meaty cut that is good for braising)
1⅔ cups (420 ml) red wine
2 tablespoons extra-virgin olive oil
2 brown onions, diced small
2 tablespoons plain (all-purpose) flour
4 carrots, peeled and cut into large chunks
2 stalks celery, halved and spiked with 3 whole cloves
5 garlic cloves, crushed
1 bouquet garni (2–3 sprigs each rosemary, thyme and bay leaf, tied together with a piece of butcher's string; or add the herbs in loose and fish them out before serving)
3 strips orange zest (peeled using a vegetable peeler)
4 cups (1 litre) beef stock
Fine sea salt
Freshly cracked black pepper

To serve
Panisse (see over page)

←

Panisse

900 ml (3½ cups) water
2 teaspoons extra-virgin olive oil, plus extra for greasing
1½ teaspoons fine sea salt, plus extra for finishing
250 g (heaped 2 cups) chickpea flour (besan)
1½ teaspoons fennel pollen
125 ml (½ cup) extra-virgin olive oil, for frying
Freshly cracked black pepper

To make the panisse:

Add the water, olive oil and salt to a medium saucepan and bring to a simmer, then slowly stream in the chickpea flour while whisking. Do this slowly, to avoid lumps from forming. A few small lumps are okay, but whisk as hard as you can to try and get some of those out. Once all the flour is incorporated, turn the heat down to low and cook, whisking every couple of minutes, until the mixture pulls away from the sides of the pan when stirred. Mix in most of the fennel pollen, reserving a pinch for the garnish.

Grease two flat entrée-sized plates (see kitchenalia note) with a little olive oil. Divide the panisse mixture between the two plates, spreading it to the edge and flattening the surface as best you can. An offset spatula (or regular spatula) can help here. Cool the panisse on your bench, then chill in the fridge, ready to fry just before serving. You can do this the day before serving.

To fry the panisse, heat a cast-iron or heavy-based frying pan, over a medium–high heat and add the olive oil. Lift the chilled and set panisse from the plate and cut each round into strips about 2–3 cm (¾–1¼ inches) wide. Fry the strips in the hot oil in small batches, about 5–6 pieces at a time, until golden brown on all sides. Set the cooked panisse aside on a cooling rack and sprinkle with the salt while it's still hot so the salt sticks. Once all the panisse are fried, sprinkle with a good crack of pepper and the remaining fennel pollen.

To finish:

When the beef is tender, remove and discard the bouquet garni and large pieces of onion. If you want a thicker sauce to coat the beef, pull out the meat and the chunks of carrot and place them on a plate. Bring the braising liquid to a simmer over a medium heat and reduce it until it reaches your desired consistency, then return the beef and carrot to the pot. You may or may not need to do this depending on the type of beef stock you use. Taste for seasoning and adjust with salt and pepper. Spoon the daube into bowls and serve with the crisp, warm panisse.

Note: The frying of the panisse takes longer than you think but it's important not to rush this by turning the heat up – the slow browning is what ensures a crisp, crunchy exterior and a smooth, custardy interior.

For some of my time at Chez Panisse, Jerome Waag was head chef. Jerome was born in France, and his mother was a beautiful cook and a great friend of Lulu Peyraud – the matriarch of Domaine Tempier (makers of my favourite rosé), and a fabulous cook herself. Alice Waters had stayed at the vineyard, not far from the seaside town of Bandol, and learned about French provincial cooking from these two women before opening Chez Panisse. Jerome later came to California – he was an artist, a chef and, eventually, the head chef of Chez Panisse. Jerome told me that his mother always shaped panisse on a small plate or saucer; the thick centre and thinning edges provided the perfect, practical shape to achieve crisp edges and a more custardy centre.

Grilled steak with horseradish cream and tomato

Makes: Enough to serve 4
Active time: 40 minutes
Inactive time: 1 hour 15 minutes

Kitchenalia: Outdoor grill,
  internal meat thermometer

Before you begin: Take your steak out of the fridge, and out of any packaging it may be in, about 1 hour before you want to start cooking. Let it rest on paper towel to absorb any excess moisture, which will help you get a nice crust.

1 x 1 kg (2 lb 4 oz) rib-eye steak, bone in (see note)
2 teaspoons extra-virgin olive oil
80 g (2¾ oz) fresh horseradish (or 3 tablespoons prepared horseradish – in which case, skip the vinegar)
1½ tablespoons white wine vinegar
½ cup (120 g) crème fraîche
Fine sea salt
Freshly cracked black pepper

To finish
1–2 juicy, ripe heirloom tomatoes, thickly sliced
2 tablespoons chopped chives
Flaked sea salt

Note: Alternate cuts to use: bone-in sirloin, rump cap, strip loin, tenderloin. The cooking time will vary between cuts, but you should look for the same finished internal temperature of 50–52°C (122–125°F) for medium rare.

Serving suggestion: This garnish of fresh tomato and horseradish cream is also wonderful with hot, grilled blue mackerel.

Even though a big steak is a real luxury, there are certain occasions that call for one. Eating outside on a beautiful summer evening is one of them. This recipe is written to cook the steak to medium rare, which is the best way to respect such a beautiful cut of meat.

Heat a charcoal or outdoor gas grill to a high heat.

Rub your steak with olive oil and sprinkle it liberally with the fine sea salt and cracked pepper. Set aside until your grill is hot.

While you're waiting for your grill to heat, peel and grate your horseradish on a microplane. Add it to a small mixing bowl with a pinch of fine sea salt and the vinegar. Allow it to sit for 5 minutes to release its aromas, then mix it with the crème fraiche. Keep this cold until ready to serve.

Place your steak on the grill and close the lid – do not touch it for 3 minutes, then flip and cook for a further 3 minutes. Flip and repeat this process twice more, for a total cooking time of about 20 minutes. Reduce to a medium heat if it appears the steak is becoming overly charred or blackened, or if you're struggling with flare-ups. You want your steak to reach an internal temperature (at the thickest part) of 50–52°C (122–125°F) for medium rare (if you don't have a thermometer handy, follow these time guides and you'll get very close to this temperature). Remove the steak from the grill and allow to rest in a warm spot for 15–20 minutes.

Slice your steak and serve it with the horseradish cream, alongside thick slices of tomato sprinkled with flaked sea salt and chives.

The *supporting* acts

"... serve forth in the order of nature itself: first *freshness*, then *flavour* and *ripeness*, and then *decay* ..."

M.F.K. Fisher, *Two Kitchens in Provence*

M.F.K. Fisher was one of the early and great proponents of fresh produce, her tales littered with descriptions of the jewels you find in the markets of the Mediterranean – produce with perfume you could bottle and beauty that belongs in an art gallery.

Still today, the heirloom varieties in these markets are a striking legacy of centuries of careful seed collection among the paysan families who worked the land and grew their own; of a time when selection decisions were based on the flavour of the fruit or vegetable, not only its virility; of a time when its ability to travel or to sit on a supermarket shelf was irrelevant. Simpler times, to be sure, but no easier.

To cultivate the land – whether for fruit, vegetables or livestock – is to become beholden to nature's relentless energy, and to correspond with an irrational yet spellbinding mistress. The months of gentle preparation, not just propagating seeds but preparing the soils, rotating crops, knowing which plant will be happy to sidle up to another; and then the anxious wait, as the weather and the seasons roll over those precious seedlings in their languid stroll to maturity. The anticipation of the perfect moment to pluck them from the earth, vine or tree, knowing that no two seasons will ever be the same – no two harvests, no two fruits. Knowing that nature is perfect in its imperfection.

For all the beauty of that immediacy and wonder, there is not a market that doesn't survive because of the tacit agreement between grower and cook (or even middleman and cook). It's a largely silent agreement that the fruit and vegetables will be respected all the way from ripe (and often before) to rot. Of course, this is also reflected in cost – it would be unfair to suggest the vegetables before or past their prime should command the same price – but for the astute cook, this is not solely about economy, it's about flavour, texture ... and respect.

Fruit that is on the firmer side will hold up better when cooked for a pie or tart, while overblown fruit is excellent for jams, reducing the reliance on sugar. Of course, when a fruit is perfect it needs nothing else, and is best eaten just as it is!

This missive is an ode to the fruit and vegetables that aren't perfect. The unfortunate but blunt reality is that this is actually an ode to practically all the fruit and vegetables you will find in the big supermarkets. It is not really a criticism, rather an acknowledgement of the reality that produce must be picked en masse, packed onto trucks, and freighted great distances before sitting on the shelf waiting for someone to choose it. We can have fun with this, for as much as the just-cooked, sprightly green bean has its place at the table, there are more notes to be played, with enormous success, across the bean spectrum.

"True *gastronomy* is making the *most* of what is available, however *modest*."

Claudia Roden,
Everything Tastes Better Outdoors

This is the time to coax flavour from water. These are the vegetables that require a little kitchen alchemy; cooked until they collapse into their sauce, having given up all they have to offer, perhaps with the help of a few culinary friends. In vegetable soups, for example, you will see that the star of the show is often cooked early with the onions, until they are releasing all their flavour, before the stock or water is added. It is also seen in dried beans that are soaked overnight before cooking (and the precious liquid that develops as you cook them), the stewed onions on your pissaladière, or even the bagna cauda, essentially a bath of warm anchovies for somewhat tired winter vegetables ...

In the home, we can do away with restaurant techniques such as routinely blanching and shocking vegetables. It's not always a bad thing for vegetables to lose their crunchy green vibrancy, instead giving way for their softer, sweeter flavours to rise up. The blanching-shocking technique produces a sameness and a "perfection", but in the process, we are robbed of the sort of flavour and excitement that you can't find in a restaurant. It's important to note that this technique was probably created to alleviate a problem in the restaurant kitchen: the inability to cook everything *à la minute*, or perhaps to ensure that an apprentice wasn't charged with hitting that elusive moment when the vegetable tastes just right. In actual fact, by blanching and then shocking vegetables in iced water, we're washing much of the gentle, salty vegetable flavour down the drain. That's not the kind of "perfect" we should be chasing at home.

If the goal of eating out is to find something you can't have at home, shouldn't part of eating at home be cooking things you can't find when you're out? Perhaps we chefs have been robbing you of flavours and textures you haven't had the chance to love. That's a shame.

Is it time to do away with the negative connotations for words such as mushy, the angst of grey vegetables, and to stop being so entitled in our expectations? If we are not perfect all the time, how can we expect it of our vegetables?

Perhaps we should apply the same thinking to our vegetables as we have to our meats? This is not just in the root-to-tip concept – using all parts of the vegetables (although I certainly encourage that too!) – rather, I want to talk about the point at which they have been picked, how long they've been stored, where they've come from. To spare a thought (and place at our tables) for the less-than-perfect vegetables, which are likely to be the majority of the vegetables you will meet in your life.

As it is with the so-called "primary" and "secondary" cuts of meat – a distinction that is a misnomer in itself – there is often a pay-off between the price of the produce and the amount of time you will spend on it. Some keys to cooking your vegetables a little longer, or dressing up those less-than-perfect ones:

· Bringing other players to the dance: most often garlic, onion, tomatoes, citrus and fresh herbs.

· Transforming these vegetables with a little help from your pantry: vinegar, sea salt, freshly cracked black pepper, honey or maple syrup, miso, cheese, butter, wine and spices like nutmeg.

· Balancing these vegetables with different texture elsewhere in the dish. They will inherently be soft, so you will want some crisp textures to balance that out elsewhere: crunchy bread, crisp crackling or chicken skin, shards of pancetta, toasted nuts or golden breadcrumbs.

When M.F.K. Fisher suggested "… serve forth in the order of nature itself: first freshness, then flavour and ripeness, and then decay …" she could have been writing the mantra for every marketeer and their symbiotic relationship with their customers. We should always celebrate and elevate the incredible produce grown in rich, living soils – the work of thoughtful and incredibly hard-working producers. That will always be the pinnacle, the dream; however, we can also find a place for the inbetweeners, a place where *your* mind and hands can help make more of produce that is on its march from ripe to rot.

It's time to bring this idea, and the culinary beauty it creates, into your home.

A FEW SIMPLE IDEAS FOR SIDE DISHES FOR FOUR PEOPLE:

Sautéed garlicky greens

Take two bunches (or one very large bunch) of silverbeet (Swiss chard) or rainbow chard. Strip the leaves from the stems and blanch them in boiling salted water. Sauté the drained leaves with 3 tablespoons of olive oil, 2 cloves of minced garlic and 1 small sliced fresh red chilli over a medium heat and season to taste. Serve with a squeeze of lemon juice.

Greens gratin

Take the stems from two bunches of silverbeet (Swiss chard) and cut them into 4 cm (1½ inch) lengths. Blanch in boiling salted water for 3 minutes, then drain and set aside. Make a light béchamel: in a small pot, melt 30 g (1 oz) of unsalted butter and stir in a scant ¼ cup (30 g) of plain (all-purpose) flour, stirring constantly until a paste forms. Add 2 cups (500 ml) of warmed whole milk, continuing to stir until the sauce thickens and comes to a gentle boil. Season the béchamel with salt, freshly grated Parmigiano Reggiano and a few gratings of nutmeg. Mix the stalks with the béchamel and spread into a gratin dish. Top with pats of butter and more parmesan and bake for 30 minutes in a 180°C (350°F) oven, until browned and bubbly on top.

Roasted cauliflower with parsley, chilli and lemon

Thinly slice a head of cauliflower (stalks and all) and toss with a light drizzle of olive oil, a sprinkle of salt and a crack of black pepper. Spread across two or three baking trays so the slices are sitting in one layer. Roast at 220°C (425°F) for 7 minutes, until the edges of the cauliflower are browned. Remove from the oven and immediately toss with 3 cloves of very finely chopped garlic, ¼ cup (7 g) of chopped flat-leaf parsley, a pinch of chilli flakes and the zest and juice of half a lemon. Serve hot or warm.

Potato purée

To make a potato purée, peel 800 g (1 lb 12 oz) of good mashing potato (floury or all-purpose, rather than waxy) and cut into large, evenly sized chunks (not too small, or they will disintegrate). Place in a pot, cover with cold water and season with salt. Bring to a boil, reduce the heat to medium and cook until a knife pierces the centre of a potato with no resistance. Drain in a colander. Heat 1 cup (250 ml) of whole milk and a decent chunk of unsalted butter, at least 90 g (3¼ oz), in the saucepan that held the potatoes. Crush the potatoes though a potato ricer (or mash with a potato masher) directly into the hot milk, stirring with a wooden spoon as you go. If desired, add a spoonful of sour cream or crème fraîche for tanginess. Stir to combine and taste for seasoning (mashed potatoes love salt – make sure you use enough).

Carrots in butter, dill and black pepper

Peel and slice six large carrots into 3 mm (⅛ inch) thick rounds. Add them to a pan with ½ cup (125 ml) water, 50 g (1¾ oz) of unsalted butter, a pinch of salt and 2 teaspoons of white (granulated) sugar. Place a lid on the pan and simmer over a medium heat for about 12–15 minutes, until the water has evaporated and the carrots are just tender. They should be glossy and glazed from the butter and sugar. Toss with chopped dill and freshly cracked black pepper.

Maple and miso sweet potato purée

A sweet and savoury side dish that would be excellent with roast chicken, duck or even grilled trout and wild salmon. This can be made a day or two ahead, kept in the fridge and then reheated.

Place a medium-sized pot (with a lid) on your stove over a medium heat. Add half the butter and allow it to bubble until it becomes brown butter (see note). Add in the sweet potato and a pinch of salt. Stir to combine, cover with the lid and turn down to a low heat. Steam for 10 minutes, stirring after 5 minutes, to begin softening the sweet potato.

Dissolve the miso in the water and add this to the sweet potato. Stir to combine. Return the lid and increase the heat to medium. Steam the sweet potato for a further 15 minutes, checking on it every few minutes and giving it a stir. Once the sweet potato is soft and falling apart, it's ready.

Purée your sweet potato in a food processor or blender with the rest of the butter and the maple syrup. Blend until smooth.

Taste for seasoning and adjust with salt. Return the purée to the pot and reheat before serving.

Note: For brown butter, simmer your butter over a low heat, allowing the liquid to evaporate. The butter will start to foam and caramelise as it melts, freeing the liquid trapped within the fat; it will go from sizzling and foaming to silent and still once there is no liquid left to evaporate. Now is when you really need to pay attention – it can go from nutty and golden to burnt very quickly. When it turns an amber shade of gold and smells deliciously nutty, it's perfect. Remove it from the heat immediately or add liquid, such as lemon juice, vinegar or water, to stop it from cooking any further.

Makes: Enough to serve 4
Active time: 10 minutes
Inactive time: 20 minutes

Kitchenalia: Food processor or blender

80 g (3 oz) cold unsalted butter
850 g (1 lb 14 oz) sweet potato, peeled and cut into large dice (about 2 medium-sized sweet potatoes)
2 teaspoons white miso
⅔ cup (170 ml) water
2 tablespoons maple syrup
Fine sea salt

Zucchini alla scapece

Makes: Enough to serve 4–6
Active time: 20 minutes

Kitchenalia: Mandoline
(alternatively, a very sharp
knife to thinly slice)

¾ cup (185 ml) white wine
vinegar (nothing fancy)
¾ cup (185 ml) water
2 teaspoons fine sea salt,
plus extra to season
4 zucchinis (courgettes), sliced
into rounds 2 mm (¹⁄₁₆ inch)
thick on a mandoline
(or with a very sharp knife)
½ cup (125 ml) extra-virgin
olive oil
5 garlic cloves, sliced thinly
on a mandoline
(or with a very sharp knife)
2 long red chillies, roughly
chopped
¼ cup (5 g) mint leaves, torn

Zucchini alla scapece is a classic preparation where zucchini (courgette) is first fried then tossed with vinegar, garlic, chilli and mint. I like to do this in reverse, where I first blanch the zucchini in a vinegar-water mix, then fry them with garlic, chilli and lots of olive oil. I would serve this at room temperature with fresh mozzarella, or as a side dish for almost anything.

Combine the vinegar and water with 2 teaspoons of salt in a medium-sized pot and bring to a boil. When boiling, add the zucchini in 3 separate batches, cooking each batch for 30 seconds once the water has returned to a simmer. Scoop the zucchini out of the water and set aside until all the zucchini is cooked.

Place a wide sauté pan over a medium–high heat and add the olive oil, garlic and chilli. When hot, add in the boiled zucchini slices. Fry until soft and beginning to fall apart. Top with the mint leaves and check for seasoning, adding more salt if needed.

Serve warm or at room temperature.

The cultural divide is often bridged across a shared table, both flavours and words sneaking their way into the kitchens of others. In this case, scapece is a derivation of the classic escabeche, an ancient yet simple method of preservation in vinegar. The origin of this word (and method) is a little more complex. Is it a derivation of esca Apicii (Apicius' dish), a nod to the famed and rather wonderful Roman cookbook author of the 1st century? Or is it a derivation of the Arabic sikbaj (sik meaning "vinegar" and baj "stew")? This second suggestion makes good culinary sense; the agrodolce flavours that the Ottomans brought with them particularly coloured the cooking of Southern Spain and Italy. Whatever its roots, this escabeche is thought to have been the cucina povera version of the fancier fish versions. Here it is, elevated to its rightful place among the best of them.

Roasted onions with blue cheese and walnuts

Makes: Enough to serve 4
Active time: 20 minutes
Inactive time: 40 minutes

4 small red onions
2 tablespoons extra-virgin
  olive oil
1 tablespoon honey
1 tablespoon white or
  red wine vinegar
60 g (2¼ oz) blue cheese
  (preferably Gorgonzola
  Dolce)
⅓ cup (80 ml) single (pure)
  cream
Fine sea salt

To finish
⅓ cup (40 g) toasted walnuts,
  roughly chopped
1 tablespoon chopped chives

The humble yet ubiquitous onion is found in every cuisine, the world over. Onions are consistent, affordable and widely available; they are also versatile, straddling the sweet-savoury divide with great success. This dish highlights their sweetness and looks gorgeous. A dish just waiting to be served on a holiday table.

Preheat your oven to 180°C (350°F).

Split your onions in half from root to tip and peel the skin off.

Heat an oven-safe pan over a high heat and add the olive oil. Place the onions, cut-side down, into the pan and sit another heavy pan on top of the onions to weigh them down. When browned well, verging on black, remove the weight and flip the onions over. Place them in the oven for 20 minutes.

Once cooked, move the onions to your chopping board and allow them to cool slightly. Meanwhile, line a baking tray with baking paper. Once cool enough to handle, cut the root end off the onions, separate the layers and lay them on the tray. Drizzle with the honey and vinegar, sprinkle with salt and return to the oven for 8–10 minutes to get nicely browned.

Remove the tray from the oven and increase the oven temperature to 210°C (410°F). Crumble the blue cheese over the onion layers and drizzle them with the cream. Return the tray to the oven for a final 7 minutes.

To serve, sprinkle the onions with the chopped walnuts and chives.

The fields surrounding the town of Gorgonzola have been used for centuries as a pit stop for tired cows on their meander to and from their summer alpine pastures. Legend suggests it was a love-struck cheesemaker who, having neglected his previously strained curds for the arms of his lover, panicked and added fresh curd to the vat the following morning. His delicious error encouraged spores of penicillium glaucum (the same mould that gives Roquefort its signature blue) to find footing between the two curds. Now produced in a region spanning Lombardy and Piedmont, Gorgonzola is predominantly sold with two levels of maturity: Gorgonzola Dolce is the softer and milder of the two; made using fresh milk and matured for two months, it is sweet, salt and spreadable. Gorgonzola Piccante is matured in underground caves for three to four months, leaving it with a firmer texture and a strong, spicy flavour.

Ghee roasted potatoes

This is a recipe of logistics – but that's where the simple recipes thrive! To roast potatoes, you could use butter, but you risk burnt milk solids under such a long and hot roast. Of course, you could use clarified butter, but then you would be missing that nutty flavour (likewise with olive oil). Since ghee is made by cooking butter until the milk has steamed away and the solids just begin to caramelise, you get all the best flavour profiles of browned butter, without any burnt butter. These potatoes have a crisp and super crunchy exterior, and a pillowy, fluffy interior. My favourite roast potato.

Peel and cut the potatoes into chunks. Place them in a pot and cover with cold water. Add a generous amount of fine sea salt to the pot along with the bicarbonate of soda, and bring to a boil. Boil until the potatoes are completely tender, without any resistance when poked with a sharp knife.

While the potatoes are cooking, preheat your oven to 200°C (400°F).

Drain the potatoes in a sieve or colander and bash them about to slightly crush them and make the edges rough (think of bouncing a tennis ball on a racket).

Place a baking pan with the ghee into the oven to heat the pan and melt the ghee. When it's nice and hot, tip the potatoes into the pan and toss them around so they're well coated. Roast for 45–60 minutes – exactly how long will depend on the variety of potato. You want them to be golden brown and crisp all over, so give them a stir and rotate your pan every 20 minutes or so.

Remove the golden potatoes from the oven and toss with the flaked sea salt. Serve hot.

Notes: Ghee is like clarified butter, only its cooking is taken a little bit further. This allows the milk solids to caramelise slightly before the butter is strained, lending ghee its characteristic nuttiness (meaning it is a close relation to brown butter, minus the solids). To make your own, place butter in a pot and simmer until all the liquid has evaporated and the butter just begins to brown. Quickly strain it through a fine mesh sieve and store in the fridge to use as needed. As you have now removed all the milk solids, it will keep indefinitely.

The bicarbonate of soda alkalises the cooking water, breaking down the surface starches and giving you that wonderful roughed-up edge on the potatoes, which crisp up when roasted. Adding a pinch of bicarbonate of soda when cooking dried beans works in a similar way (see note on page 197).

Makes: Enough to serve 4–6
Active time: 10 minutes
Inactive time: 1 hour 30 minutes

Before you begin: Ghee is readily available at supermarkets, but it's also simple to make at home (see notes).

1 kg (2 lb 4 oz) potatoes (Dutch cream is my choice here)
Pinch of bicarbonate of soda (baking soda)
Scant ½ cup (80 g) ghee (alternatively, use clarified butter or duck fat)
Fine sea salt
Flaked sea salt, to finish

Long-cooked green beans

Makes: Enough to serve 4
Active time: 20 minutes
Inactive time: 40 minutes

¼ cup (60 ml) extra virgin
    olive oil
1 small brown onion, diced
5 garlic cloves, minced
1 large juicy, ripe tomato, or
    1 x 400 g (14 oz) tin whole
    peeled San Marzano
    tomatoes
½ cup (125 ml) dry white wine
¼ cup (7 g) oregano leaves
600 g (1 lb 5 oz) green beans,
    stem-ends trimmed off
Fine sea salt

To finish
Juice of half a lemon
Good-quality extra-virgin
    olive oil

Libby and I have discussed at length the merits of long-cooking vegetables. We believe that if we can get people to see the beauty in something that was once a vibrant, tropical green but has now yielded to the tones of olive trees, we may, indeed, have a culinary revolution on our hands.

If you find yourself with perfect, young, tender haricot verts, this is not the recipe for them. This is for the large, overgrown green beans – most green beans found on our shop shelves.

Heat a medium-sized pot with a tight-fitting lid over a medium heat and add the olive oil. Add in the onion and garlic and sauté with a pinch of salt until they are soft and sweet, but have no colour, about 10–15 minutes.

Dice the tomato (or crush the tinned tomatoes with your hands) and add to the pot. Add in the white wine and oregano and simmer for about 2 minutes.

Add in the green beans with a really good pinch of salt and cover with the lid. Drop the heat to low and simmer for about 30–40 minutes, until the beans are completely soft and yielding. Give them a stir every 10 minutes. If at any point the beans are becoming dry and the tomato is sticking, add ¼ cup (60 ml) water and continue cooking.

Turn off the heat and check the beans for seasoning. I always find these beans need a lot of salt, so adjust accordingly. Add a squeeze of lemon juice and finish with a generous drizzle of good-quality olive oil. Serve hot, warm or at room temperature.

Roasted cabbage with charred chilli and curry leaf butter

Makes: Enough to serve 4
Active time: 30 minutes
Inactive time: 30 minutes

Kitchenalia: Indoor grill pan
(or open flame),
food processor

2 large long red chillies
20 g (¾ oz) cold unsalted
butter, plus an extra
50 g (1¾ oz)
25 curry leaves
Zest and juice of 1 lime
1 large garlic clove, grated
on a microplane
1 tablespoon extra-virgin
olive oil
½ large head of cabbage,
cut in half
Fine sea salt
Flaked sea salt, to finish

The buttery popcorn flavour of curry leaf works so well with chilli and sweet, caramelised cabbage. This is a delicious side for grilled chicken or pan-fried fish, but it is also hearty enough to be the centrepiece, served with steamed rice.

Char the chillies over an open flame or on a dry grill pan. When they are blackened all over, place them in a small bowl and cover the bowl with a plate or aluminium foil so they can steam. When they are cool enough to handle, peel off the skin and remove the seeds.

Preheat your oven to 220°C (425°F).

In a small saucepan, heat the 20 g (¾ oz) of butter over a medium heat. When the butter is foamy, add in the curry leaves and let them pop and sizzle. When they stop sizzling, remove half of the curry leaves and set them aside for your garnish. Pour the butter into the bowl of a food processor. To the bowl, add the chillies, lime juice and the garlic, with a good pinch of fine sea salt. Add in the remaining cold butter and process until smooth, stopping to scrape down the sides as needed. Set aside.

Heat a large oven-safe skillet over a high heat. Add the olive oil and, once it's hot and smoking, add the cabbage halves. Let them blacken on one side before flipping them over to the other and then popping the whole pan into the oven. Roast for 15–20 minutes, until the cabbage is soft, sweet and well-browned.

Cut each cabbage wedge in half, so you have four portions. Slather the wedges with the curry leaf butter and garnish with the lime zest and reserved crisp curry leaves. Season with the flaked sea salt and serve hot.

Caramelised fennel gratin

No one can deny that the top of a gratin is the best part. Baking this delicious gratin in a baking tray increases the amount of surface area, resulting in more of that crunchy, golden and bubbly top. Take care to follow the ratios of the vegetables to get the best result.

Heat a large sauté pan over a low–medium heat and add the butter and onion, along with a pinch of salt. Sweat the onion, stirring every few minutes, until it becomes completely caramelised, about 30 minutes. If it looks like it's sticking to the pan or burning before caramelising, simply add 2 tablespoons water and cover with a lid, slightly ajar (this is to allow the onions to steam and cook through by preventing the water from evaporating too quickly). You can continue to add water as often as needed until the onion has fully caramelised.

Preheat your oven to 180°C (350°F).

When the onion is caramelised, add in the fennel and another good pinch of salt and cover the pan, again with the lid slightly ajar. Sweat the fennel with the onion until the fennel has released all its water and the pan has dried up, about 15–20 minutes. Taste for seasoning and adjust with salt.

Transfer the onion and fennel to a small and shallow baking tray, spreading it to the edges. Pour the cream over the fennel and onion. Sprinkle the thyme leaves and both grated cheeses over the top and bake for 20 minutes. Rinse out your sauté pan to use again.

While the gratin bakes, toss the breadcrumbs with the olive oil and a pinch of salt in your cleaned sauté pan. Toast over a medium heat until golden and crisp. Set aside.

After 20 minutes, remove the gratin from the oven and sprinkle it with the toasted breadcrumbs, going all the way to the edges. Top with freshly cracked pepper. Return the gratin to the oven for a further 10 minutes, until the breadcrumbs are a deep golden and the gratin is bubbling.

Sprinkle with the extra thyme leaves and flaked sea salt and serve hot.

Makes: Enough to serve 4–6
Active time: 25 minutes
Inactive time: 1 hour 20 minutes

40 g (1½ oz) unsalted butter
400 g (14 oz) brown onions, thinly sliced (about 3 small onions)
800 g (1 lb 12 oz) fennel, thinly sliced (about 2 large bulbs)
200 ml (7 fl oz) single (pure) cream
1 tablespoon thyme leaves, plus extra to garnish
¼ cup (25 g) freshly grated Parmigiano Reggiano
⅓ cup (25 g) grated Comté or Gruyère
1 cup (60 g) breadcrumbs (panko or sourdough)
1 tablespoon extra-virgin olive oil
Fine sea salt
Freshly cracked black pepper
Flaked sea salt, for finishing

Grilled asparagus with pine nut salsa

Makes: Enough to serve 4
Active time: 30 minutes

Kitchenalia: Outdoor grill
or indoor grill pan

Before you begin: Heat your outdoor charcoal grill. If using an indoor grill pan, make sure it's hot before grilling the asparagus.

2 bunches fat asparagus

Pine nut salsa
Heaped ⅓ cup (60 g) pine nuts
1 cup (30 g) basil leaves
loosely packed
¼ cup (60 ml) extra-virgin olive
oil, plus extra for brushing
1 garlic clove, grated on
a microplane
Heaped ¼ cup (30 g) freshly
grated Parmigiano Reggiano
Zest and juice of half a lemon
Fine sea salt
Freshly cracked black pepper

Seasonal adjustment: When asparagus is not in season, I love to toss this salsa through warm cooked butter beans (both tinned cannellini-style beans and the long, yellow beans that look like yellow green beans).

At first glance, this is grilled asparagus tossed in pesto, but by changing the traditional proportions of the pesto, increasing the amount of pine nuts and decreasing the amount of basil and olive oil, you get a delicious nutty salsa that works wonderfully well on asparagus.

Trim the woody asparagus ends by holding each spear in both hands and snapping it wherever it wants to break naturally. It should be the bottom third of the spear. Do this with all the asparagus, then set aside.

For the salsa, toast your pine nuts in a dry skillet over a medium heat until golden all over, then set aside to cool. Crush the cooled pine nuts in a mortar and pestle, then remove and set aside. Crush the basil in the mortar and pestle with a pinch of salt until it makes a paste. Add the crushed pine nuts back into the mortar, along with the olive oil, garlic, parmesan and a crack of pepper and stir to combine (or mix everything together in a mixing bowl if your mortar isn't large enough). You should end up with a thick salsa. Set aside.

Heat an outdoor grill or a cast-iron grill pan on your stove to a high heat. Brush the asparagus spears with olive oil and grill until nicely charred on all sides, but still crunchy and not flimsy.

Place the asparagus and the pine nut salsa in your serving dish and toss to combine. Finish with the lemon zest and juice. Taste for seasoning and serve warm.

Long-cooked peas with tarragon and verjus

Makes: Enough to serve 4
Active time: 10 minutes
Inactive Time: 20 minutes

¼ cup (60 ml) extra-virgin
    olive oil
1 large French shallot,
    thinly sliced
3 garlic cloves, minced
    (preferably young garlic)
1⅓ cup (200 g) shelled peas
    (see note)
¼ cup (60 ml) verjus
¾ cup (185 ml) water
2 tablespoons chopped French
    tarragon leaves
Fine sea salt

Note: Frozen peas work for
this recipe but if it's spring, try
to find fresh.

Like the Long-cooked green beans on page 240, this recipe illustrates the magic of letting some things cook for a bit longer. Peas that were once starchy and bright green give way to sweetness and savouriness and yes – a little army-green colour. I don't mind this at all, especially at home, when all I really care about it is how delicious something is.

Heat a medium-sized pot with a tight-fitting lid over a medium heat. Add the olive oil with the shallot and garlic and sauté for 3–4 minutes.

Add in the peas, verjus, water and a good pinch of salt and place the lid on the pot, turning the heat down to low.

Simmer the peas for 20 minutes. Check them after about 15 minutes to ensure the water hasn't evaporated too quickly. If it has mostly gone, add ¼ cup (60 ml) water and keep cooking until you hit 20 minutes.

To finish, stir in the tarragon and taste the peas for seasoning. Serve hot.

Tarragon, derived from the French *estragon* (meaning "little dragon"), is a complicated little herb to grow: some sun, some shade; well-drained soil; too humid and she'll succumb to fungal disease, too dry and she's gone. A perennial in the true sense, she disappears over winter, yet even invisible she's sensitive to the frost. She won't grow from seed, nor self-seed (but will grow from a cutting), and if you don't dig her up every few years to separate her entangled roots, she'll choke herself!
All this is likely why her Russian cousin has found such footing. Do not be drawn in by this imposter. Slightly muddy and drab of flavour, Russian tarragon has nothing on the sprightly anise flavour of French tarragon. Subtle yet alert, bitter yet sweet – she's a wonder. Chicken's best culinary friend. Mine too.

Chère estragon,
Je t'aime,
Danielle

Sweet-and-sour cabbage

This is a great way to use up the tough outer leaves from a head of cabbage. Don't slice the cabbage too thinly if you want to retain some crunch.

Slice your cabbage into strips 2–3 mm (about ⅛ inch) thick with a knife and toss it together with the 1 tablespoon of fine sea salt. Place it in a colander or sieve in your sink to drain for 20 minutes. Rinse the cabbage under cold running water, then squeeze it between your hands to get as much water out as possible and set aside.

Mix the sugar and rice wine vinegar together and set aside.

Heat a large wok or wide sauté pan over a high heat. When the wok is hot, add the oil, garlic and chilli (if using), followed immediately by the cabbage. Stir to combine and leave to cook for a minute. Add in the sugar-vinegar mix, stir and cook for another minute. Taste for seasoning and adjust with salt. Serve hot.

Makes: Enough to serve 4
Active time: 10 minutes
Inactive time: 20 minutes

Kitchenalia: Wok (alternatively, use a wide sauté pan)

Half a large head of Savoy cabbage (or round red or green cabbage)
1 tablespoon fine sea salt, plus extra for seasoning
1½ tablespoons white (granulated) sugar
¼ cup (60 ml) rice wine vinegar
¼ cup (60 ml) neutral oil
4 garlic cloves, minced
1 small red birdseye chilli, or ½ teaspoon dried chilli flakes (optional)

Pastry *and* pudding

*Baking
for karma*

"I have discovered no panacea for the troubles which afflict humanity – unless it is that a meal *shared* round the *kitchen table* serves both as a *celebration* of the *good times* and a *comfort* in times of trouble."

Elisabeth Luard, *Family Life*

And then, like a big game of musical chairs, the music stopped, for everyone.

In March 2020, I, like so many others, found myself cocooned in my home until Covid's raging storm passed. When I think back on this time, I think about the fear, anxiety and sadness we were all holding onto – and yet, that unusual comfort of knowing that while we were apart, we were all in the same place, our homes. I can now also see how fortunate that was.

Like so many, I took solace in my kitchen. Most of the ideas for this book were percolating then, even if I didn't know it. Farmers' markets were closed; at first, even staple ingredients were hard to come by, and we all had to make do with what we had. Some of us (like this out-of-work chef) had more time on our hands, while others, such as health workers and parents home-schooling their kids, had (a lot) less. In those early days I was making chickpea pasta, pumpkin and coconut soup, and baking. So much baking. I was sharing a lot of these recipes virtually – it brought me great joy to see people following those ideas and cooking those meals. I still think those earliest recipes were some of my best.

Birthdays were especially difficult: no one to celebrate with, and no candles to blow out. One of my nearest and dearest friends, Georgie, has her birthday in April. We were mere weeks into the lockdown, and the realisation that I couldn't give her a big hug or share glasses of Champagne with her on her birthday really hit me hard. I couldn't imagine what she was feeling. I took to doing the one thing I knew I could share. You will find my Chocolate cake with dark chocolate and cream cheese frosting on page 296 – it's a super moist, rich cake that is a perfect birthday cake for the chocolate-lovers in your life, which Georgie and I both are. I packed it into an open-top box, dropped it on her doorstep, lit the candles and watched from my car as she opened the door. We both cried. These weren't tears of sadness, but tears of relief that neither one of us was alone.

Baking has been my therapy over the years. Where savoury recipes require analysis, tasting along the way, and much more thought, I've always found comfort in a well-written sweet recipe. It's my time to think while also working, which is the greatest of ways to work things out. Follow these instructions as exactingly as you can, and you will be rewarded.

Possibly the greatest part of this therapy session is that I know it will result in brightening someone's day. A cake is always best eaten the day it's made, and I don't know too many people that can – or should! – have a whole cake in one day (although, see the Strawberry, ricotta and spelt loaf on page 266), so my favourite thing to do is to give it away fresh out of the oven.

Cakes are also baked to celebrate the special moments in our lives. It is such a joy to be able to make a birthday cake for someone you love. No matter how good a bought one is, there is nothing that can nourish the spirit like a homemade cake.

There are also the desserts that are made for entertaining. A beautiful galette or freshly baked tart, a warm chocolate cake, a boozy trifle, fruit and cookies, or a perfectly set panna cotta. These all require a bit more technique, and I've spent years tweaking and finessing these recipes to ensure they work.

The following three recipes are my pastry essentials. I use them often and like to keep them handy. Use the Flaky pastry recipe for both sweet and savoury baking – it's my most-requested recipe, and yet every time I make it, I learn something new. The ratios have not changed, but I find I'm always tweaking the method to ensure flaky, crunchy success.

To me, baking is meant to be shared. Cakes are baked to take to your children's school bake sale, to leave on your neighbour's doorstep, to take to a friend's house for tea; to share after dinner, sending your friends home with extra slices for breakfast. Share for karma, share for love, share to make someone's day a little brighter. This is one of the many powers of food.

A note on ovens:
All oven temperatures listed are fan-forced unless otherwise stated. If you require the conventional oven temperature, increase the given temperature by 15–20°C (25–35°F) degrees, according to the manufacturer's instructions.

A note on eggs:
All recipes have been tested and developed using large, 600 g (1 lb 5 oz) per dozen eggs unless otherwise specified.

Flaky pastry

Makes: Enough dough for
1 large galette
Active time: 20 minutes
Inactive time: 2 hours

Kitchenalia: 30 cm (12 inch)
round pizza tray (or baking
tray), pastry brush (for
when cooking)

340 g (11¾ oz) plain
(all-purpose) flour,
plus extra for dusting
1 tablespoon white
(granulated) sugar
1 teaspoon fine sea salt
250 g (9 oz) cold unsalted
butter, diced
120–160 ml (4–5¼ fl oz)
ice-cold water

Notes: To make a great flaky pastry,
you want to see pieces of butter
in the dough when you roll it out.
If the butter is diced too small,
the pastry becomes short and
crumbly, rather than flaky. Layered
pieces of butter become the pockets
where steam expands and pushes the
sheets upward, creating a puff-
pastry-like quality.

Keeping everything – ingredients,
bowl and your hands – as cold as
possible while you work is really
important here. This is much easier
in winter; in summer, you'll need to
work faster and move the ingredients
and bowl in and out of the fridge or
freezer throughout the process, right
up until the pastry goes in the oven.

Serving suggestions: Use this
pastry dough to make the Pissaladière
(see page 72), the Pumpkin, leek and
Gorgonzola galette (see page 58) or
the Plum galette with fennel crème
Anglaise (see page 277).

This is the only flaky or shortcrust pastry recipe that I use: tarts, quiches, pies, flans – it does them all. The ratio of butter to flour is important, as is not overworking the dough and keeping everything as cold as possible while you work. The moisture in the butter steams as the dough cooks, lending the pastry a rich flavour and a delicate, slightly crumbly texture.

The only variable is the water needed. This depends on the flour you're using (flours around the world are all so different) and the humidity in the air, thus the varying measurement. This recipe yields enough for one large galette, plus some trim, which can be frozen to be used at a later date. I keep a collection of trim in my freezer, and when I have enough, I thaw it all and press it together to form a new galette. It works a treat.

Place the flour, sugar and salt in a mixing bowl and stir to combine. If it's a hot day, put the bowl in the fridge or freezer to chill for 5–10 minutes.

If your hands are very warm, dip them in ice water before proceeding. Add the cold, diced butter and use your fingertips to break it up. You're not looking for an even consistency here, you want some large chunks of butter as well as some little pieces. Flatten the chunks of butter by crushing and smearing them between the palms of your hands to create little sheets. (Alternatively, you can dump everything onto your bench and press the butter down into the bench.)

Make a well in the centre of the mixture. Pour 120 ml (4 fl oz) cold water into the well and use your hands to mix the water into the flour, bringing the dough together to form a ball. If it still has some dry, floury spots, add another 20 ml (1 tablespoon) water, and work the dough until it feels like it will stick together without feeling sticky and wet.

Cut the dough in half, stack one piece over the other and press down – this creates layers in your pastry. Repeat this once more, then press the dough into a disc. Wrap the disc in baking paper followed by aluminium foil (to ensure the dough doesn't dry out) and leave it in your fridge for at least 2 hours, but up to 48 hours. If you're not using the dough straight away, pop it into the freezer instead (you will need to thaw it in the fridge overnight before using).

Pull the dough out of the fridge and place it on a well-floured bench. When it has warmed enough to be slightly pliable, use a rolling pin to roll it from the centre, turning as you go, to create a rough circle. Use a liberal amount of flour to prevent the dough from sticking to your bench. Continue rolling and rotating until the dough is about 3 mm (⅛ inch) thick. Trim the dough and leave it on a baking-paper-lined baking tray (ideally a round pizza tray), rolled out, in your fridge until you're ready to assemble and bake, or use it straight away.

Sweet tart shell

This unusual recipe for pastry uses honey, white and brown sugar to produce a beautifully burnished and crisp, yet tender, tart shell. It even stays crisp the next day after a night in the fridge – the holy grail!

In the bowl of a stand mixer fitted with the paddle attachment, combine the butter and both sugars on low speed, stopping and scraping down the bowl with a spatula as needed. You are not trying to aerate here, so this will happen in about 30 seconds. Add in the honey and mix to combine.

Mix the flour and salt together in a separate bowl.

Add the flour mix to the stand mixer and bring the dough together on a low–medium speed, stopping and scraping the bowl as needed to bring it together evenly.

Scoop the dough onto a large sheet of baking paper laid out on your bench and cover it with a second sheet of baking paper. Use a rolling pin to roll your dough to a thickness of 2 mm (1/16 inch) – very, very thin! If your dough is too soft, making it difficult to roll evenly, place it in the fridge for 15 minutes to firm up slightly, then continue to roll. Place the rolled sheet of dough in the fridge for 10 minutes to chill.

Remove the top sheet of baking paper and proceed to peel off as much of the pastry in one piece as you can from the bottom sheet. Lay the pastry into your fluted tart tin. It will tear and break into pieces, but you can patch that up and puzzle it back together in the tin as you go.

The important thing here is to take your time. This is the longest step in the process, but the resulting super thin, crisp shell is a thing of beauty. You'll have excess dough that we'll use later to patch any cracks that appear while baking (any excess beyond that can be shaped into a disc, wrapped and frozen for a few smaller tarts another day). Press the dough into the fluted edges, leaving an overhang of around 1 cm (1/2 inch) (this will help guard against shrinkage as the dough relaxes). Place in the fridge to chill for 30 minutes.

Preheat your oven to 155°C (310°F) fan-forced.

Remove the tart shell from the fridge. At this point, you can trim the overhanging dough by running a small paring knife along the edge of the tin. See if you can't make the edges a tiny bit thinner by lightly pushing the dough upwards slightly past the edge of the tin with your finger. This ensures you won't have a shrunken tart shell. Cover the dough with a sheet or two of aluminium foil and gently press it into the pastry, being sure to cover the base and the sides. Weigh the base of the pastry down using pie weights or dried rice or beans, or a mixture of both.

Bake for 35 minutes, then carefully remove the foil and pie weights. Use the excess dough to patch up any cracks that have appeared (there may not be any). Bake for a further 10–15 minutes, until the base is completely and evenly golden. Remove the pastry from the oven and leave it to cool in the tin before you proceed to fill it.

Makes: Enough dough for 1 fluted tart shell, ranging from 23 cm (9 inches) to 30 cm (12 inches) depending on the tart you're making
Active time: 25 minutes
Inactive time: 1 hour 30 minutes

Kitchenalia: Fluted tart tin with removable base, either 23 cm (9 inches) or 30 cm (12 inches), stand mixer fitted with the paddle attachment

150 g (5½ oz) unsalted butter, at room temperature
35 g (1¼ oz) soft brown sugar
35 g (1¼ oz) white (granulated) sugar
50 g (1¾ oz) honey
250 g (9 oz) plain (all-purpose) flour
1 teaspoon fine sea salt

Serving suggestions: Use this sweet tart shell to make the Raspberry and mascarpone tart (see page 268), the Meyer lemon tart (see page 271) and the Fig and hazelnut frangipane tart (see page 272).

Vanilla bean crème diplomat

Makes: 1.5 litres (6 cups)
Active time: 25 minutes
Inactive time: 2 hours

Before you begin: You can do most of the work for this recipe the day before, simply finishing it by whisking through the whipped cream just before you serve.

550 ml (19 fl oz) whole milk
110 g (3¾ oz) white (granulated) sugar
45 g (1½ oz) cornflour (cornstarch)
135 g (4¾ oz) egg yolks (about 7–9 egg yolks) (reserve egg whites – see serving suggestions)
1½ teaspoons vanilla bean paste
½ teaspoon fine sea salt
30 g (1 oz) unsalted butter
350 ml (12 fl oz) thickened (whipping) cream

Crème diplomat – a thickened custard with whipped cream folded through it – can feel a bit old-fashioned, but I have found so many uses for it that I feel the need to bring it back! It's creamy, it's sweet, it's easy to work with and it's totally delicious.

Place the milk in a saucepan over a low heat and warm until scalding (steaming, with tiny bubbles at the edge of the pot).

In a mixing bowl, combine the sugar, cornflour, egg yolks, vanilla bean paste and salt. Set a sieve over another mixing bowl.

When the milk is scalding, slowly and steadily stream it into the egg yolk mixture to temper the eggs, whisking as you go to avoid lumps forming. Scrape the custard from the mixing bowl back into the saucepan and place over a low–medium heat. Heat, whisking constantly, until you have a very thick paste.

Pour the mixture through the sieve and into the mixing bowl, then whisk for a further 2 minutes. Add in the butter and whisk until completely melted. Place the custard in an airtight container with a sheet of plastic wrap or baking paper sitting directly on the surface to prevent a skin from forming. Refrigerate for a couple of hours, until well chilled. This part can be done a day ahead.

Once the custard has completely chilled, use a whisk to whip the cream to soft–medium peaks. Fold the whipped cream through the custard. Keep the finished crème diplomat in the fridge until ready to use.

Serving suggestions: You'll see this crème diplomat recipe come into play in the Raspberry and mascarpone tart (see page 268), the Polenta chiffon cake with vanilla cream and strawberries (see page 286) and the Apricot pavlova with apricot kernel cream (see page 292). The pavlova makes excellent use of the egg whites you'll have left over from this recipe, as does the recipe for Ricciarelli (see page 288).

Blood orange, rosemary and olive oil cake with citrus compote

This is a perfect winter cake: the fruitiness of the oil, the freshness of the citrus, and the herbal tones of the rosemary. It's taken years to get this recipe right. I've had so many olive oil cakes that have fallen short of my expectations: some too dense and lacking the lightness and joy of a butter cake; others where the olive oil feels more like a gimmick than a boon. Time has taught me that it's the eggs that are the key – you need a lot! Consequently, this is a rather large cake (8 eggs will do that) requiring a bundt (ring) tin to ensure it cooks through to the centre without becoming dry on the edges. These tins make for a fabulous-looking cake – definitely a worthy investment!

To make the cake:

Preheat your oven to 155°C (310°F) fan-forced. Grease a large bundt tin with olive oil (ideally, olive oil spray) followed by a dusting of flour. Tap out any excess flour.

Cut the stem end off the two blood oranges and process them, skin and all, in a blender or food processor to a fine pulp. Set aside.

In a bowl, combine the flour, baking powder, rosemary, almond meal and salt. Set aside.

Add the sugar and eggs to the bowl of a stand mixer fitted with the whisk attachment, and beat on a medium–high speed until light, airy and fluffy. This will take about 6–8 minutes. With the machine running, slowly stream in the olive oil, followed by the vanilla extract, then the puréed oranges. Stop the machine and dump in the flour mixture. Turn the machine on to low and mix until just combined with no lumps of flour remaining. Pour the batter into the tin.

Bake for 50–60 minutes, until a skewer inserted into the tallest part of the cake comes out clean. Allow the cake to cool completely in the tin before tipping it out.

To make the citrus compote:

Peel the zest off the oranges using a vegetable peeler. Use a small paring knife to slice away any white pith from the zest, then cut the zest into long, thin slivers, as thin as you can get them.

Add the zest slivers to a small saucepan with the sugar, water and salt and cook over a low heat for about 15 minutes, until the syrup thickens and the zest candies. Set aside to cool.

While the syrup cools, use a small paring knife to remove all the white pith from the oranges, then cut the segments out (see note over page). Stir the orange segments into the cooled syrup.

To serve, slice and serve the cake with the citrus compote and a spoonful of yoghurt.

Makes: 1 bundt cake, enough for 12–14 slices
Active time: 40 minutes
Inactive time: 1 hour

Kitchenalia: 27 cm (10¾ inch) bundt (ring) tin, blender or food processor, stand mixer fitted with the whisk attachment

Cake
2 blood oranges (or navel oranges)
450 g (1 lb) plain (all-purpose) flour, plus extra for dusting
2 tablespoons baking powder
2 tablespoons chopped rosemary
60 g (2¼ oz) almond meal
1 teaspoon fine sea salt
320 g (11¼ oz) white (granulated) sugar
8 eggs
320 ml (11 fl oz) extra-virgin olive oil, plus extra for greasing
1 teaspoon vanilla extract

Citrus compote
3 blood oranges (or navel oranges)
110 g (3¾ oz) white (granulated) sugar
250 ml (9 fl oz) water
Pinch of fine sea salt

To serve
Greek-style plain yoghurt

⟶

Note: When carefully cut, citrus segments are elegant and refined – a world apart from the orange quarters on a sports field! Using a small, sharp knife, run the blade along the inside of the dividing membranes of the orange, popping out each neat, naked segment as you go. Turn the membranes over like the pages of a book as you make your way around the orange. Don't forget to squeeze the juice that is left in the core into the syrup.

Claudia Roden famously brought the orange cake from the shores of the Mediterranean into our kitchens. The Greeks grow wonderful oranges – they add yoghurt to their *portokalopita*, a bubbly, bouncy affair, doused in orange syrup. In Tuscany, the *schiacciata alla fiorentina* is made for Carnival – it traditionally includes lard from the recently slaughtered family pig, and an indulgence of vanilla in celebration (or perhaps defiance) of the impending Lent. The Portuguese make their *bolo de laranja* in a bundt tin, while in Valencia it's a *coca de llanda*, the *llanda* referring to the baking sheet it's cooked on. In Morocco, where the streets are festooned with citrus, you're as likely to find it made with vegetable oil as olive, and with lemons as often as oranges. A romantic reverence for citrus is an imperative for a happy kitchen, and an orange cake is a great way to celebrate that.

Cherry and walnut cake

Makes: 1 cake, enough
for 8–10 slices
Active time: 15 minutes
Inactive time: 1 hour

Kitchenalia: 23 cm (9 inch)
round springform cake tin,
stand mixer fitted with
the whisk attachment

150 g (5½ oz) plain
(all-purpose) flour
1 teaspoon baking powder
½ teaspoon fine sea salt
220 g (7 oz) white (granulated)
sugar, plus an extra
2 tablespoons for
sprinkling
2 eggs
2 teaspoons vanilla extract
100 ml (3½ fl oz) neutral oil,
plus extra for greasing
90 g (3¼ oz) chopped walnuts
400 g (14 oz) pitted fresh or
frozen cherries (or berries)

The crisp, crackly top, contrasted by the tender crumb underneath is what makes this simple cake extra delightful. It is also excellent made with raspberries, or with blueberries and blackberries, in place of the cherries. The fruit can be fresh or frozen – it's very flexible. It also happens to be dairy-free. Morning or afternoon, with tea or with coffee – this is a great cake to add to your repertoire.

Preheat your oven to 160°C (320°F) fan-forced. Prepare your springform tin by greasing the sides with oil and wrapping the base with baking paper. Clip the sides in place and trim any excess paper to stop it from burning while baking.

In a mixing bowl, whisk together the flour, baking powder and salt to ensure there are no lumps. Set aside.

Add the sugar and eggs to the bowl of a stand mixer fitted with the whisk attachment, and beat on a high speed until the mixture is pale yellow, light and fluffy. This will take about 7–8 minutes. Stop and scrape the sides of the bowl with a spatula as needed.

With the machine running on high, add in the vanilla, then slowly drizzle in the oil. Turn the machine off and add in the flour mixture. Turn the mixer back on to a low speed and whisk to combine.

Remove the bowl from the machine. Use a spatula to fold in the walnuts and cherries, then pour the batter into the tin. Sprinkle the extra sugar over the top before placing the cake in the oven.

Bake for 50–60 minutes, until a skewer inserted into the centre of the cake comes out clean. Leave the cake in the tin to cool, then slice and serve.

Apple and nut crumble cake

A cake that's particularly perfect for the cooler months, when apples are that bit sweeter, the warmth of spice is that much more enticing and the need for a baked treat is that much stronger. A simple ingredient list that makes for a most satisfying dessert or morning tea. This recipe also employs an interesting technique whereby the dry ingredients are added to the butter and sugar before the wet ingredients go in – a bit of extra insurance to create a smooth, creamy, emulsified cake batter.

Before you begin: Leave your butter out on the bench overnight to ensure it's at room temperature when you're ready to bake. Alternatively, warm a ceramic bowl in a low oven, then place it upside down over the butter and leave for 10 minutes.

Preheat your oven to 160°C (315°F) fan-forced. Prepare your springform tin by greasing the sides with butter (or olive oil spray) and wrapping the base with baking paper. Clip the sides in place and trim any excess paper to stop it from burning while baking.

To make the crumble topping, combine all the ingredients in a bowl and use your fingertips to mix everything together, ensuring there are no white floury bits. Set aside.

For the cake, add the butter and sugar to the bowl of a stand mixer fitted with the paddle attachment, and beat on a high speed until the mixture is light, fluffy and almost white in colour. This will take about 5–7 minutes. Stop and scrape the sides of the bowl with a spatula as needed.

In a separate bowl, combine the flour, baking powder, cinnamon, nutmeg and salt. Set aside.

Crack the eggs into a small bowl and add in the vanilla extract and milk. Whisk to combine, then set aside.

Once the butter and sugar are creamed together, stop the mixer. Tip in the dry ingredients and mix on a low speed until combined, about 30 seconds. Add in the egg mixture and mix on a low speed until a smooth batter forms. Stop once during this mix and scrape the bowl to ensure an even batter. When you have a smooth batter, stop and remove the bowl from the mixer; use a spatula to stir in the apples and lemon zest.

Pour the batter into the tin and top with the crumble mix, being sure to distribute it evenly.

Bake for 60–70 minutes, until a skewer inserted into the centre of the cake comes out clean. Allow the cake to cool completely before removing the ring of the tin. Slice and serve.

Makes: 1 cake, enough
    for 10 slices
Active time: 20 minutes
Inactive time: 1 hour 15 minutes

Kitchenalia: 23 cm (9 inch)
    round springform cake tin,
    stand mixer fitted with
    the paddle attachment

150 g (5½ oz) unsalted butter,
    at room temperature, cubed,
    plus extra for greasing
250 g (9 oz) white
    (granulated) sugar
240 g (9 oz) plain
    (all-purpose) flour
1½ teaspoons baking powder
1 teaspoon ground cinnamon
½ teaspoon freshly grated
    nutmeg
¼ teaspoon fine sea salt
3 eggs
2 teaspoons vanilla extract
120 ml (4 fl oz) whole milk
3 apples (Granny Smith
    preferred), peeled, cored and
    thinly sliced
1 tablespoon lemon zest (about
    1 lemon)

Crumble topping
100 g (3½ oz) finely chopped
    nuts (walnuts, hazelnuts,
    almonds, pecans)
50 g (1¾ oz) unsalted butter,
    at room temperature
50 g (1¾ oz) soft brown sugar
25 g (1 oz) plain
    (all-purpose) flour
½ teaspoon ground cinnamon
Pinch of fine sea salt

Pineapple and coconut cake with cream cheese frosting

Makes: 1 cake, enough for
   12–16 slices
Active time: 20 minutes
Inactive time: 1 hour

Kitchenalia: 35 x 23 x 5 cm
   (14 x 9 x 2 inch) cake tin
   (approximately), stand
   mixer fitted with the paddle
   attachment

1 x 430 g (15¼ oz) tin crushed
   pineapple in juice
3 eggs
330 g (11¾ oz) white
   (granulated) sugar
1 teaspoon vanilla extract
150 ml (5 fl oz) neutral oil
90 g (3¼ oz) unsweetened
   desiccated coconut
320 g (11¼ oz) spelt flour
   (see note on page 266)
½ teaspoon baking powder
2 teaspoons bicarbonate of
   soda (baking soda)
½ teaspoon fine sea salt

Icing
120 g (4¼ oz) unsalted butter,
   at room temperature
250 g (9 oz) block cream
   cheese, at room temperature
175 g (6 oz) icing
   (confectioners') sugar, sifted
1 teaspoon vanilla extract
Pinch of fine sea salt
110 g (3¾ oz) coconut flakes
   (see note)

This cake reminds me of home. Growing up, we used to have something similar that must have had bran mixed into the batter, giving it a slightly nutty flavour. I've mixed desiccated coconut and wholemeal flour to give it that lovely nuttiness I remember so intensely from my childhood. Using tinned pineapple means that you can make this cake all year round.

Before you begin: You can make this cake dairy-free by omitting the icing and simply serving it with coconut yoghurt and a dusting of icing (confectioners') sugar. Keep the finished cake and any leftovers in the fridge.

Preheat your oven to 160°C (315°F) fan-forced. Grease and line the base and sides of your cake tin with baking paper.

In a mixing bowl, whisk together the pineapple (including the juice), eggs, sugar, vanilla and oil. In another mixing bowl, combine the desiccated coconut, flour, baking powder, bicarbonate of soda and salt. Tip the dry ingredients into the wet and whisk to combine.

Pour the batter into the tin and bake for 30–40 minutes, until a skewer inserted into the centre of the cake comes out clean. Remove from the oven and allow to cool completely in the tin.

To make the icing, beat the butter in the bowl of a stand mixer fitted with the paddle attachment until uniform and light. Beat in the cream cheese, followed by the icing sugar, vanilla and salt.

Lift the cake onto a platter or board, removing the baking paper from underneath. Spread the icing over the cake and finish with the coconut flakes. Cut into squares and serve.

Note: For a stronger toasted-coconut flavour, toast the coconut flakes on a baking tray in a 160°C (315°F) fan-forced oven for about 5 minutes.

Strawberry, ricotta and spelt loaf

Makes: 1 loaf, enough for
    8–10 slices
Active time: 20 minutes
Inactive time: 1 hour 30 minutes

Kitchenalia: 21 x 11 cm
    (8¼ x 4¼ inch) loaf tin,
    stand mixer fitted with
    the paddle attachment

Before you begin: Leave your butter and eggs out on the bench overnight to come to room temperature. Alternatively, carefully place your eggs (in the shell) into a glass of lukewarm water, where they will come to temperature in about 10 minutes. To speed up the butter softening, warm a ceramic bowl in a low oven, then place it upside down over the butter and leave for 10 minutes.

225 g (8 oz) spelt flour
    (see note)
1½ teaspoons baking powder
½ teaspoon fine sea salt
60 ml (2 fl oz) whole milk
100 g (3½ oz) ricotta
3 eggs, at room temperature
1 teaspoon vanilla extract
250 g (9 oz) strawberries
    (1 punnet)
1 tablespoon lemon zest
    (about 1 lemon)
175 g (6 oz) unsalted butter,
    at room temperature or
    slightly warmer
    (but not melted)
250 g (9 oz) white
    (granulated) sugar
1 tablespoon raw sugar

This butter cake is so heavenly that when I first tested it, my partner and I devoured the entire thing in one day! Butter-based cakes can be tricky to master, but they are oh-so-good when you do, and a foundational kitchen skill to boot! It's crucial that your ingredients are at room temperature; you are bringing together disparate items – flour, eggs, butter and sugar – that don't necessarily want to be friends. Your best chance for a successful emulsion is to give them as much in common as possible – in this case, their temperature. As with mayonnaise, if some of your ingredients are too cold or too warm, the mixture will split (not the end of the world, but the cake will be a little denser and oilier, rather than light and fluffy).

Preheat the oven to 160°C (315°F) fan-forced. Line your loaf tin with baking paper, allowing the sides of the paper to extend past the edges of the tin.

Combine the flour, baking powder and salt in a bowl. In a separate bowl, combine the milk and ricotta. Set both bowls aside.

Crack the eggs into a small bowl (do not whisk) and add the vanilla extract. Set aside.

Hull and chop half of the strawberries and mix them with the lemon zest in another bowl. Hull and cut the remaining strawberries into rounds. Set both lots of strawberries aside, keeping them separate.

Add the butter and white sugar to the bowl of a stand mixer fitted with the paddle attachment and beat on a high speed until the mixture is light, fluffy and almost white in colour. This will take about 5–7 minutes. Stop the machine and scrape down the sides as needed.

With the machine running, add the eggs, letting one slide in at a time, and waiting until each egg is fully incorporated before adding in the next.

Stop the machine, add in half the flour mixture and turn the machine on to low speed to just combine. Add in the milk-ricotta mixture and mix until combined. Finally, stop the machine again and add in the remaining flour mixture, along with the chopped strawberries and lemon zest. Return the machine to a low speed and mix until it all just comes together.

Pour the batter into the tin and top with the rounds of strawberries. Sprinkle the raw sugar over the strawberries and bake for 70–80 minutes, until a skewer inserted into the centre of the cake comes out clean.

Let the loaf cool in the tin before tipping it out. Slice and serve.

Note: Spelt flour is worth seeking out – I love the nuttiness it gives to cakes – but if you can't find it, swap it for wholemeal or plain (all-purpose) flour.

Raspberry and mascarpone tart

Makes: 1 x 30 cm (12 inch) tart,
enough for 12–14 slices
Active time: 1 hour
Inactive time: 5 hours

Kitchenalia: 30 cm (12 inch)
fluted tart tin with removable
base, stand mixer fitted with
the paddle attachment

Tart
1 baked Sweet tart shell
(page 255)
1 batch Vanilla bean crème
diplomat (page 256), using
350 g (12 oz) mascarpone in
place of the whipped cream
500 g (1 lb 2 oz) fresh
raspberries, left whole
(about 4 punnets)

Raspberry compote
200 g (7 oz) fresh
or frozen raspberries
75 g (2½ oz) white
(granulated) sugar
Juice of 1 lemon
Pinch of fine sea salt

I can't stand desserts that are just a façade. This tart tastes as good as it looks – and it looks really good! Lay the raspberries out like I've done here if you have the patience (I promise it's therapeutic), or simply toss them onto the tart. It will be gorgeous either way.

Before you begin: This makes a large and impressive tart. To make a smaller, 23 cm (9 inch) tart for 8–10 people, reduce the ingredients of the tart by 25 per cent (you'll have leftover pastry dough to store in your freezer). You can make the tart shell dough and line the tin a day in advance. You can also make the raspberry compote a day ahead.

You'll need to prepare a Sweet tart shell (see page 255) as well as a batch of Vanilla bean crème diplomat (see page 256), replacing the cream with mascarpone (see ingredients list).

Prepare your Sweet tart shell (allow it to cool) and the Vanilla bean and mascarpone crème diplomat.

To make your raspberry compote, set a small saucepan over a low heat and add the raspberries, sugar, lemon juice and salt. Simmer until soft and thick, about 15–20 minutes. Pass through a sieve to get rid of the raspberry seeds. Once cooled, spread the compote across the entire base of the baked tart shell, getting all the way to the edges.

Top with the crème diplomat, spreading it out in an even layer.

To finish, top the tart with the fresh raspberries set in concentric circles, or simply tumble them onto the tart to cover the crème diplomat. Refrigerate the completed tart for at least 2 hours (but up to a day in advance) to allow everything to set. Serve cold from the fridge.

Meyer lemon tart

A classic lemon tart is rather like a little black dress – it never goes out of style. Meyer lemons are a sweeter, less sour, relative of regular lemons. I love them for this dessert but you can, of course, use regular lemons if you can't find Meyers.

Before you begin: You'll need to prepare a Sweet tart shell (see page 255) for this recipe.

Prepare your Sweet tart shell and allow it to cool.

Now make your lemon curd. In a small, non-reactive (stainless steel or enamel-lined) saucepan, combine the lemon zest and juice, sugar, eggs, egg yolks and salt, whisking well to ensure the egg is incorporated.

Preheat your oven to 130°C (250°F) fan-forced.

Set a fine mesh sieve over a heatproof mixing bowl and set aside. Place the saucepan holding the lemon mixture over a low heat while continuously whisking. Make sure you whisk thoroughly and get into the edges. Continue to heat until the mixture thickens and reaches a temperature of 68°C (155°F) on your thermometer – this will take about 10 minutes. Immediately pour the mixture through the sieve into the bowl using a rubber spatula to gently push it through. Discard any coagulated bits. The curd will still be quite a thin liquid at this point.

Gently whisk the butter into the hot curd a few pieces at a time. Continue to whisk until the butter has completely melted. Pour enough curd straight into your baked, cooled tart shell to come about 1 cm (½ inch) from the top of the shell (see notes).

Bake the tart for 20–25 minutes. The filling will still be wobbly when you take it out.

Allow the tart to cool at room temperature. It is at its peak served within a few hours. Alternatively, you can chill the tart in the refrigerator for several hours if you don't intend on serving it straight away, but it will lose a little of its suppleness. Slice and serve cold, with whipped cream or crème fraîche.

Notes: If making the 23 cm (9 inch) tart, you'll have plenty of curd so fill the tart with the curd right to the top, without it spilling over the pastry. You may have extra curd, depending on the thickness of your pastry, that you can refrigerate and save to serve with scones or cake – it will hold for over a week.

The Ricciarelli recipe (see page 288) is the perfect destiny for your leftover egg whites.

Makes: 1 tart, the larger enough for 12–16 slices, or the smaller enough for 8–10 slices
Active time: 50 minutes
Inactive time: 2 hours 30 minutes

Kitchenalia: Fluted tart tin with removable base, either 23 cm (9 inches) or 30 cm (12 inches) wide, and 3.5 cm (1½ inches) deep, thermometer, stand mixer fitted with the paddle attachment

1 baked Sweet tart shell (page 255)

Lemon curd for 23 cm (9 inch) tart
Zest of 4 Meyer lemons
280 ml (10 fl oz) lemon juice (about 5–7 lemons)
225 g (8 oz) white (granulated) sugar
8 large eggs
4 egg yolks
Pinch of fine sea salt
190 g (6¾ oz) unsalted butter, cubed

Lemon curd for 30 (12 inch) tart
Zest of 6 Meyer lemons
375 ml (13 fl oz) lemon juice (about 8–10 lemons)
300 g (10½ oz) white (granulated) sugar
10 large eggs
6 large egg yolks
Pinch of fine sea salt
250 g (9 oz) unsalted butter, cubed

To serve
Whipped cream or crème fraîche

Fig and hazelnut frangipane tart

Makes: 1 tart, the larger enough
  for 12–16 slices, or the smaller
  enough for 8–10 slices
Active time: 1 hour
Inactive time: 2 hours 30 minutes

Kitchenalia: 30 cm (12 inch)
  fluted tart tin with removable
  base (see note), stand mixer
  fitted with the paddle
  attachment, food processor

1 baked Sweet tart shell
  (page 255)
11–12 ripe figs, cut in half
1 tablespoon white
  (granulated) sugar

Hazelnut frangipane
140 g (5 oz) hazelnuts
80 g (2¾ oz) soft brown sugar
1 tablespoon water
130 g (4½ oz) unsalted butter,
  at room temperature
80 g (2¾ oz) white
  (granulated) sugar
Pinch of fine sea salt
2 eggs, at room temperature
2 teaspoons vanilla extract
80 g (2¾ oz) plain
  (all-purpose) flour

To serve
Crème fraîche

We really amp up the hazelnut flavour by first making a hazelnut praline, which is then used to make a traditional frangipane. The combination of figs with hazelnuts in a crisp, sweet tart shell is pure bliss – the smells coming out of your kitchen will leave you intoxicated (in the best way).

Before you begin: You'll need to prepare a Sweet tart shell (see page 255) for this recipe.

The frangipane can be made a day or two in advance and kept in the fridge, but it will need to come out of the fridge at least 30 minutes before using, so you can easily spread it into the tart shell. The baked tart is best eaten on the day it's made.

Prepare your Sweet tart shell and allow it to cool.

For the hazelnut frangipane, preheat your oven to 150°C (300°F) fan-forced. Place the hazelnuts on a baking tray and toast them for 30 minutes. If using hazelnuts with the skin still on, once toasted, tip them into a tea towel and use the tea towel to rub as much of the skin off as possible. Leave the oven on.

Line a baking tray with baking paper and set it aside. In a small stainless-steel saucepan, heat the brown sugar and water over a low–medium heat, stirring occasionally using a heatproof spoon or spatula, until it's smoking and has turned a deep shade of amber. Add in the hazelnuts and stir to coat. If your caramel turns grainy after adding the hazelnuts, simply continue to cook it until the sugar melts again and forms a glossy sheen on the nuts. Carefully tip the praline onto your baking tray, spread it out, and allow to cool completely.

Once cool, break the hazelnut praline into pieces and process them in a food processor until a thick paste forms. Combine the praline paste in a bowl with the butter, white sugar, salt, eggs and vanilla. Add in the flour last and stir to just combine. Set aside.

Increase your oven temperature to 160°C (320°F) fan-forced.

Spread the frangipane over the base of the tart shell, smoothing it out with an offset or regular spatula. Nestle the figs into the frangipane, cut-side up. Sprinkle the tablespoon of sugar over the figs and bake for 50–60 minutes, until the top is golden and the figs are jammy.

Allow the tart to cool, then serve with crème fraîche.

Note: For a smaller tart, simply use a 23 cm (9 inch) fluted tart tin with a removable base and halve the frangipane recipe and the number of figs. Reduce the baking time to 40–50 minutes.

Strawberries in rosé with vanilla shortbread

Makes: 16 shortbread
  and enough strawberries
  to serve 6
Active time: 20 minutes
Inactive time: 10 hours

Kitchenalia: 23 cm (9 inch)
  fluted tart tin with removable
  base, food processor

Before you begin: You will need to
macerate half the strawberries with
the sugar and rosé in your fridge
overnight to really extract as much
strawberry flavour as possible. The
shortbread can be baked a day ahead
and kept in an airtight container.

Strawberries
500 g (1 lb 2 oz) strawberries
  (about 2 punnets)
2 teaspoons white
  (granulated) sugar
60 ml (2 fl oz) good-quality
  rosé wine
½ teaspoon orange zest
  (optional)

Shortbread
225 g (8 oz) plain
  (all-purpose) flour
75 g (2½ oz) white
  (granulated) sugar, plus
  an extra 1 tablespoon
1 vanilla bean, split and seeds
  scraped (see note)
150 g (5½ oz) cold unsalted
  butter, cubed
¼ teaspoon fine sea salt
1 egg yolk
2 teaspoons vanilla extract

This is an elegant and simple dessert. Be sure to make this when strawberries
are at their absolute peak – late spring and into summer.

To prepare the strawberries:

Hull and slice half the strawberries into quarters or eighths, depending on
their size. Combine the strawberries with the sugar, rosé and orange zest
(if using). Cover and leave in your fridge overnight.

On the day of serving, hull and slice the remaining strawberries to the
same size as the macerating strawberries and toss the two batches
together. Allow to sit for at least an hour, or as long as 3 hours.

To make the shortbread:

Preheat your oven to 160°C (320°F) fan-forced.

Combine the flour, sugar, vanilla bean seeds, butter and salt in the
bowl of a food processor. Process until the mixture resembles coarse
breadcrumbs. Add in the egg yolk and vanilla extract and pulse a few
times until the dough comes together.

Press the dough into your fluted tart tin, going all the way to the edges
and ensuring the top is flat. Use a knife to score the dough into 16 wedges.

Bake in the oven for 30–35 minutes, until the dough is lightly golden
around the edges. Remove from the oven and dust the top with the extra
tablespoon of sugar. Allow to cool, before slicing through where you've
scored the dough.

To assemble:

Divide the strawberries, with their juices, between small bowls and serve
with a piece of shortbread alongside.

Note: Reserve the vanilla bean pod and mix it in with the soaking strawberries
as soon as you've used the seeds for the shortbread.

Seasonal adjustment: This shortbread is also lovely served with a scoop of seasonal
fruit ice cream, or simply with perfectly ripe stone fruit, such as peaches.

Plum galette with fennel crème Anglaise

This is my favourite sweet galette. The combination of tart plums with the earthy sweetness of fennel seed has haunted me since I first tasted it at Chez Panisse. The stone fruit of California is some of the best in the world – my favourite variety was a cross between a plum and an apricot called Flavour King (how could you not love?!). In Australia I've grown to love blood plums, a variety with a deep, dark crimson flesh that makes for an exceptional galette.

Nature must agree with me on this combination. When these plums are at their best, it's the moment for wild fennel to be growing on roadsides, along highways and train tracks. I was once told that early settlers in California spread fennel seed as they travelled so they could find their way back a year later. Most people don't know that you can cut that wild fennel, give it a good wash and cook with it. It's beautiful, fragrant and, best of all, free. Simply lay the whole seedheads on a baking tray and leave them to dry, then store the seeds in a glass jar. In lieu of wild fennel, I've written this recipe using shop-bought fennel seeds.

Before you begin: Make your Flaky pastry (see page 254) a day ahead, or at least several hours in advance, so it has plenty of time to chill. You can make the dough, roll it out and leave it refrigerated until you're ready to cook. You also want the fennel seeds and the cream to infuse overnight (at least 8 hours). The crème Anglaise, in its entirety, can be made a day ahead.

To make the fennel crème Anglaise:

Toast the fennel seeds in a dry pan over a medium heat until fragrant and just beginning to smoke. Transfer the toasted seeds to a mortar and pestle and crush them slightly. Mix with the milk and cream, cover tightly and leave in the fridge overnight.

The following day, set up a sieve over a bowl and set aside. Heat the fennel-infused milk and cream in a small saucepan over a low–medium heat until it starts to steam.

Combine the egg yolks, salt and sugar in another bowl. Slowly stream the hot cream and milk mixture into the yolks while constantly whisking.

Return the custard to the pan and place it over a low heat. Cook, stirring constantly with a wooden spoon, until it becomes thick enough to coat the back of the spoon. Strain it through the sieve into the bowl, to remove the fennel seeds, then stir in the extra 100 ml (3½ fl oz) cream and the vanilla paste. Immediately transfer to an airtight container, cover with a lid and refrigerate until well chilled.

Note: Vanilla bean paste and vanilla extract are interchangeable here. I like using paste in this crème Anglaise because I like to see the vanilla bean seeds but that's purely an aesthetic choice.

Makes: 1 large galette,
   enough for 10–12 slices
Active time: 45 minutes
Inactive time: 9 hours

Kitchenalia: Round 30 cm
   (12 inch) pizza tray,
   pastry brush

Galette
1 round Flaky pastry (page 254),
   rolled out to a thickness of
   3–4 mm (about ⅛ inch)
1 kg (2 lb 4 oz) blood plums
50 g (1¾ oz) unsalted butter,
   at room temperature
50 g (1¾ oz) white
   (granulated) sugar
50 g (1¾ oz) almond meal
1 tablespoon plain
   (all-purpose) flour
1 egg, plus 1 egg beaten with
   1 teaspoon water (egg wash)
2 teaspoons vanilla extract
   (see note)
½ teaspoon almond extract
Pinch of fine sea salt
2 tablespoons raw sugar
1 tablespoon caster
   (superfine) sugar

Fennel crème Anglaise
3 tablespoons fennel seeds
150 ml (5 fl oz) whole milk
150 ml (5 fl oz) single (pure)
   cream, plus an extra
   100 ml (3½ fl oz)
100 g (3½ oz) egg yolks
   (from about 5–6 eggs)
Pinch of fine sea salt
70 g (2½ oz) white
   (granulated) sugar
1 tablespoon vanilla bean paste

To make the galette:

Preheat your oven to 200°C (400°F) fan-forced.

Cut the plums in half and remove the stones. Reserve and dice any bits of fruit that cling to the stone and set aside. Cut each plum half into 2–3 wedges and set these aside, too.

In a mixing bowl, beat the butter and white sugar together using a wooden spoon or spatula. Add in the almond meal, flour, 1 egg, the vanilla and almond extracts and the salt. Mix to combine. This is a simple frangipane.

Place your pastry round onto a round pizza tray (or baking tray) lined with baking paper. Spread the frangipane on the base of your flaky pastry round, leaving a 3–4 cm (1¼–1½ inch) clean border. Spread the diced plum over the frangipane, then lay the plum wedges in concentric circles, slightly overlapping. Fold the edge of the pastry over the plums, creating a 3–4 cm (1¼–1½ inch) crust. Use a pastry brush to brush the crust with the egg wash, then sprinkle it with the raw sugar. Finally, sprinkle the caster sugar over the plums.

Transfer the galette to the oven and immediately turn the heat down to 180°C (350°F) fan-forced. Bake for 40–50 minutes, until the galette is deeply golden and the fruit is viscously bubbly.

Leave the galette to cool on a cooling rack, being sure to remove the baking paper from underneath to keep the pastry from going soft. Cut into slices and serve with the cold fennel crème Anglaise.

Seasonal adjustment: This galette recipe works brilliantly with apricots in place of plums. In winter, swap the fennel seeds in the crème Anglaise for a couple of tablespoons of Armagnac or a teaspoon of ground cinnamon, and the plums for apples or rhubarb.

There is absolute simplicity, almost naivety, in one of my favourite moments of kitchen alchemy: it's the moment in making a galette when the fruit starts to give up its jamminess, juices bubbling, the fruit threatening to collapse just as the edges of the pastry become golden and flaky. A galette has remained a seasonal staple of the Chez Panisse kitchen for a reason, and it was a tradition that I brought with me when I came to Australia. This buttery pastry galette, rich and crisp, is the ultimate blank canvas for the best of the season. It is the most wonderful of recipes, or indeed concepts, that deserves a place in every kitchen: so versatile, so forgiving; so therapeutic to make, so impressive to serve. If you are only going to have one pastry recipe in your arsenal, this is it.

Blackberry and chocolate trifle

This is a beautiful holiday or celebratory dessert, and is particularly wonderful when you can find delicious fresh blackberries. I especially love that it's made in its entirety a day ahead, so I don't have to worry about dessert on a day that might involve a lot of other cooking. Even better, it's easily transported in its dish, and honestly, looks and tastes great, no matter how you put it together. The ultimate party dessert.

Before you begin: To make this easier, you can make all or some of the components a day ahead (sponge cake, compote and pudding). You could also swap the sponge cake for a shop-bought sponge or Italian pandoro. You'll want this trifle to sit for at least 8 hours so it all soaks together. Heads up: making a trifle requires lots of mixing bowls – best to clean them as you go, so you can reuse them.

To make the sponge cake:

Preheat your oven to 180°C (350°F) fan-forced. Prepare your baking pan by lining the base and sides with baking paper. The lining doesn't need to be perfect, as the cake will be torn into pieces when you assemble.

In the bowl of your stand mixer fitted with the whisk attachment, whisk the eggs and sugar together on a high speed until light, fluffy and voluminous. This will take about 5 minutes.

In a separate bowl, mix the flour, baking powder and salt.

When the eggs and sugar are ready, stop the machine. Tip in the flour mixture, add the vanilla and whisk on a high speed, until just combined.

Pour this batter into your tin and bake for 20 minutes, until a skewer inserted into the centre of the cake comes out clean. Set aside and leave to cool in the tin.

When the cake has cooled, slice it through the middle, in half, so you have two thin sheets of cake.

To make the blackberry compote:

Combine the blackberries, sugar and the 200 ml (7 fl oz) water in a medium-sized saucepan set over a medium heat. Bring to a low simmer and cook, stirring every few minutes, until it has thickened and is bubbly, about 10–15 minutes. Pour the compote into an airtight container and set aside. Rinse out your saucepan and return it to the stove.

In the saucepan, combine the gelatine powder with the extra 2 tablespoons water. Stir to dissolve. Allow this to sit for 5 minutes, then place the pot over the lowest-possible heat to just melt the gelatine, gently swirling the pan so it melts evenly. As soon as the gelatine has completely melted and no granules remain, scrape the gelatine liquid into the hot blackberry mixture. Add the lemon zest and juice and stir to combine. Allow the compote to cool, then cover and chill in the fridge until set. This will take at least 2 hours. The finished texture will be like a thick blackberry jam.

Makes: Enough to serve 12–14
Active time: 1 hour 30 minutes–2 hours
Inactive time: 8 hours 30 minutes

Kitchenalia: 35 x 20 cm (14 x 8 inch) baking pan (approximately), stand mixer fitted with the whisk attachment, glass trifle bowl

Sponge cake
4 eggs, at room temperature
165 g (5¾ oz) white (granulated) sugar
100 g (3½ oz) plain (all-purpose) flour
1 teaspoon baking powder
¼ teaspoon fine sea salt
2 teaspoons vanilla extract

Blackberry compote
500 g (1 lb 2 oz) fresh blackberries (about 4 punnets) halved, or use frozen
220 g (7¾ oz) white (granulated) sugar
200 ml (7 fl oz) water, plus an extra 2 tablespoons
2 teaspoons gelatine powder
Zest and juice of 1 lemon

Chocolate pudding

3 tablespoons cocoa powder
  (see note)
2 tablespoons cornflour
  (cornstarch)
60 ml (2 fl oz) whole milk,
  plus an extra 500 ml (17 fl oz)
1 egg, plus 2 egg yolks
¼ teaspoon fine sea salt
100 g (3½ oz) white
  (granulated) sugar
50 g (1¾ oz) cold unsalted
  butter, cubed
140 g (5 oz) 70 per cent dark
  chocolate, broken into pieces
1 teaspoon vanilla extract

To assemble

500 ml (17 fl oz) thickened
  (whipping) cream
100 ml (3½ fl oz) amaretto
250 g (9 oz) fresh blackberries
  (about 2 punnets)

To make the chocolate pudding:

In a mixing bowl, combine the cocoa powder, cornflour, the 60 ml (2 fl oz) of milk, the eggs, egg yolks and salt. Whisk until smooth and set aside.

In a medium-sized saucepan, heat the extra 500 ml (17 fl oz) of milk with the sugar until scalding and steamy.

Slowly stream the hot milk into the mixing bowl while whisking constantly, then scrape the custard from the bowl back into the pan. Place the pan over a low heat and continue to stir with a whisk until the custard begins to bubble. Turn the heat off and add in the butter, chocolate and vanilla. Mix to completely melt the butter and chocolate.

Pour the pudding into an airtight container and cover with a piece of baking paper, pressing it directly onto the surface of the pudding to prevent a skin from forming. Leave in the fridge until completely chilled.

To assemble:

Whip the cream to soft peaks either by hand using a whisk, or in the bowl of a stand mixer fitted with the whisk attachment. Set aside.

Begin assembling by covering the bottom of your trifle bowl with a few pieces of torn cake. Drizzle one third of the amaretto onto the cake. Top that with one third of the blackberry compote, followed by one third of the chocolate pudding and, finally, one third of the whipped cream. You don't need to create completely smooth layers – I prefer to dot everything in spoonfuls, being sure to drop a few spoonfuls at the edge of the glass bowl, so you can see the layers of the finished trifle.

Repeat this step twice more, making for three layers in total, finishing with a last layer of whipped cream (add the top layer of cream just before serving if it's piled too high to be able to cover the bowl). At this stage, cover the bowl and refrigerate the trifle overnight, or for at least 8 hours.

Top the trifle with the fresh blackberries just before serving.

Note: Dutch-process cocoa has a deeper, richer colour and a more intense chocolate flavour, while regular cocoa powder is redder in colour, contains less fat and therefore is a little less intense in chocolate flavour. Dutch-process cocoa is treated in a way that raises its pH levels, making it more neutral and less acidic. If the packaging does not say "Dutch process" you can assume it's regular cocoa powder. This is important, because when baking you are often relying on the reaction of bicarbonate of soda (baking soda) and baking powder with acids in the batter to create the gases that give your cake its rise. The different cocoa powders can be used interchangeably in any recipe where leavening is not required – as is the case with this pudding, as well as in icings, custards and mousse – but in cakes, such as the Chocolate cake with dark chocolate and cream cheese frosting (see page 296), they can react quite differently. Keep away from drinking chocolate, which contains added sugars and may result in an overly sweet pudding or cake.

Sticky toffee chocolate and prune cake

A cake similar to sticky toffee date pudding, but with deeper, more wintry notes of chocolate and prune. The only tricky thing is that you must serve this dessert warm, but I give you some notes on that below. This is a comforting and rich way to end a winter meal.

Preheat your oven to 160°C (315°F) fan-forced. Line the base of your cake tin with baking paper and grease the sides with butter. Set aside.

Combine the prunes, rum (or tea) and water in a small saucepan and bring to a simmer over a low–medium heat. Once simmering, turn the heat off, cover the pan and set it aside for 10 minutes.

In a mixing bowl, combine the flour, cocoa powder, baking powder, bicarbonate of soda and salt.

In another bowl, combine the sugar, egg, vanilla and milk.

In a food processor or blender, blend the prunes and their cooking liquid with the butter. The warm prune mixture will melt the butter as it blends. When completely smooth, whisk this into the sugar-egg mix, then pour it all into the bowl of the dry ingredients. Whisk until there are no lumps, then pour the batter into the cake tin.

Bake for 30–40 minutes, or until a skewer inserted into the centre of the cake comes out clean.

While the cake bakes (or ahead of time), prepare the toffee sauce. Combine the sugar, cream and butter in a small saucepan. Bring this to a simmer over a low heat and continue simmering for about 10 minutes, whisking it every few minutes. Finish with the vanilla extract and the pinch of salt.

While the cake is still warm, remove it from the cake tin and place it on your serving plate or on a cake stand. Use a chopstick or skewer to poke a few holes in the top of the cake, then pour half of the hot toffee sauce over it. Reserve the remaining sauce to serve on the individual slices.

Lightly whip the cream to very soft peaks, either by hand using a whisk, or in the bowl of a stand mixer fitted with the whisk attachment.

Slice the cake and serve warm on plates, with a drizzle of the warm toffee sauce and a dollop of the whipped cream.

Notes: This cake must be served warm – if you can time its baking to serve straight from the oven, even better! An easy way to do this: before dinner, mix and combine your dry ingredients and your wet ingredients, keeping them separate. All you need to do then is combine the two, pour the mixture into the prepared baking tin and pop it in the oven just before you sit down for dinner. You can also make your toffee sauce in advance; you'll just need to warm it through again over a low heat before pouring it over the cake. If you time this well, your cake will be just out of the oven and still warm when you're ready for dessert.

If you want to bake the cake ahead, you can warm it in a 100°C (200°F) fan-forced oven for about 10 minutes just before serving. Pour half the toffee sauce onto the cake, cover it and place it in the oven. Pour the remaining hot toffee sauce over the cake as you are serving.

Makes: 1 cake, enough
for 8 slices
Active time: 40 minutes
Inactive time: 40 minutes

Kitchenalia: 20 cm (8 inch)
round cake tin, food processor
or blender

170 g (6 oz) pitted prunes
80 ml (2½ fl oz) rum
(or steeped black tea)
125 ml (4 fl oz) water
130 g (4¾ oz) plain
(all-purpose) flour
40 g (1½ oz) Dutch-process
cocoa powder
1 teaspoon baking powder
¼ teaspoon bicarbonate of
soda (baking soda)
¼ teaspoon fine sea salt
160 g (5¾ oz) soft brown sugar
1 egg
1 tablespoon vanilla extract
100 ml (3½ fl oz) whole milk
60 g (2¼ oz) unsalted butter,
plus extra for greasing

Toffee sauce
150 g (5½ oz) soft brown sugar
300 ml (10½ fl oz) single
(pure) cream
50 g (1¾ oz) unsalted butter
1 teaspoon vanilla extract
Pinch of fine sea salt

To serve
150 ml (5 fl oz) thickened
(whipping) cream

Vanilla panna cotta with cherries

Makes: Enough to serve 8
Active time: 30 minutes
Inactive time: 9 hours

Kitchenalia: Dariole or
    individual brioche moulds
    (optional)

Panna cotta
900 ml (30 fl oz) single
    (pure) cream
80 g (2¾ oz) white
    (granulated) sugar
3 vanilla beans, split and
    seeds scraped
1 strip lemon zest (peeled using
    a vegetable peeler)
2¼ teaspoons gelatine powder
3 tablespoons water

Cherries
225 g (8 oz) fresh cherries,
    pitted
70 g (2½ oz) white
    (granulated) sugar
125 ml (4 fl oz) water
1 teaspoon vanilla extract
½ teaspoon almond extract
3 tablespoons lemon juice

A perfectly wobbly and mildly sweet panna cotta is one of the great desserts. It's as much about texture as it is about flavour. This is a dessert to carry you through the seasons: with citrus in winter, poached pears in autumn, strawberries in spring, and almost any stone fruit in summer. If unmoulding a panna cotta makes you nervous, simply set and serve it in little bowls – you won't be able to appreciate the wobble as much, but the flavour won't be compromised in the slightest.

Before you begin: The amount of vanilla bean in this recipe is luxurious – you can cut it down to one vanilla bean and still have a delicious panna cotta.

A few maraschino cherries served with each panna cotta is a lovely, and easy, option if you can't get your hands on good fresh cherries.

For the panna cotta, combine the cream, sugar, vanilla beans (pods and seeds) and lemon zest in a small saucepan and place over a low heat. Stir continuously and heat until the cream begins to steam, then turn off the heat and allow it to sit while the flavours steep for at least 30 minutes. Scoop out the lemon and vanilla bean pods. (Tip: rinse and dry the vanilla bean pods and store them with your sugar for vanilla-scented sugar.)

In a small saucepan, sprinkle the gelatine over the water and whisk to combine. Leave it to sit for 5 minutes while the gelatine absorbs the water. Add a ladleful of the cream mixture into the hydrated gelatine and warm over a low heat until the gelatine has completely dissolved. Whisk this into the cream mixture, pour into a jug and place in the fridge. After about 1 hour, the mixture should have started to cool. Give it a gentle whisk to redistribute the vanilla bean seeds so they don't all end up on the bottom. Alternatively, to speed this process up, you can chill the mixture over a bowl of ice whilst constantly stirring until it has noticeably thickened.

Pour the panna cotta mixture into individual dariole moulds, or pour it into little custard pots or ramekins that you'll serve the dessert in, avoiding the need to unmould. Cover tightly with aluminium foil or beeswax wrappers and leave in the fridge overnight to set.

To prepare the cherries, put the cherries in a glass jar. Heat the sugar and water in a small pot, bring it to a boil and stir until the sugar has completely dissolved. Stir in the vanilla extract, almond extract and lemon juice, then pour over the cherries. Allow to cool before you seal the jar and leave it in the fridge overnight.

When ready to serve, either unmould each panna cotta (see note) onto a dessert plate, or serve them in the vessels you chilled them in. Spoon some marinated cherries and their syrup over each panna cotta. Serve cold.

Note: To help unmould each panna cotta, you can soak a tea towel in very hot water and wrap it around the base of the mould for a few seconds to help release the sides, before flipping it out.

Polenta chiffon cake with vanilla cream and strawberries

Makes: 1 cake, enough for
10–12 slices
Active time: 50 minutes
Inactive time: 2 hours

Kitchenalia: 2 x 20 cm (8 inch)
round cake tins, cake stand,
stand mixer fitted with the
whisk attachment

Before you begin: You will need
to prepare a batch of the Vanilla
bean crème diplomat (see page 256)
for this recipe, which can be made
a day ahead.

5 eggs, separated, plus
1 extra egg white, at
room temperature
200 g (7 oz) plain
(all-purpose) flour
1 tablespoon baking powder
1 teaspoon fine sea salt
250 g (9 oz) white (granulated)
sugar, plus an extra 35 g
(1¼ oz)
80 g (2¾ oz) polenta
160 ml (5¼ fl oz) whole milk
100 ml (3½ fl oz) extra-virgin
olive oil
1½ teaspoons vanilla extract
Zest of 1 lemon
Pinch of cream of tartar

To assemble
150 g (5½ oz) strawberry jam
500 g (1 lb 2 oz) fresh
strawberries (about
2 punnets), hulled and
diced small, reserving some
whole strawberries to top
the cake
1 batch Vanilla bean crème
diplomat (page 256)

This cake may just be one of my favourite recipes in the whole book. It's fun to make and so incredibly delicious. The taste of pure, joyful, summer. The chiffon cake is ethereally light and spongy but this means that, structurally, it won't tolerate being made too far in advance. Make all the elements ahead of time, but assemble them only an hour or two before serving. You can keep the assembled cake refrigerated until you're ready to serve.

Preheat your oven to 160°C (315°F) fan-forced. Line the bases of your two cake tins with baking paper, leaving the sides ungreased. Set aside.

Pour the egg whites into the bowl of a stand mixer and the yolks into a mixing bowl.

In a separate, large bowl, sift together the flour, baking powder and salt then whisk in the 250 g (9 oz) of sugar and the polenta. Set aside.

Add the milk, olive oil, vanilla and lemon zest to the egg yolks and whisk to combine.

Using your stand mixer fitted with the whisk attachment, start whipping the egg whites with the cream of tartar on a medium–high speed. When they become foamy, add the extra 35 g (1¼ oz) of sugar, 1 teaspoon at a time, and waiting about 30 seconds in between each addition. This should take about 5 minutes. Turn the machine off and whisk a few times by hand to smooth out the consistency.

Pour the egg yolk mixture into the dry ingredients and whisk to combine. Fold in the whipped egg whites in three additions, folding from the bottom each time. Divide the batter between the two cake tins and bake for 50–55 minutes, until a cake tester or skewer inserted into the centre comes out clean.

Remove the cakes from the oven and invert them onto a cooling rack. The edge of the cake tin should be higher than the top of the cake, but if the cake is taller than the tin, invert each cake by balancing the edge of the upside-down tin on four small ramekins, allowing the cake to hang. Leave the cakes like this to completely cool for about an hour.

To assemble, slice each cake horizontally into two even rounds, leaving you with four rounds. Place one round on your cake stand and evenly spread one third of the jam over it, all the way to the edges. Top the jam with one third of the chopped strawberries in one even layer. Top the strawberries with a heaped ½ cup of the crème diplomat and spread it almost to the edges. Add the next cake round and repeat with the next two layers, then top with the final cake round. Scoop the remaining crème diplomat onto the top of the cake and use a spoon or spatula to create beautiful swoops. Sprinkle the cake with a few reserved strawberries, either whole or cut into rounds. Chill the cake in the fridge until you're ready to serve.

Note: The pinch of cream of tartar stabilises the tiny bubbles in the whipped egg whites, so that when they are folded into the cake, they hold their shape for longer. Without it, your cake would collapse in the centre.

Ricciarelli

Makes: 20 biscuits
Active Time: 20 minutes
Inactive time: 1 hour 15 minutes

Kitchenalia: Food processor
(optional)

250 g (9 oz) blanched almonds
(or almond meal)
220 g (7¾ oz) caster
(superfine) sugar
Zest of half a lemon
Zest of half an orange
65 g (2½ oz) egg white
(from about 3–4 eggs)
¼ teaspoon bicarbonate
of soda (baking soda)
Pinch of fine sea salt
1 teaspoon almond extract
Icing (confectioners') sugar,
for coating

A perfect end-of-dinner biscuit that sits as happily alongside a glass of amaro, as it does a cup of tea or coffee. These biscuits are best made a day ahead, so are perfect for entertaining. This is also an excellent recipe to keep in mind for when you have an excess of egg whites.

Before you begin: Swap the whole almonds for almond meal if you don't have a food processor. I like to grind blanched almonds myself because I think they have more flavour, but your biscuits will be delicious either way.

Blitz the almonds, sugar and citrus zests together in a food processor until it turns to citrus-scented almond meal (if using almond meal, simply mix these ingredients together in a mixing bowl). Transfer to a mixing bowl and add in the egg white, bicarbonate of soda, salt and almond extract. Stir to combine until a thick dough forms.

Shape the dough into 20 small balls, then toss them through the icing sugar to coat well.

Place the biscuits on a baking-paper-lined baking tray and leave them on your bench for about an hour to dry.

Preheat your oven to 160°C (320°F) fan-forced.

After drying, press the biscuits to flatten them slightly and shape into an oval. This should create some cracking on the surface, which is ideal.

Bake for 12–14 minutes, until the biscuits under the icing sugar appear golden brown.

Remove the biscuits from the oven and transfer them to a cooling rack to cool. Store in an airtight container.

A sophisticated biscuit to indulge your childhood nostalgia, this version of ricciarelli is all chew and tenderness, propped up with notes of almond and undertones of citrus zest. These biscuits hail from Siena, where they were traditionally reserved for Christmas time, but they are related to the better-known macaroon. The almond-oval shape is thought to have been inspired by the shape of the Sultan's slippers – a biscuit literally designed to tell a story, in this case, of the Crusades in the Holy Land. Do not feel you need to have such tales of grandeur or conquests to indulge.

Coffee granita with whipped cream

This is a great dessert for after lunch on a hot summer's day. Serve with a chilled nip of amaretto or Frangelico for an affogato-like experience. This dessert is also great with the Ricciarelli (see opposite page).

Dissolve the sugar in the hot coffee and pour it into a small, shallow dish. Leave it to cool, then place it in your freezer.

After the first hour in the freezer, take a fork to the granita and stir it to break up any ice crystals that have formed. Do this every 30–60 minutes, until you have a slushy-like texture.

You can then leave this in the freezer until you're ready to serve. Place your dessert glasses into the freezer so they're nice and cold.

Just before serving, lightly whip the cream by hand, so you can easily control how far you take it. You want something that holds its shape but only just.

To serve, scoop the granita into your chilled dessert glasses and top with whipped cream.

Note: Simply double or triple the recipe to serve more people. The granita will take slightly longer to freeze, so it might be good to get started on it a day before serving.

Makes: Enough to serve 2
(easily scaled up; see note)
Active time: 20 minutes
Inactive time: 5 hours

50 g (1¾ oz) white
(granulated) sugar
180 ml (6 fl oz) hot, freshly
brewed espresso coffee
100 ml (3½ fl oz) single
(pure) cream

Ricciarelli, Coffee granita with whipped cream

Apricot pavlova with apricot kernel cream

Makes: 1 pavlova, enough
    to serve 10–12 slices
Active time: 1 hour 15 minutes
Inactive time: 15 hours

Kitchenalia: 19 cm (7½ inch)
    round plate (to use as
    a stencil), stand mixer fitted
    with the whisk attachment,
    hammer

Apricots
15 apricots, halved,
    pits removed and reserved
    (see Before you begin)
100 ml (3½ fl oz) white wine
    (or Muscat de Beaumes-
    de-Venise if you're feeling
    extravagant! If so, omit
    the honey)
3 tablespoons honey

There is a small treasure inside the pits of apricots and other stone fruit known as the *noyaux*. These kernels have a bitter almond flavour, which perfumes the cream for this pavlova beautifully. This is a real stunner for an Australian Christmas, when the apricots should be at their peak.

Before you begin: My suggested order for approaching this recipe is as follows. One day in advance, prepare the apricot kernels, infuse the cream and roast the apricots (keep them refrigerated). Make the custard part of your crème diplomat a day in advance, simply leaving the cream that's infusing to be added on the day of serving. You could also make and bake your meringue the day before, just leave it in the oven overnight. You want to assemble the pavlova just before serving as it doesn't like to sit for a long period of time.

You'll need to infuse the cream for the Vanilla bean crème diplomat (see page 256) with the apricot kernels. Freeze your apricot pits for several hours to make the shell more brittle. Next, place them in-between two tea towels. Use a hammer on a sturdy bench top (something that won't crack when hit with a hammer!) and crack them lightly. You'll know how much force to use after doing a couple. You ideally want to just crack the husk without smashing the white kernel inside, but it's fine if you do. Separate the white kernel and discard the husk. Place the kernels into a bowl with the 350 ml (12 fl oz) of thickened (whipping) cream called for in the recipe. Cover and refrigerate overnight. The following day, strain the cream, discard the kernels and proceed with the Vanilla bean crème diplomat recipe as written.

To prepare the apricots:

Preheat your oven to 200°C (400°F) fan-forced. Place the apricot halves on a baking tray, cut-side down, splash them with the wine and drizzle with the honey. Roast for 20–25 minutes, basting them a few times to ensure they don't burn. Bake until the apricots are jammy, but not falling apart. Allow to cool, then refrigerate on the tray, covered with aluminium foil (if the tray doesn't fit in your fridge, carefully transfer the apricots to an airtight container so they're sitting cut-side down in a single layer).

Notes: It's easier to separate eggs when they're cold, so do this before you start; use the yolks in your Vanilla bean crème diplomat, then leave the egg whites to come to room temperature to use for your meringue.

While apricot kernels have been used for centuries by the frugal cook to impart a delicious whisper of wild almond, it is prudent to note that they do contain a tiny amount of cyanide (!) and are not to be consumed in their entirety regularly or en masse.

To make the meringue:

Ensure there is a rack in the centre of your oven and remove any racks that may be above it. Preheat your oven to 150°C (300°F) fan-forced.

Place the egg whites and salt in the bowl of a stand mixer fitted with a whisk attachment. Beat on high until the egg whites hold soft peaks. Add in the sugar, 1 tablespoon at a time, over the course of about 5–6 minutes. Continue to beat for 2 minutes after you've added the last of the sugar. The egg whites should be voluminous, hold stiff peaks and be very glossy. Reduce the speed of the mixer to low and add in the vinegar and cornflour. Mix until fully incorporated, then turn off the mixer.

Take a flat baking tray and cut a sheet of baking paper to fit it. Use a roughly 19 cm (7½ inch) plate and a marker to trace a circle on the sheet of baking paper. Dab a small amount of meringue into each corner of your baking tray, then flip the sheet of baking paper over (to avoid the pavlova touching the ink) and press it down in the corners so the meringue holds the paper down.

Scoop the meringue into the centre of the traced circle and push it out to fill the circle, trying to stay within the lines. Shape into a dome with a flat top, about 8 cm (3¼ inches) high. An offset spatula will help with this.

Carefully place the tray in the oven, gently shut the oven door and immediately turn the heat down to 100°C (200°F) fan-forced. Bake for 1½ hours without opening the oven door. Then, still without opening the door, turn the oven off and leave the meringue in the oven for 4–5 hours – or overnight (with the oven light on, if possible, to keep the oven dry and slightly warm) if you are making this for the following day.

To assemble the pavlova:

Place the meringue on a plate, platter or cake stand. Use a small serrated knife to cut out the flat top of the meringue. Scoop as much of the crème diplomat into the cavity as will fit without spilling over; you will probably have a little left over to serve on the side. Top the pavlova with the roasted apricots and any of their syrup (keep the leftover apricots to be served alongside each slice), then sprinkle with the toasted almonds.

Notes: To avoid a collapsing pavlova, be sure to use caster (superfine) sugar and not white (granulated) sugar. I learnt this the hard way during a late-night pavlova baking session.

I like to use Chinese black vinegar as it gives the meringue the slightest off-white tone, which I prefer to a stark white meringue, but any white vinegar will also work.

Mix almond extract through your finished crème diplomat if it doesn't have a strong almond flavour (kernels can vary in how pungent they are).

Meringue
140 g (5 oz) egg whites, room temperature (from about 4 eggs)
Pinch of fine sea salt
220 g (7¾ oz) caster (superfine) sugar (see notes)
1 teaspoon Chinese black vinegar (see notes)
1 tablespoon cornflour (cornstarch)

To assemble
1 batch Vanilla bean crème diplomat (page 256) made with apricot kernel-infused cream (see Before you begin)
30 g (1 oz) almonds, toasted and halved
½ teaspoon almond extract (optional, see notes)

Apricot pavlova with apricot kernel cream

Chocolate cake with dark chocolate and cream cheese frosting

Makes 1 cake, enough
for 12–14 slices
Active time: 30 minutes
Inactive time: 2 hours 30 minutes

Kitchenalia: 25 cm (10 inch)
round, deep cake tin, stand
mixer fitted with the paddle
attachment

75 g (2½ oz) Dutch-process
cocoa powder
175 g (6 oz) soft brown sugar
150 g (5½ oz) white
(granulated) sugar
225 ml (7¾ fl oz) hot, freshly
brewed coffee (decaf and/or
instant also work here)
2 teaspoons vanilla extract
140 ml (4½ fl oz) neutral oil
2 extra large eggs
240 ml (8 fl oz) whole milk
1 teaspoon white wine vinegar
250 g (9 oz) plain
(all-purpose) flour
2 teaspoons bicarbonate
of soda (baking soda)
1 teaspoon baking powder
1 teaspoon fine sea salt

Icing
200 g (7 oz) 70–80 per cent
dark chocolate, broken into
pieces (see notes)
3 tablespoons Dutch-process
cocoa powder
170 g (6 oz) unsalted butter, at
room temperature, plus extra
for greasing
125 g (4½ oz) icing
(confectioners') sugar, sifted
Pinch of fine sea salt
1 teaspoon vanilla extract
250 g (9 oz) block cream
cheese, at room temperature

This makes a gorgeous, large single-layer cake that's perfect for birthdays and celebrations. A classic to make over and over again. Between the moist, tender chocolate cake and the decadent ganache-like icing, this is one for chocolate-lovers, a club to which I belong.

Preheat your oven to 160°C (315°F) fan-forced. Prepare your cake tin by buttering the sides and lining the base with baking paper. Set aside.

In a large mixing bowl, combine the cocoa powder and the sugars. Pour in the hot coffee and whisk to ensure there are no lumps. Add in the vanilla, oil, eggs, milk and vinegar, then whisk until smooth. Lastly add in the flour, bicarbonate of soda, baking powder and salt and, again, whisk until smooth.

Pour the batter into the cake tin and bake for 55–70 minutes, until a skewer inserted into the centre of the cake comes out clean. Allow the cake to cool completely in the tin (about 1 hour).

To make the icing (I like to do this once my cake is fully cooled, so I can ice it straight away), melt the chocolate over a double boiler (see notes) until completely melted, then set aside to cool.

In the bowl of a stand mixer fitted with the paddle attachment, combine the cocoa powder, butter, icing sugar, salt, vanilla and cream cheese and beat on medium–high speed until light and fluffy, about 2–3 minutes. Stop and scrape the sides of the bowl as needed. Pour in the melted chocolate and stir to combine.

To finish, invert the cake onto a cake stand or platter and remove the round of baking paper. You can slice the top of the cake off using a serrated knife to create a flat layer, or leave it as is. Scoop the icing onto the cooled cake and spread it all the way to the edges. If making a layer cake, add half the icing to the top of one of the cakes, spreading it all the way to the edges, then lay the second cake on top and scoop the remaining icing onto the cake, again, spreading all the way to the edges. Slice and serve.

Notes: If I'm baking this cake for kids, I use a 40 per cent milk chocolate instead of the dark chocolate for the icing.

To set up a double boiler, place a small mixing bowl holding whatever it is you're melting over a saucepan of boiling water, ensuring the base of the bowl isn't touching the water. Stir occasionally until everything has completely melted.

Optional adjustment: For a layer cake, divide the batter between two 21 cm (8¼ inch) round cake tins and bake for 40–45 minutes.

The pen and the wooden spoon

I have fallen swiftly on many occasions: there was a sea urchin with buttered baguette on the port of Cassis; a glass of L'Anglore at Septime; an early-morning coffee granita in Salina, piled high with cream and served with an orange-spiked brioche; bone marrow in London; anchoïade in Rayol; my first Pantescan caper. Love at first bite is common, but my friendships tend to be more of an acquired taste, blossoming over time ... that was, until I met Dani.

I can remember the day we met with incredible clarity. Such a sunny disposition, so many similar ideas, a shared table and a shared appreciation of the joy that brings; so much said, and so much left to say. If you have ever eaten Danielle's food, you will better be able to imagine the person she is – her cooking is a mirror of her personality. I had found a friend for life.

Nearly a decade on, when our publisher suggested I might help to write this incredible book, we both jumped at the idea. We knew it would be a delight, we knew we would learn a lot – I have always loved time shared in Danielle's kitchen. And yet, I'm not sure we anticipated the way it would grow our friendship and our respect for each other's work.

Perhaps unusually, both writing and cooking are quite solitary events ... right up to the moment where the book starts appearing on strangers' bookshelves and the plates are sent out to strangers' tables. You make a lot of decisions, you think a lot, you question yourself, you strip the ideas back to their bones, and then maybe add one or two back in, only to take them out again. It's an incredibly personal process. It's also often quite lonely. It's been so lovely to share.

Happily, the more we have talked, debated and questioned, the more we have realised how similar our styles are, albeit across two different *métiers*. Our shared curiosity, our love for refining an idea, for distilling it down to its essence, our love for all that came before.

In this book, we have worked to share that which is solitary – not just with each other, but with you. We wanted to create something that was truly designed to help. We wanted recipes that warrant your attention; we wanted recipes that would become a part of your life. We wanted to explain our reasoning, and to explain the thoughts behind the choices and the romance of good cooking, alongside the rules.

We hope you love it as much as we do.

—*Libby*

How to cook an octopus ...

Collating your favourite recipes necessitates a little soul-baring. More than a menu in a restaurant, which may change with the whims of the season, the producer, or even just your mood, a cookbook tells a rather detailed (and permanent!) story of who you are.

This book felt particularly so. After that long lockdown, when I had more time than ever to cook in my own kitchen, with somewhat limited ingredients (and certainly no access to all the wonderful producers who coloured so much of my restaurant cooking), this book was borne out of careful thought regarding what makes beautiful cooking in a home. Just like the clothes in your closet or the jewellery in your drawer, cooking is a way to wear your art. It represents a snapshot of what you like and don't like, and what's important to you. Now that the recipes are all here, on these pages, you'll be able to see quite a bit about who I am.

These recipes range from very simple, everyday foods to more elaborate options for entertaining. Either way, they're designed to bring happiness to your table. They lean on the history and romance we find all around us, particularly in our travels. On reflection, they are largely classic: they highlight the fruit, vegetables, meat or fish that you have before you; they take into account the foibles and complications of imperfect produce. I like food that isn't cluttered, and that tastes of itself – you will see that among this collection. And while I use butter and olive oil with delicious abandon, I do like the end result to be light. I don't like to feel weighed down after a meal. I also enjoy cooking that asks a little of me – the act of cooking is very much my therapy, so I like food that requires my hands, mind and heart.

Beyond the dishes I love to cook, I thought a lot about you, dear reader. I created a list of questions:

"Does this recipe share a useful technique or highly adaptable method?"

"Is it clear and easy to replicate in a home kitchen?"

"Is it a joy to make?"

"Can all the ingredients be found at your local grocery store?"

"Does it celebrate food?"

and most importantly,

"Is it so delicious that I couldn't possibly leave it out?"

All the recipes in this book answered each of these questions with a resounding *yes*. I did also try to think about the people around you. I like recipes that will please a crowd, that children and adults alike will enjoy (although, as I'm an avid chilli lover, you may find you need to adjust the heat for younger palates!). While I was hoping you would find pleasure and reward in the process, and the delight of sharing something you've created with others, I also want their happy response to drive that pleasure home.

Sadly for our eight-legged friend, he didn't make the cut. You see, while a cookbook will inevitably reflect the writer, it will also be a capsule of time – none of us are static in our thoughts, ideas and tastes. At one point, while writing this book, I became gripped by the idea that I must teach people the easiest, sure-fire way to cook octopus. So many people are bewildered by octopus. With the recipes out there equal parts superstition and knowledge, it's no wonder people are confused! Alas, after several tests, and finding a method that worked successfully at home, I realised that no matter how great this recipe might be, most people wouldn't have easy access to quality octopus, and even if they did, it would be unlikely to become a staple, nor was it necessarily one for everyone – so out it came.

But ... just in case you were wondering:

How to cook an octopus:
Add your octopus to a large pot and cover it by 3–4 cm ($1\frac{1}{4}$–$1\frac{1}{2}$ inches) of cold water. Add a good pinch of salt, half an onion, two garlic cloves, a stalk of celery, a split carrot, a few good glugs of olive oil, a pinch of chilli flakes and a few strips of lemon zest. Bring it up to a gentle simmer without ever boiling. Place a lid on the pot and simmer for 30–40 minutes, then turn off the heat. Leave the octopus to cool in the liquid, then drain it and leave it to dry. From here, you can slice your octopus and serve it cold, or proceed to brush it with olive oil and char it on a hot grill or in a pan.

What you have before you are my favourite recipes from my home – I hope they will also become favourites in yours.

—Danielle

Acknowledgements

The greatest joy in writing this book was being able to collaborate on it with my dear friend and writer, Libby Travers. Libby was one of my first friends in Australia, and to say we hit it off is an understatement. She felt like a friend I'd had for ages, but actually we'd just met. We bonded over food, and spent many nights eating, drinking and conversing into the wee hours of the morning. The late nights have gone, and Libby has since moved to France and started a family, but we still retain that same connection I felt when we first met. When my publisher Jane Willson asked who I might like to collaborate with on the writing of this book and suggested Libby, the decision was already made in my head. Luckily, Libby was keen too. Although the recipes in this book are mine, Libby's beautiful words capture the spirit of my food like no one else can, and all those little nuances make a world of difference. I am forever grateful that she took this project on with me, and I sincerely hope we can do it again.

To Harriet Davidson, who is the most thoughtful and kind editor I have ever worked with. I had the great pleasure of cooking with Harriet at Fred's and so, again, the idea that I might work with someone who tangibly knows my food and my voice is the greatest gift. She knows all the right questions to ask, and has even played a role in the cover of this book, sourcing the gorgeous tablecloth from French artisan Sarah Espeute. She has an incredible eye for beauty, and a thoughtful and inquisitive brain. Everything you want in the person who is checking the details in your writing. I am sure she will one day be writing books of her own, and I look forward to that day.

To Jane Willson, my publisher. Thank you for gathering the best possible team of people to bring this one together. I am forever grateful for your support and guidance. This book would not exist without you. Please can we do it again?

To Justin Wolfers, who has the title of Editorial Manager, but in my mind has been so much more. I felt completely held throughout the book-making process. Thank you, Justin, for putting up with my missed deadlines and still managing to keep it all on track *and* with a smile on your face.

To Sarah Odgers, who has managed the design of this book, and to Emily O'Neill, who has done such a wonderful job executing it. I can't believe you took my stupid Pinterest board and turned it into this crazy beautiful book. Your brilliance knows no bounds!

To the photoshoot team: Alan Benson (photographer), Emma Knowles (stylist), Jimmy Callaway (home economist) and Sarah Atton (food prep).

Those weeks together shooting the nearly 100 recipes will remain some of the most fun weeks of my career. I am so grateful you were able to lend your talents (and hard work) to this book, and I feel you can really see this all coming together in the photos. As with most creative projects, the people are what make the magic happen. I think we made some magic in these photos. Looking at them will forever bring me joy, not just because I think they are stunning but because, in each one, I can remember the feeling I had in those days working with you.

On a personal note, I would like to thank my partner Dan, who probably knows the dishes in this book better than I do. Thank you for your thoughtful feedback and for your love. I could not have done this without you.

To my immediate family, Mom, Dad, Christie, Marty, Charlie, Mia and my dearly departed brother Manny. The simplest way of summarising what you mean to me is that without you, I am nothing. Thank you for your encouragement and support with everything I do. I love you all to the moon and back, forever and ever.

Food inspiration can come from many forms these days: a photo on social media, a conversation with another cook, recipes handed down through the generations, a perusal of a new or old cookbook. It's hard to pinpoint where the inspiration for a recipe begins and ends, and often they are an amalgamation of all of those things. The food writers I return to time and time again for inspiration are Alice Waters, Claudia Roden, Diana Kennedy, Edna Lewis, Elizabeth David, Flo Braker, Ina Garten, Lulu Peyraud, Marcella Hazan, Martha Stewart, Niloufer Ichaporia King, Rose Gray, Rose Levy Berenbaum, Ruth Reichl, Ruth Rogers, Samin Nosrat, Skye Gyngell and Tamar Adler; unsurprisingly, all women. I thank all of them, and others who have been brave enough to write recipes and send them out into the world. Food has always been about generosity for me; I think sharing your knowledge is one of the most generous acts you can do. Where a direct line of inspiration can be drawn, I have tried to credit in the recipes themselves.

Cookbooks are made by teams of people, not just one. For everyone named here, there are many others behind them. I thank you all from the bottom of my heart for believing in me and making something that we can all be so proud of.

Index